CHRIS HOY
THE AUTOBIOGRAPHY

CHRIS HOY

THE AUTOBIOGRAPHY

CHRIS HOY

HarperSport

An Imprint of HarperCollins*Publishers*

HarperSport
an imprint of HarperCollins*Publishers*
77–85 Fulham Palace Road,
Hammersmith, London W6 8JB

www.harpercollins.co.uk

First published by HarperCollins*Publishers* 2009
1 3 5 7 9 10 8 6 4 2

A catalogue record of this book
is available from the British Library

ISBN 978-0-00-731131-6 (hardback)
ISBN 978-0-00-731134-7 (paperback)

Printed and bound in Great Britain by
Clays Ltd, St Ives plc

Mixed Sources
Product group from well-managed
forests and other controlled sources
www.fsc.org Cert no. SW-COC-1806
© 1996 Forest Stewardship Council

FSC is a non-profit international organisation established to promote the
responsible management of the world's forests. Products carrying the FSC
label are independently certified to assure consumers that they come
from forests that are managed to meet the social, economic and
ecological needs of present or future generations.

Find out more about HarperCollins and the environment at
www.harpercollins.co.uk/green

To my mum and dad, Carol and David

Contents

INTRODUCTION

The Danger of Disappearing
up my Own Orifice

On the day after I won my third gold medal at the Beijing Olympics I was visited by a small posse of Scottish journalists, and asked a question I have never been asked before, or since.

'In the last 24 hours everyone has offered their opinions of Chris Hoy,' said Gary Ralston of the *Daily Record*. He may have been stroking his chin as he contemplated how he was going to phrase the next part of his question – I could tell that it wasn't going to be of the more familiar 'How does it feel?' or 'Has it sunk in yet?' variety.

'I wonder,' continued Gary. 'What does Chris Hoy think of Chris Hoy?'

There was only one answer to that. 'Chris Hoy thinks that the day Chris Hoy starts talking about himself in the third person is the day that he disappears up his own arse.' It maybe wasn't the response that Gary was looking for, but he, and the others, looked reasonably happy with it, and it duly featured in their stories the following day. (Thankfully, it also got me out of having to offer up a cringe-worthy response to the actual question.)

I bring it up because it popped into my head when thinking about this book. I asked myself: what kind of book would

I like to read? Personally, I'm not a huge fan of the straight-forward 'then-I-did-this-and-then-I-did-that' life story. What I like, particularly in a book about sport, is an insight into what it's actually like to compete at a high level, and what it takes to get there, and stay there – ideally sprinkled with a few semi-humorous anecdotes. In essence, I want to know how a sports person does what they do. I want to know *why*, too, but most of all I want to know *how*.

It's the way I've always been. At school, I enjoyed subjects where the answers tended to be 'no' or 'yes'. I liked logical subjects – maths, the sciences – which involved some kind of puzzle and a definite or correct conclusion or answer at the end of it. I liked there to be a 'right' answer, I suppose, but I also enjoyed the process of working towards it.

I wouldn't want this book to read like a science manual or maths paper. But I hope that it can go some way to explaining 'how'. If I were an aspiring athlete, or just a fan of sport – and without referring to myself in the third person – I think that is the kind of book I would enjoy reading.

In any case, I am still just as interested in the question of 'how?' as I was when I was a 16-year-old, and making my first, tentative and very nervous pedal strokes around the forbiddingly steep-looking banking of the Meadowbank Velo-drome. As I look ahead to the London Olympics, with the knowledge that, just to make the British team, never mind win another gold medal, I will probably have to be a better athlete in 2012 than I was in 2008, the question remains as pertinent as ever.

The irony, of course, is that, while I say I like 'right' answers, in reality there seldom is a definitive answer. Training and competing are less an exact science and more an endless puzzle; they are a creative process of trial and error – and a process I enjoy, even though I know that the correct answer one season can be the wrong one the following year.

After 25 years of competing as a cyclist, on BMXs, mountain and road bikes, and finally on the track, I would like to think that I have stumbled on some 'right' answers; if I have been paying attention then I should have learnt something. Yet at the same time, if I thought I had all the right answers, I'd be screwed. I know that I wouldn't get near the team for 2012, never mind challenge for a gold medal, if I thought for a second I could just carry on doing the same things.

So the search, the working out of the puzzle, continues. The answers or solutions to some problems remain elusive, while for others the nature of the problem, or challenge, changes; the variables do what the name implies: they vary. I'm getting older, for one thing – I'll be 36 by the time the London Games come around – and my rivals are getting younger, if only in relation to me. And so I have to go back to the drawing board, come up with new ideas, and then work even harder.

For me, it's the puzzle and the inherent unpredictability of sport that keeps it fun – and endlessly fascinating. I hope this book can reflect that and, for aspiring athletes and armchair fans alike, prove interesting.

CHRIS HOY

THE AUTOBIOGRAPHY

CHAPTER 1

The Art of Throwing
Up in Secret

Beijing, Tuesday 19 August 2008

It was 8.30 when I woke up and hauled myself out of bed. I was lucky, having my own room in the athletes' village. Jason Kenny, my neighbour in the room next door, had been sharing with Jamie Staff. However, Jamie, whose Olympic Games had started and finished with our gold medal-winning ride in the team sprint the previous Friday, had moved out, so now Jason too had his own space.

It was the final day of the track cycling programme: day five. I had raced on all four days so far, and I could feel it in my legs. First thing in the morning they were stiff and painful, having so far made 14 flat-out efforts in the course of long and draining days at the track.

I could also see the fruits of those efforts, though: two gold medals, from the team sprint and keirin, in the bedside cabinet. I permitted myself the odd sneaky look, though it felt like a bit of a guilty pleasure. I didn't feel I could – or should – enjoy them until my Games had finished.

That would be today, a day that might even end with a third gold, in the individual sprint. But, bizarrely, there was every chance that my neighbour and team-mate, the afore-mentioned Jason Kenny, could be the opponent to stand in the way of what, I had been told by journalists a couple of days earlier, would be a historic achievement. No British sportsperson had won three gold medals in a single Olympic Games in a century, I was told. That was news to me: I hadn't even allowed myself to contemplate the possibility of winning three Olympic titles prior to Beijing, let alone start considering any historical significance. And this morning that was certainly the case: the team sprint and keirin had gone, they were finished. I was focused only on the day's racing.

The individual sprint starts with a qualifying round – a time trial over 200 metres – and then proceeds over three days with man-against-man contests. Now, two days in, I had made it to the semi-finals. These and the final were both best-of-three rounds, so I would have six more races at most, if I got through my semi and if both rounds went the distance. At 8.30 in the morning, moving my legs slowly and painfully out of bed, then hobbling stiffly towards the shower, I didn't know how I would cope with that. By bluffing, I imagined.

Though I had my own room, Jason and I shared the apartment, and the shower. Not at the same time, I should clarify. But Jason, being more of a morning person than me – which isn't saying much – was in there first, and so I waited, then showered, before joining Jason to ride down to the canteen for breakfast.

It's not as though it was far. It was only a few minutes' journey, but cyclists abide by a set of absolute golden rules. Never stand when you can sit. Never sit when you can lie down. And never walk when you can cycle. At this stage of the competition, in particular, it is a case of trying to preserve all the energy and strength you can.

We freewheeled down to the canteen in silence, arriving at the entrance and locking up our bikes. It might be the

Olympic athletes' village, with stricter security than the Pentagon, but you still lock your bike. You can never be too careful – especially with a £3,000 road bike.

Looking back now, this would have been a quite surreal scene: Jason and I heading off to breakfast together, like best mates, as if there were nothing out of the ordinary about the day ahead. It probably helps that Jason must be one of the most relaxed people in the team, if not the sport: nothing seems to faze him, and he is famous for his languid and laidback style (off the track, I should point out: on it, his reactions are a little bit faster).

Both of us knew there was a chance that, just a few hours later, we would race each other for an Olympic gold medal, in arguably the most prestigious of the track cycling events, the sprint. We had qualified first and second in the initial 200m time trial two days ago, and we had both progressed reasonably comfortably to the semi-finals – separate semi-finals, with the German rider Max Levy as Jason's opponent, and Mickaël Bourgain of France as mine. Beat them and we'd be meeting again a few hours later, in an Olympic final.

But neither of us mentioned any of this. We didn't talk about racing at all. We just chatted about the usual things, and spent breakfast engaged in the activity that occupies so much of your down time at the Olympics: people watching. This is a particularly entertaining and enjoyable pastime in the athletes' village, where you get famous names, some extraordinary shapes and sizes, which inspire games of 'guess the sport.'

Thus did Jason and I pass this very ordinary hour on this most surreal of days, before returning to our apartment, to prepare for the 40-minute bus journey to the Laoshan Velodrome, on the outskirts of Beijing.

First, though, I paid a visit to the British team's sprint coach, Jan van Eijden. Jan, from Germany, was the world sprint champion in 2000. He retired in 2006 and came to work for us the following year, having been poached from the Eurosport commentary box by our head coach, Shane Sutton, who reckoned Jan had the ingredients to become a top coach. Though he wasn't the fastest in the world, Jan consistently won head-to-head 'match' sprint races. Tactically, I would argue that he is the best sprinter of the last decade. And Shane was right, as he often is (and sometimes isn't): Jan's knowledge and experience make him a brilliant tactical coach, and a real asset to the British team. Added to which is the fact that he is very upbeat and virtually always smiling. So he – like the incredible force of nature that is Shane Sutton – is also good for morale.

But this morning I wasn't going to see Jan to have my morale lifted, or to ask, in the eventuality of us meeting in the final, how I might beat Jason. I knew he wouldn't discuss Jason's tactics – and in any case, I wasn't thinking of Jason … yet. I was thinking of my semi-final opponent, Bourgain.

Before any race, we watch videos of our opponent in action. So Jan got his computer out, and together we watched every sprint race I had ever ridden against Bourgain. We looked for potential weaknesses (his, but also mine). I'd watched all these videos numerous times before. But this, I suppose, was like looking over your notes before an exam. It's probably not going to make much difference ('if you don't know it now, you'll never know it,' as the mantra used to go before exams), but, as in the anxious pre-exam wait, you think that you should be doing something. It feels better than doing nothing.

The videos for Beijing were prepared by our performance analysts: there were hours and hours of races on film, over 300 gigabytes' worth; files and files, comprising a complete library, with every opponent racing and just about every scenario you could imagine. But the analysts' work goes way beyond just having all this stuff on film. They've studied it and worked out things like, 'If Bourgain is leading with half a lap to go there's an 80 per cent chance he'll win the race ...' or 'When he's behind his opponent with two laps to go, there's a 30 per cent chance he'll win.' All these statistics and data ('the numbers', as we call them) have been prepared by the Great Britain team's performance analysts – go to any World Cup meeting and you'll see them sitting quietly at the back of the stand with a tripod, filming every single race.

The thing is, a head-to-head match sprint race will often come down to intuition and what we call track craft – the fast/slow feinting and cat-and-mouse tactics that you see between two riders – but it's reassuring to have the statistics to back it all up; it can give you extra confidence in your game plan.

As Jan and I sat and watched the footage of my previous races against Bourgain, we focused on a couple in particular. One was at the same Laoshan Velodrome, at the Beijing World Cup the previous December. At that point, I was still taking my first, tentative steps as a sprinter. At 31, I was a bit old, really, to be trying something new – or so the accepted wisdom went. Match sprinting – since it demands the explosive acceleration of a Usain Bolt coupled with the quick reflexes and agility of an Olga Korbut – was seen as a young man's game (and I'm no Olga Korbut). But having lost my specialist event, the kilometre, I was determined to add another string to my bow.

And that's really all I was thinking back in December 2007, at that World Cup in Beijing. The team sprint remained my priority as I looked ahead to the Olympics, while the keirin, in which I was also a relative novice, and the sprint gave me other options. My thinking was that if I could do all three events, I'd increase my chances of being selected for the team sprint. But at that point the idea that I could challenge for a medal in all three seemed like a pipe dream. I was expecting to be competent and competitive, nothing more.

And I still had some distance to go, if my meeting with Bourgain in the quarter-final of the 2007 Beijing World Cup was anything to go by. He beat me in two straight rides. Both rides were quite close, as it happens, but the bare statistics don't lie. Two-nil is a comprehensive beating. And it was to be expected: Bourgain, a 28-year-old Frenchman best described as a 'pure sprinter,' was certainly one of the top two or three in the world, having medalled in every world championship since 2004.

The other race Jan and I watched was from two months later, when I met Bourgain again, this time at the World Cup in Copenhagen. This was the race that offered the first sign that I might yet make it as a sprinter. Shane Sutton, in typically excitable and enthusiastic style, told me it was 'the turning point – the moment you became a sprinter'. Reminiscing about it months later, he seemed even more convinced about this. 'What was the critical race?' he'll ask – expecting whoever he is asking to reply that it was my defeat of reigning world champion Theo Bos, the Dutchman who dominated sprinting in recent seasons, in the quarter-final of the world championships in Manchester a few weeks after that Copenhagen World Cup.

He loves it if you respond: 'Bos in Manchester.' It allows him to counter with: 'Nah, mate – Bourgain in Copenhagen.'

He's right. I was riding in Copenhagen purely to try and qualify an extra British sprinter for the Olympics. My own ticket to Beijing rested on the keirin; I had to beat my old rival Arnaud Tournant, another Frenchman, to win the series, and thus qualify for Beijing.

The meeting had started on the Friday evening with the team sprint, and we had a terrible night, giving one of our worst performances in this event in recent years. While the French dominated, again, we could only qualify fourth, and then lost out to the Netherlands – led by Bos – in the ride for the bronze medal.

The next day was better: I reached the final of the keirin, which proved a bit of an epic. Tournant was just as keen to win, since that would guarantee him his Olympic place, and he and his team-mate, Grégory Baugé, both laid it on thick in the final, launching a series of attacks but ultimately failing to overake me, as I led from the front to win the race and the series, and secure my ticket to Beijing.

Competing in the sprint, on the third day, felt a bit like doing my duty for the team. Thanks to the keirin I was now guaranteed my Olympic place, which I was delighted about. But I didn't know if I'd ride all three events in Beijing. To be honest, I didn't know if I had it in me, and worried that I could spread myself a little too thinly by attempting such a full programme.

Added to this general uncertainty was the fact that there was a fourth event to do in Copenhagen: the lucrative Japanese invitational keirin, with its £10,000 first prize. I was doing that, too – well, that prize was quite an incentive – and I knew that by Sunday evening my legs would be in bits.

But first up in the morning was the 200-metre time trial that acts as the qualifier for the sprint, and determines the subsequent draw. I was third with 10.2 seconds, behind yet another of those fast Frenchmen, Kévin Sireau, with Bourgain second. I progressed fairly smoothly through a few rounds before my meeting with Bourgain in the semi-final.

In the first race I didn't ride well. It was the same problem that I often encountered in these head-to-head races. Though I had the raw speed, my tactics were a bit dodgy. OK, I'm being kind to myself. Basically, I only had one strategy. All the decent rides I'd done so far had seen me going from the front, setting a fast pace, trying to take the sting out of my opponent's tail, and then countering them when they made their move. It was a very one-dimensional way to ride, and it only worked if I could get to the front in the first place. And – not surprisingly, given that my opponents would have studied me in competition, just as I studied them – they were getting wise to it. So Bourgain beat me. One-nil.

I came off the track feeling pretty tired, and pretty discouraged. To add to my general dejection, I was then sick as I sat on the stationary rollers, keeping my legs spinning – and the lactic acid at bay – between races.

I could feel that something wasn't right, and called Jan over, asking him to discreetly fetch a bucket, or some other water- (or vomit-) tight container. 'But make sure no one can see what you're doing,' I told him; I didn't want any of my opponents to see that I was suffering so badly. Jan carried out the task to perfection, providing and then dispensing with the container before anyone saw anything. I should point out that vomiting is not uncommon; the repeated sprint efforts create such high lactic acid concentrations that they can, literally, make you sick.

My little bout of sickness didn't distract Jan from the mission that remained ahead of me: to beat Bourgain. 'He knows you can do that,' he said, referring to my one and only tactic. 'You gotta go from the back!'

I had tried going from the back in previous sprint matches, but I found it difficult to commit. What would happen is that my opponent would stall, I would hold back a little, and then we'd both end up 'jumping' – that is, opening our sprint – at the same time. The whole point of coming from behind is that you should have the element of surprise. But to gain the advantage you have to jump first, preferably without your opponent seeing you. If you both jump at the same time, and are going at more or less the same speed, it's extremely hard to come around the other rider, since he has the inside line, and therefore less distance to travel.

'Look,' said Jan. 'You're one-nil down, so you've got nothing to lose. I don't care about the outcome. I just want to see you try to execute this race tactically.'

Why did I lack the confidence to go from the back? The problem, I think, was that I had bought into the misconception that the guy at the front controls the race. It's very difficult to hold back, to be patient and sit a couple of lengths behind someone, maintaining your place high on the banking and waiting for the right time to make your move. But what Jan kept drilling into me was the idea that the guy at the back can be the one dictating the tactics; and, as he told me now, my second-round match against Bourgain offered the ideal opportunity to test this theory. As he kept saying, I had nothing to lose.

I knew it was true, but it's a difficult mindset to take into a race. I was determined, however, to follow Jan's instructions, to force Bourgain to the front and then attack him. From behind I was able to force him to commit early, while I waited and waited and – going against my instincts – waited some more. Coming into the bell lap I was quite a bit down, but he was going full gas, while I was still winding it up. Even coming off the back straight I was still about a length behind, but I was gaining, and I remember thinking, I'm going to pass him here. And I did, eating up the gap on the home straight, crossing the line first and thinking: that was easy. Although it only levelled the contest at 1–1, I knew that was the turning point. Suddenly, I had the momentum – the upper hand.

There was only a 10-minute break between the second and third rides – hardly even enough time to vomit – and I was feeling completely exhausted by now; as if I didn't have another effort in my legs. But I suspected that Bourgain – though he hadn't had as busy a weekend as me, missing the previous day's keirin – would be feeling pretty tired as well. It's at this stage of the competition that the mind games come in. You're in the track centre, warming up in full view of your opponents, and the trick is to appear less tired than you actually feel (and, if you're going to throw up, to do so secretly).

I rode slowly around the track centre, preparing for that third ride, with Bourgain himself following the same routine just yards away, and then I made sure I went up to the start first. I wasn't going to be seen delaying it, buying some more recovery time. When we were called, I was straight there, and I made sure I didn't slouch in the chair as we waited to go to the line.

When Bourgain came and sat beside me he was shaking his legs out, and stretching them, clearly trying to revive them. Beside him, I sat perfectly still and bolt upright, trying to send out the message that I was fresh, that I was up for it. A pre-race ritual is the presentation of the 'pegs' that determine the starting order: peg one means you are on the inside, and lead the sprint off, with peg two giving you the rear position. I picked peg one and sprang up, heading straight to the start. My legs were screaming, but it was all about bluffing it at this point. I've no idea whether any of this psychological warfare had any effect.

Following Jan's advice again, I used the same tactic in the third ride. Once I had forced Bourgain to the front he tried to get me to go past him again, slowing right down, almost coming to a standstill. I could have gone early – and in previous races probably would have panicked and done exactly that – but I stuck to the tactic of sitting patiently behind him, keeping high up the banking, forcing Bourgain to make the first move. Then, again as in the second ride, I swept past him to win, and make the final.

I lost the final to Sireau – after another embarrassment, when I managed to fall off the rollers while 'revving out' during my pre-race warm up, pedalling at about 250rpm, and clattering very noisily to the floor – but I didn't mind too much about losing. Like Bourgain, Sireau had had a day off the previous day. He was relatively fresh, whereas I was on my last legs. It was the race against Bourgain that had been important. To have executed it the way Jan wanted me to – that was the breakthrough.

Shane knew it immediately. So did I. I don't mean that I suddenly thought I could win the sprint title at the world championships, far less the Olympics, but I felt I'd cracked it, to a certain extent. There was this mythology around the sprint – it seemed like a bit of a black art. As a kilo rider, I was seen as a bit of a diesel engine, with plenty of power, but without the gift of great acceleration, and no tactical nous. If I beat someone in a sprint I was often told it was 'just gas' – just power – though Shane had always told me I could be a good sprinter, if I just put my mind to it.

Defeating Bourgain was significant because I was beating a tactically 'better' rider, and someone who'd qualified faster than me. It wasn't gas – I was doing what a successful sprinter has to do: imposing myself on the race, and on my opponent. Match sprinting is cycling's equivalent of a boxing match, with two opponents going head-to-head, or toe-to-toe; it is as much a battle of wills, and confidence, as a test of speed. Finally I had beaten an accomplished sprinter, and it came simply from not letting my opponent do what he wanted to do.

Four weeks later I surprised a lot of people by beating Theo Bos, also by two rides to one, on my way to reaching the final of the sprint at the world championships in Manchester. I then went on to surprise more people – including myself, I think – by beating Sireau in the final to become the first British rider since Reg Harris to be crowned world sprint champion. Harris, whose legendary status is acknowledged in the shape of an impressive bronze statue overlooking the home straight at the Manchester Velodrome, won the last of his five world sprint titles in 1954. Fifty-four years we had waited to claim the title again – and I was as shocked as anyone.

And now here I was in Beijing, with a chance of adding the Olympic sprint title – something no British cyclist, not even the great Harris, had ever achieved. Given all that was at stake it was just as well, really, that as I ate breakfast with Jason, then spent time talking tactics with Jan, I didn't allow myself to think about the possible ramifications of success. It is one of the golden rules in the British team, drilled into us by our psychiatrist, Steve Peters: focus on the process, not the outcome.

Even now, with only hours left of the Olympic track cycling programme, I didn't for a second consider the possibility of three gold medals, or the reaction back home to the success we – Team GB in general, the British cycling team in particular – were enjoying in Beijing. Any thoughts I might have had about how life could change in the event of winning that third gold medal would have been about as helpful as a puncture.

At this point, there was only one thing occupying my mind: my semi-final against Bourgain …

CHAPTER 2

Pimped-up Rides
and Broken Hearts

As a sports-obsessed seven-year-old boy Olympic gold medals
were a long way from my thoughts, but bikes were not. Bikes
were in my thoughts all the time during my childhood in
Edinburgh; they occupied every waking hour, with the
evidence plastered all over my school jotters, which were
filled with poems about bikes, essays about bikes and detailed
drawings of my 'dream machine'.

It's probably more accurate, however, to say that cycling
occupied every waking hour when I wasn't thinking about
football, and obsessing over my favourite team, Hearts (as in
Heart of Midlothian), or later, when I was a teenager, when I
wasn't thinking about rugby, and then rowing.

You get the picture: life revolved around sport. I have no
idea how I found the time to do anything else. Such as chess,
for example. Chess was my first passion, and in my first day
at school, George Watson's College in Edinburgh, I made a
point of asking the head teacher how I might join the school
chess club. I had been introduced to the game at the age of
four by my uncle Derek, who had what was then an unbelievably modern piece of kit – an electronic chess board. I
think I was fascinated both by the game and the novelty of

the technology, and played my dad all the time; he let me win initially, before his competitive instincts kicked in. Sadly, my chess playing became a casualty of my all-consuming interest in more physical pursuits. But I'm really not sure I was Grandmaster material.

There's a story which has been told quite a few times now about how I was inspired to take up BMXing after seeing the bike chase scene in *E.T.*, when it came out in 1984, and I was an impressionable seven-year-old. In fact, it has now appeared in the media so often that I'm sure many people's instinctive reaction would be to assume that it isn't true – or am I betraying my relatively newfound cynicism?

It comes as a relief to be able set the record straight at last. It's true. I was inspired by *E.T.* to take up BMXing. So thank you Elliott, thank you Steven Spielberg … though I suspect my love affair with cycling would probably have blossomed anyway, sooner or later.

Whether it would have started without BMXs is another question. I really don't know. All I know is that – thanks originally to what I saw in *E.T.* – BMXs looked like great fun. What's more, they were the epitome of cool for a seven-year-old kid.

It wasn't just the bikes – though they were pretty cool. The padded outfits, complete with motorcycle-style helmets, were cool too, and the tracks were magical places, even the rudimentary ones, of which there were a few in Edinburgh. Not too far from my parents' home, in Murrayfield, there were cinder tracks at Lochend and Danderhall. Lochend had been virtually destroyed, and Danderhall didn't have a proper gate, but they were still great fun to tear around on our bikes. The nearest track with a proper start gate was in Livingston, a new town about 15 miles west of Edinburgh, and six or seven of us would travel out there midweek, usually on a Wednesday evening, to do gate practice – the start was critical in a BMX race, and it was my killer weapon.

My mum got me my first bike, for a fiver from a church jumble sale, and my dad went to work upgrading it – pimping my ride, you could say. As a youngster my dad, David, had been quite into bikes himself, or, more accurately, into taking them apart and reassembling them. He built himself a bike out of old parts, which he used for his paper round in Edinburgh (he grew up there too), and when I became interested in bikes he was delighted, because it allowed him to indulge his passion. As I got better and better bikes – having broken the original one doing jumps on a home-made ramp in the garden – my dad's role as mechanic became even more important. Once a week he'd strip the bike down, clean all the parts, and put it back together, often using the kitchen table as his workbench. My mum, Carol, was remarkably understanding ... most of the time.

But at that time the BMX was vying with football for my attention and affection. George Watson's, a mixed-sex independent school, both primary and secondary, owed much of its reputation to its illustrious rugby-playing former pupils – the Hastings brothers, Gavin and Scott, foremost among them. I played football, which was, if not frowned upon, then not exactly a core part of the curriculum. But we were allowed to play for one year, before being introduced to rugby, and when I was eight I was part of the school team.

We were unusual – ahead of our time, perhaps – in that we had a female coach, even if Miss Paton probably assumed the position by default. I don't think any other teachers were particularly interested in football, so I think it fell to her to run the team. And yes, we had the mickey taken out of us by other teams for having a female coach in those unenlightened times, but she was clearly a fan of the beautiful game.

As were we too, but that didn't stop us from being rubbish. I cringe now in recalling some of the beatings we suffered at the hands of other schools. We weren't just beaten; we were usually – to use a good Scottish word – gubbed. A seven-nil defeat by Juniper Green sticks in my mind for some reason, but I don't know why, because that wasn't too unusual. There was only one team in the whole of Edinburgh that we seemed to be able to beat: poor, hapless Bonaly.

Despite all that, I loved football. I played midfield, though positions were fairly arbitrary. We played on these big old pitches, with no nets in the goal. It was ridiculous, no concession being made to the fact that we were about four feet tall, with tiny little legs. On the full-sized pitches we looked like the Lilliputians from *Gulliver's Travels*, and games would consist of the ludicrous spectacle of 20 eight-year-olds chasing the ball, like bees swarming around honey. It didn't matter what position you were supposed to play in, there was only one place to be – as close to the ball as possible. It was like one of those medieval games of street football, involving hundreds of people, a free-for-all with no organization. As for passing – forget it. Poor Miss Paton, who could often be seen enjoying a cigarette on the touchline, wasn't really able to impart any tactical instructions, or strategy – though I suppose you could say that we were allowed to express ourselves!

As well as playing myself, after a fashion, I became absolutely obsessed with Heart of Midlothian, the team that played about half a mile from my house, at Tynecastle Stadium. 'H-E-A … R-T-S, if you cannae spell it, then here's what it says … Hearts, Hearts, glorious Hearts,' as the club song goes. I was a committed Jambo – Jambo being an abbreviation of 'Jam Tarts', the team's other name – and occasionally went to games with the son of our local butcher, Bob the butcher. I didn't go with my dad, because he was a supporter of Hibs, or Hibernian, the other Edinburgh club. When I didn't go to games I'd listen on the radio, or watch the results coming in on the BBC's teleprinter at 4.45 in the afternoon.

The Hearts score that spewed out of that machine could make or break my Saturday evening. Not that, as a seven-year-old, I had particularly exciting plans most Saturday evenings.

The worst season was 1985/86, and it had a profound effect on me. I was nine going on ten, and at the zenith of my Hearts obsession. Now, anyone who knows anything at all about Scottish football, and especially Hearts, will not need to be told about the 1985/86 season. But for a nine-going-on-ten-year-old it was traumatic, to say the least.

The players, scores and games are burnt into my memory, engraved on my consciousness. To this day, I can still name the 1985/86 team: Henry Smith, Walter Kidd, Sandy Jardine, Craig Levein, Brian Whittaker, Gary Mackay, Neil Berry, Kenny Black, John Colquhoun, Sandy Clark, John Robertson.

These players, whom I wouldn't hesitate to call my boyhood idols – with John 'Robbo' Robertson, Gary Mackay and John Colquhoun particular favourites – took Hearts to the top of the Scottish Premier Division, and within one game of winning the league title for the first time in 26 years. There was no better time to be a Jambo. And, ultimately, no worse time. On the final day of the season Hearts were leading Celtic by two points. All they needed was a draw against mid-table Dundee. All they needed to do, most of us imagined, was to turn up.

In those days, it was two points, rather than three, for a win. Going into that final day, Hearts also had a goal-difference advantage on Celtic – they were on plus-28, with Celtic on plus-24. So if, in the worst-case scenario, Hearts lost and Celtic won their game against St Mirren, the Glasgow club would have to do so by at least three goals, unless Hearts lost by more than one. Got that?

On the day, Celtic won 5–0. And Hearts lost 2–0. The impossible, in other words, happened. And thousands of scarves and

T-shirts, already emblazoned with 'Heart of Midlothian, League Champions 1985–86', had to be discarded. Talk about snatching defeat from the jaws of victory. And don't even get me started on the conspiracy theories …

I was crushed – and if I hadn't been, then I would be a few days later, when Hearts faced Aberdeen in the Scottish Cup Final, only to lose 3–0. It was bordering on cruelty. And, to be honest, I don't know if I ever really rediscovered my passion for football. These days, I couldn't name a single player in the Hearts team, which is a shame, because I would have liked to keep my interest going. But I feel that football has changed so much, and that a lot of what was so great about it – games packed with genuine and committed fans watching players they could identify with – has disappeared.

If anything positive came of the experience of following Hearts through that rollercoaster season, then it was in the form of an important lesson, and a good one to learn when you're young. It could be summed up thus: don't get your hopes up; don't take anything for granted; expect nothing. These, as I would find out, would be useful mottos for any Hearts fan, or, for that matter, Scotland fan – when it came to either football or rugby.

There's a postscript to my interest in, or obsession with, that legendary Hearts team – and they remain club legends, in part because we're still waiting for a first league title since 1960.

Ten years later, John Robertson came into the Texaco garage where I, by now an 18-year-old about to head off to university, was working. 'Robbo' had been my ultimate hero, as he was to most Hearts fans – he is the most prolific goal-scorer in the club's history. And here he was walking across the forecourt and into my shop! I was completely star-struck, and as he walked towards me I realized something else: he was tiny. He could barely see over the counter.

Still, it was quite a thrill to meet my boyhood hero, even if I was a little over-awed. In my flustered state I think all I managed to say was, 'Pump four, mate? That'll be sixteen quid.'

After our brief and largely unsuccessful foray into football, rugby took over. Rugby was a big part of the culture of the school, though there was no particular pressure to play, and it wasn't cliquey, as I know it can be at some schools. Watson's was a nice school, with a good atmosphere. There was a real cross-section of people among the teachers and pupils, and I felt fortunate to go there.

My parents weren't wealthy – Dad working in the building industry, eventually as a chartered surveyor, Mum as a nurse – and I know they had to make sacrifices to send my sister, Carrie, and me there. Not that they were explicit about that to us, but we were made aware that we were lucky to go to a good school, and we both knew, I think, that we shouldn't waste the opportunities available to us there. I tried to do the best I could, because I was also aware, from a young age, that although sport seemed the most important thing in my life, ultimately education would be more important. After all, as I was later told by my school's careers adviser, 'You're not going to make a living out of sport.' (OK, so this turned out to be bad advice … but I wasn't to know it at the time – and neither, to be fair, was he.)

As far as the rugby went, there was no pressure to play, either from the teaching staff or from my peers. I suppose some implicit 'pressure' was applied by the roll call of illustrious rugby players among the school's former pupils, headed by the Hastings brothers. But there are other notable alumni, too, including Martin Bell, the Olympic skier, Martha Kearney, the broadcaster, the MPs Malcolm Rifkind, David Steel and Chris Smith, the mountaineer Robin Smith, the architect Sir Basil Spence, and Mylo, the singer-songwriter. A pretty eclectic bunch – and even the three politicians all represent different parties.

When I was at school, there were future Scottish rugby internationals Jamie Mayer, Marcus Di Rollo and Jason White, who would go on to captain the national side.

When I started playing rugby we were coached by Mr French, a Rangers fan, but still a good guy. In those days it was straight into the full game, no mini rugby to break us in. And initially it was similar to the football in many regards, with 15 of us all chasing after the ball. Loosely speaking there were backs and forwards, but we didn't stick too rigidly to that.

That said, I quickly settled on the position of stand-off, and I became the kicker. There was a lot of pressure involved in being the kicker. As with the football, there was no concession made to the fact we were small, with puny legs: we played on full-size pitches, with full-size goals. So kicking was a challenge, and my record wasn't quite as impressive as Chris Paterson's.

Like Paterson, I often managed 100 per cent, but that would be either 100 per cent over, or 100 per cent missed, with the ball invariably skidding along the ground. If I got the first conversion over, then I was fine; it would relax me, and I'd have a good game. But the kicking tended to mirror the game: if I kicked well, I played well; if I kicked badly, I found that it played on my mind and destroyed my game. I had some horrendous games.

It's funny, though, that kicking seems to be something that attracts the individualist. Think of Jonny Wilkinson and Paterson, and you tend to think of them obsessively practising the art of kicking, long after their team-mates have left the training pitch. Paterson has even spoken in the past about being given a hard time at school for spending so long on his own, practising his kicking. As an aspiring young rugby player I was similar, I suppose. If I'd kicked badly in a match, the following day would see me in one of our two local parks, with my dad, practising until it got dark – or until my dad got bored.

But the problem – and this would be something of a recurring theme for me in my sporting life – was that all that practice didn't really make much difference. Nobody ever really showed me *how* to kick. My dad knew the basics, but I had no one to help me with my technique. It's a bit like having a bad golf swing: you can practise as much as you like, but without expert help you're not going to get any better. It was also like golf in another sense, though. If I stuck one through the posts every once in a while it gave me a real buzz – and kept me practising just a little bit longer.

My kick-offs were just as erratic as my conversion attempts. I had this knack of picking out the biggest guy in the opposing team, and I'd be confronted with the sight of this – relatively speaking – huge second row catching it and running straight back towards me. Thus, within the first minute of most games, I'd suffer a big bang to the head. But I only suffered concussion on one occasion, in training. I'd broken through and was running towards the try line; and I thought I was clear, so I throttled back as I neared the posts, and was cruising towards the line, oblivious to the fact that an opposing winger had chased me all the way. He dived and clipped my ankles, and I, clutching the ball to my chest, hit the ground like a sack of spuds. The ball 'broke' my fall, but it caused a whiplash effect, my head bouncing off the ground. I had no idea where I was, what day it was or what I was doing.

Remarkably, the only other serious injury I suffered on the rugby pitch was a broken thumb. It was the first and only time my dad missed a game – an omen, perhaps. I was in fourth year at secondary school, it was on the eve of my first important exams, the Standard Grade (the Scottish equivalent to 'O' levels) prelims, when, in the early minutes of a game against Heriot's, I went to hand off a big prop and felt my thumb bend right back. It was excruciating, but I gave it a shake and carried on playing. Until the next scrum, when I received a pass. Suffice to say that the resulting scream could probably be heard by my parents, who were out of town for the weekend. The result was an arm in plaster from hand to elbow, which meant I was assigned a 'scribe' – some poor sixth year – for the exams. This wasn't as inconvenient as it sounds, because I remember my 'scribe' being pretty helpful with the multiple-choice questions on my Chemistry paper. If I said 'C' he'd say: 'Do you want to think about that r-e-a-l-l-y c-a-r-e-f-u-l-l-y?'

The high point of my rugby career came when I was selected to captain the Edinburgh Schools under-15 team against the North of Scotland. It felt amazing to pull on the navy blue kit – which bore an uncanny resemblance to the Scotland jersey – for a match played up in Inverness, and which we won, with me kicking three out of three conversions. Eat your heart out, Chris Paterson. It was quite an eye-opener playing with kids from other schools, and there was a seriousness of purpose about us; it came, I suppose, from the sense of pride, and responsibility, we all felt representing not only our schools, but our city. I remember a prop from Musselburgh displaying a particularly impressive attitude for a 14-year-old. After he scored the first try he jogged back with the ball, and threw it at me – hard – with the instruction: 'Make it count!' No wonder I felt such relief at seeing that first one sail through the posts. He was a big guy.

And I, by contrast, was small for my age. I had been big for my year in primary school, but found myself being overtaken by a lot of the others in high school. By third year, my last year in the rugby team, I was the second smallest in the team, which put me at a serious disadvantage. By the time I was 15 everyone had been growing and I hadn't really started – I was a little shrimp, a Smurf. Only the scrum-half was smaller than me, and I used to take a real pasting in games.

I loved going to rugby matches as well, and attended virtually all of Scotland's Five Nations home games, sitting in the schoolboy enclosure and then running on to the pitch at the end of the match. After one game against Ireland, which Scotland won, I was the first on to the pitch – a sign of my promise as a sprinter, possibly – and ran up to Damian Cronin, the big second row, as he was filmed leaving the pitch. I ended up on TV, very visible in my yellow anorak, with my mop of almost matching hair, patting Cronin on the back.

One of the greatest games in Scotland's history – and arguably my greatest sporting memory – was the 1990 Five Nations decider against England at Murrayfield, the national stadium that was a stone's throw from my house. It was the Grand Slam decider, with both teams in contention, but England almost certain to win. Or so they thought.

Scotland, led out by David Sole, set the tone by entering the field at a slow, almost funereal, pace. England, led by Will Carling, had looked super confident, but – as crazy as it sounds – the way that Scotland walked on to the pitch seemed to say: we're in charge. It gave them the impetus, and they sustained that in the game itself; you could see and almost feel how pumped up the Scotland team was as they got stuck into their opponents, and they won 13–7 to give Scotland the Calcutta Cup, Triple Crown and Grand Slam. All in all, it was a pretty good afternoon – one of the proudest in Scotland's sporting history.

Watching Sole's slow march gives me goosebumps, even now, but the irony was that, having attended so many games at Murrayfield, I missed that one. I had a ticket, but I had faced a huge dilemma: go to the game or compete in a BMX race in Paris. I opted to travel to France, but I watched the video of the game when I got home the next day, and watched it again and again, until the tape wore out.

Eighteen years later, I had the honour, and the unforgettable experience, of making my own appearance at Murrayfield for a Scotland international. It was the 2008 Autumn Test against the mighty All Blacks, who had just finished their haka when I was expected to perform the daunting task of delivering the match ball.

My only hope was that it would prove more successful than my previous 'guest' appearance on a rugby pitch, during the half-time break of an Edinburgh Gunners match in 2002, following my gold medal at the Manchester Commonwealth Games.

On that occasion, having been introduced and interviewed in the middle of the pitch, I was asked if I was a big rugby fan.

'Oh yeah,' I said. 'I played at school, went to Murrayfield a lot – I love it.'

'OK, Chris, a final question,' said the MC. 'Who are you supporting today?'

'Well, no surprises there, I'm an Edinburgh boy, so I'm backing THE REIVERS!'

I was hoping to get a big cheer from the 5,000 in the crowd. Instead, and much to my surprise, there was a stunned silence, then a chorus of boos. Unbeknown to me, six months earlier, the city's professional rugby club had changed its name from the Edinburgh Reivers to the Gunners. Which might sound innocuous enough, but in the highly politicized and heavily factionalized world of Scottish rugby, it was significant – they had only been the Reivers after an amalgamation, of sorts, with the Borders regional team. And now the name had been reassigned to the Borders;

so 'the Reivers' referred not to Edinburgh, but to their bitterest rivals. What I had done was a bit like shouting 'Come on, City!' at Old Trafford – though fortunately rugby supporters are a little less partisan, and a lot more forgiving.

There was no such *faux pas* at Murrayfield in November 2008. Wearing a Scotland shirt with '3' and 'Hoy' on the back, and with my three Olympic gold medals hanging from my neck, I was introduced to the crowd and walked into a wall of noise, plonking the ball down in the middle, then turning to the Scotland team and making what I hoped would be a series of rousing, fist-clenched gestures. I may even have shouted 'Go onnnnnnnn!' or something similarly encouraging. There was nothing planned or rehearsed about it; it was completely spontaneous, inspired by the noise of the crowd and the exhilarating sense of anticipation, expectation and sheer drama inside Murrayfield Stadium. It didn't work, unfortunately – Scotland lost, after a decent performance – but the response from the crowd had a similar effect on me to that of David Sole's famous slow march: the hairs on the back of my neck stood up. I was stunned. In all my previous visits to Murrayfield, most of them in the schoolboy enclosure, I could never have imagined that one day a cyclist would receive such a reception.

My souvenir Scotland shirt now hangs in a frame in my house, a memento of an unforgettable experience, and a reminder of my boyhood dream of one day playing for my country.

The time has probably come to admit that it is the closest I'll ever get to fulfilling it.

CHAPTER 3

Smells of Sandwiches
and Mars Bars

Yes, my childhood revolved around sport – so far, adulthood hasn't been much different – and bikes were the dominant theme. My BMX career, which started when I was seven, ran along parallel lines to my football, then rugby, and almost outlasted both. I retired from BMX when I was 14, and stopped playing rugby the following year.

But my burgeoning interest in BMX coincided with a very difficult time for my family, following the deaths, within a week of each other, of my grandma and grandpa – my dad's parents. To appreciate how profound an effect this had on me, not to mention my dad, mum and sister Carrie, I should describe our living arrangements, which were fairly unusual. We lived in the top-floor flat of a townhouse in Murrayfield, a nice suburb of Edinburgh, and, in the style of a big Italian family (not that we have a drop of Italian blood, as far as I know), we shared the house with my grandparents, who lived downstairs in a separate flat with a shared entrance. In other words, to enter our house I had to go through my grandparents' front door, which meant I saw them all the time.

It was the type of house, in the kind of setting, that presented myriad opportunities for boys' own-style adventures. There was a decent-sized garden at the back, with a disused railway line over the wall at the end; a place that was, inevitably, out of bounds. I was always warned not to play on the railway line, that it was 'dangerous,' which naturally heightened my curiosity. Back in those days it was little more than a stretch of wasteland, overgrown and quite wild, though the platform from the old railway station, which was right behind our house, remained. These days, it has been tarmaced and is a popular cycle track, though I'm sure 8-year-old kids are still told to stay away. When I wanted to get round this rule, I didn't clamber over the wall at the end of the garden – that was too obvious – instead, I sneaked around the side of the house, entering by the old platform, with my sister sometimes a partner-in-crime and willing accomplice in the illicit adventure.

Poor Carrie. She is two years older than me, and could be a little bit bossy, as elder sisters are prone to be towards baby brothers; and I could be a little brat, as baby brothers are prone to be towards elder sisters. We always got on well and still do, but I could be a bit sneaky as a young kid and I would frequently land her in trouble. If she was being bossy, and I was winding her up by resisting her commands, I had a knack of being able to make her snap at precisely the moment that Mum or Dad would appear on the scene. In they'd walk, to Carrie screaming and shouting, and me sitting there looking put-upon, an imaginary halo floating above my head. Still, Carrie and I were always playing together, and we had a lot of fun, especially in the garden, and up at the top of the road – where we *were* allowed to play – in an area we called 'the Conkers,' a clearing with huge chestnut trees. As we got older Carrie and I only became closer and closer, even as our own interests diverged. She was more into art than sport, and she loved reading, going on eventually to work in publishing. She was always highly intelligent, and became 'Dux' of our school, though, despite her talents, she has never seemed to have any ego at all. That can be seen in her support for me throughout my cycling career, which has been incredible, from attending all my major events, to, afterwards, spending hours producing beautiful albums of the press cuttings and photographs. These are no Pritt Stick jobs – they are stunning coffee table-sized books, and priceless mementos which have to be seen, and flicked through, to be fully appreciated.

My parents bought the family house in 1969, when they were newly married – and they remain there to this day, forty years on. It has proved a solid investment, then, though their friends questioned that at the time, since it meant – according to my dad – that they couldn't afford furniture and didn't go out for more than a year. After a year, so the family legend goes, they bought a fridge and went to the cinema. Or should that be 'the pictures'?

The story of how they bought the house was unusual, too. It was owned by a wealthy friend of my grandma – my dad's mum – who allowed my parents to live in the top-floor flat while they were looking for property; the arrangement was for six months. But in the midst of that she decided to sell, and offered them first refusal. The house was valued at around £5,000 and my parents, who had fallen for it, really pushed the boat out to buy it.

The house was far too big for the pair of them, but, with the shared entrance, it was impossible to rent out one of the floors. A solution presented itself a year later, when my dad's parents, Jerry and Mary, lost the house in which they lived. My grandpa was the manager of a grocery depot, and he and my grandma lived in a flat above the warehouse, which was in Leith, and thus explains my dad's allegiance to the Leith football team, Hibernian. The flat came with the job, and when grandpa retired, in 1970, they had to move. So it was that they came to live with my parents in Murrayfield, occupying the first floor, while we – not that I was born quite yet – lived upstairs.

Having my grandparents downstairs was fantastic, the perfect scenario for a young kid. There was the security aspect; if we were playing in the garden, or on the street, they could keep an eye on us (most of the time), as well as my parents. And of course, it meant I saw them all the time, frequently as I rushed past after coming in their – and our – front door, before dashing up the internal stair that led into our flat. After dinner I'd often sneak downstairs for some biscuits from my grandma, though my abiding memory of evenings with my grandparents was the intense heat. Like a lot of older people, they had the heating up to the maximum, and their living room was like a sauna. When I went back upstairs it wasn't the crumbs around my mouth that gave away the fact I'd been scoffing biscuits, it was my rosy cheeks.

I loved having my grandparents downstairs, though, inevitably, being so young, I didn't fully appreciate how much I loved having them downstairs until they were gone. They died, as I have said, within a week of each other in 1984, my grandpa first and then my grandma, when I was eight. It was my first experience of dealing with a family death, and the sadness and sense of upheaval were exacerbated by the fact we were so close, in both senses of the word. Coming home from school and not passing my grandparents on my way upstairs was very strange and a hard thing to deal with; it meant everything changed instantly, and in more ways that I anticipated.

It was a tough time for my parents, but they also had a pressing, and practical, problem: what to do with the house. It was too big – and too expensive – for my parents, Carrie and me, so they had to sell the bottom flat. The problem, however, was the shared front door.

My dad worked in the building trade, having not gone to university but straight into an apprenticeship. Eventually he did go to university, in his fifties, to do a surveying degree – he actually graduated the year before me – but when I was in primary school he ran a building company, with a team of three or four builders, though I think he did a lot of the work himself. He was very hands-on, and he's got great practical skills. The trouble is – and I hope he won't mind me saying – it takes him an age to get things done. He is great at taking on jobs, especially for other people; he can't say no. If he has a fault, it's that he over commits, and takes on more than he can manage.

When my grandparents died business for my dad was far from booming: it was a tough time for industry, the property industry especially. So my dad decided to take a year out, more or less, and take on a big project: turning the house into two flats, with separate front doors.

I can understand if my mum felt some trepidation – for the reasons discussed above, and because, though he did jobs for other people to perfection, our house was often a bit of a building site by contrast. Still, in the aftermath of his parents' death, he got started on this project. First he removed the internal staircase, which led up to our flat. Then he built an external staircase, with a new front door. Where the internal stair had been, he built two new rooms. And then, to make the ground-floor flat attractive to prospective buyers, he built a double garage, which – much to my disappointment – reduced the garden by about half.

It was like a *Grand Designs* project, and I can imagine Kevin McCloud, had the TV programme existed back then, wandering into our house-cum-building site, saying: 'I just wonder if he's taken on too much here.' It really was like a construction site for much of that year, and at one point the plumbing was disconnected upstairs. Initially we still had a toilet downstairs, but then that was cut off, too. For about three days we had to visit the Texaco garage at the bottom of the road, each time with some spurious excuse for returning, in order to use the toilet there. On the plus side, we were never out of milk, since that was the standard purchase to justify all the toilet trips. After the best part of a year, though, my dad had managed to convert the house into two separate flats. And 25 years later, as he likes to joke, the job is … very close to completion.

Mum, meanwhile, was a night owl. As a nurse she worked the night shift in the sleep department at the Edinburgh Royal Infirmary, which meant she left at eight in the evening and got home at seven in the morning. She'd sleep during the day, and, when I came in from school at about four I'd put the kettle on, make her a cup of tea and wake her up. If that makes me sound like a model child, I should confess that, lurking towards the forefront of my mind, was the thought of dinner. I don't know how Mum did it, but she would get up, do the housework, make our dinner, and then go back to work: that was her life, really. Carrie was good at helping around the house, but it makes me a bit embarrassed to think of my contribution, given how hard my mum and dad worked. If I picked my scattered clothes up off my bedroom floor, that was me mucking in and doing my bit.

I know that I had a privileged upbringing – not financially, but in a far more important way, with my family providing the most stable foundation. We weren't exactly the Waltons – more like the Simpsons – and there'd be nagging and arguments, but they would blow over, and it was a happy home; or, for the first eight years of my life, two homes, each as happy as the other, and one considerably hotter.

* * *

It was around the time of my grandparents' death that I began to get really serious about BMXing. Though I was serious about football and rugby, my commitment to BMX was on another level. It had to be, because what started as a bit of fun on my pimped-up old bike from the church jumble sale soon developed to the point where I was no longer just riding local tracks, and competing against riders from the Edinburgh area, but joining sponsored teams, riding fancier bikes, and travelling first to England, then to Europe, in search of ever more serious competition.

The race that sticks most firmly in the memory is the 1986 world championships in Slough, near London. Glamorous, eh? Slough these days stands almost as a euphemism for dreary and boring, a suburban town where nothing much happens, thanks to it being the setting for *The Office*, Ricky Gervais's satirical comedy, though the town had an image problem long before that, the poet John Betjeman writing: 'Come friendly bombs, and fall on Slough! It isn't fit for humans now ...'

Well, Slough will always evoke entirely different emotions, and more colourful memories, in me. As far as I was concerned, Slough in 1986 was the height of glamour, and the centre of the universe, because it hosted the biggest BMX world championships in the sport's young history. Around 1,600 riders – many of them having travelled over from America – descended on Slough for the meeting; there were 64 in my under-11 age group alone, which is a figure worth reflecting on. Could any other sport attract such a large field for an international event in such a young age category? But these were the glory days of BMX. If the *E.T.* chase scene had reflected this latest craze, then it had also acted as a catalyst, because BMX grew hugely in popularity from the mid to the late 1980s, before hitting a sharp decline.

For me, those 1986 championships were a defining moment. They gave me a glimpse of what might be possible and shaped my desire to carry on; to up the ante and see how far I could go. I'd been racing for two years, and doing quite well, but Slough was my first international race. I was going well; I could feel it, and I felt confident as I lined up, alongside seven fellow ten-year-olds in my heat. I won, qualifying for the eighth-finals (the stage before the quarter-finals), and then won again, going through to the quarters. And I breezed through them, finishing second – with the top four going through.

I was in the semi-finals of the world championships. Now it was really serious, because to make the final was the big thing. And here's one reason why: all the finalists would have single-digit number-plates (i.e. 1–8, as opposed to some messy double- or triple-digit number) at the following year's championships. There was huge kudos in that.

Let me describe a BMX race. Or, rather, let the eight-year-old me describe a BMX race (copyright: my school jotter from p4M, mistakes as original):

My Weekend

I enjoy doing BMX. BMX stands for Bicycle Motocross. I race on my bike, there are jumps you go over and the corners are banked. Scotia is my favourite BMX shop [and also my sponsors, so I already understood that it was a good idea to namedrop my sponsors at every opportunity]. Yesterday I went racing at Glasgow. Gate two seemed to be putting me into third place (the gate is a thing at the start wich you put your front wheel against and somone says 'Riders Ready, Pedels Ready, Go' and pushes the gate down). You pick a card and it will have a number, 1, 2, 3, 4, 5 or 6. So I got third. Scotia are taking me training on Thursdays. I have done a picture of a track on the next page.

Just for the record, this got a big red tick and 'very good'.

Giving another flavour of the sport, a few pages later, under the heading 'My Favourite Place', I find another tenuous excuse to shoe-horn my obsession into my school work (see also 'My Holiday', and numerous other 'My Weekends'):

> My favourite place is at the Derby BMX track. You get to watch the famous riders and get their autographs. There is a commentator who tells you who is in the lead over a microphone. When you are on the start you feel very nervous! Once you are racing you can not really hear the people cheering because you are concentrating so much on the race. There is a smell of sandwiches and Mars bars [do these actually smell? I think I meant burgers and hot dogs, which, when I smell them now, evoke the BMX races of my childhood]. When I crash, if I fall on my mouth I have a mouth guard but dirt can get in your mouth. It tastes horrible! Especially when the ground is wet!

Only a tick and 'good' this time. Obviously not my best work.

A BMX track is ridiculously short (this is me writing as a 33-year-old again, in case you weren't sure) – only around 400 metres long, sometimes shorter. It's over within 30 seconds. You line up eight abreast, behind the start gate, feeling unbelievably nervous. It's intense. Before you are traffic lights, which give the signal to start.

When the gate drops, you're away. 'On the "B" of the bang', as Linford Christie would say; or, perhaps more accurately in this instance, the 'G' of the green light. You start in lanes, but as soon as the gate drops it's a free-for-all and you're into the first bend after around 30 metres. Often this will be a ninety-degree bend, with a U-bend after that, and three or four jumps located in between. It can be physical – it's not officially a contact sport, but in fact it is, so you're jostling with your rivals to hold position, and fighting for the best line into the corner.

But the start determines so much, which is why I used to travel the 15 miles to Livingston one evening a week, to practise on the only track in the Edinburgh area with a proper start gate. That wasn't all: I would also practise on the street outside our home every evening. A bit like the goal-kicking for rugby, it was something I could practise on my own, honing my reflexes, experimenting with different pedal start positions, and working on accelerating my bike up to speed as quickly as possible, using lampposts on the street as markers for distance. And all that practice seemed to pay off: starts became my strength, my killer weapon.

So, back to Slough – where, incidentally, the other riders included Iwan Thomas, the future 400-metre runner, and, in my age group, a young German called Jan van Eijden, who, 20 years later, would become my sprint coach (see chapter one), as well as numerous other future track cycling champions, among them Australian Darryn Hill, the 1995 world sprint champion, and my future friend and team-mate, Craig MacLean. By the semi-final stage Jan had been knocked out – he only made it to the quarters, which shows the depth of talent there was in BMXing, given the career he went on to have as a cyclist. But I was still in the competition, preparing for my biggest moment – and with confidence, because I had progressed pretty smoothly to this point.

Bang! The start gate dropped and the race started in the usual frantic fashion. Four from the semi would qualify for the final, and I made a reasonable start, lying third going around the second U-bend. Coming out of that last corner, still in third, and, with a place in the final in my sights, we negotiated the final jump. Get over that OK and I'm there: in the final. But disaster struck. Hitting the ground after the jump, my foot slipped off the pedal, and I crashed onto the crossbar – which hurt, but wasn't as painful as it would have been had I been a little older than 10.

But it was incredibly bad timing, and there followed one of the most frustrating experiences I've ever had in a bike race. I was still moving, but somehow couldn't reconnect my foot and pedal; despite my desperate attempts, the pedal remained empty. And the more I panicked, the less likely I was to rectify this situation. It's a bit like when you're really late and in a hurry, trying to unlock your door – that's when you're most likely to fumble and drop your keys.

Paradoxically, time seemed both to stand still and speed up. As I tried to focus on getting my foot back on the pedal, one rider came past me on my left. Then, around 10 metres from the line, a second passed me on my right. My slip of the foot had cost me two places. It had also cost me my place in the final. I crossed the line fifth, just out of the qualification places.

I was inconsolable. And I couldn't get the race out of my head, re-running it over and over again – not only in my head, but on TV. One of the dads had recorded it on an early video camera, which was about the size of an outside broadcast unit, with the battery in a backpack that wouldn't have looked out of place on a week-long safari. His video of the race was a bit shaky, but I sat and watched it again and again, thinking: maybe this time my foot won't slip off the pedal. It was a source of huge regret for me. I had really, really, *really* wanted to make the final. Not just for the kudos of the single-number bib at the following year's championships, but because each of the finalists was presented with a small trophy. And I loved getting trophies.

After the race I was in tears. My dad tried to console me, telling me I'd ridden a good race, that I'd been unlucky and would have lots more opportunities in the future. Dad came to all my races – despite, for quite some time, being in the midst of his *Grand Designs* project back home – and he couldn't have been more supportive, which was in contrast to some of the parents you'd see at these races. While I was crying because I was disappointed, others cried because their parents put pressure on them and reacted badly when they didn't live up to the expectations they had for them. I saw kids being smacked on the head, their parents shouting, 'What did you do that for?' Then you'd see the bottom lip begin to tremble, and the tears start.

As we drove home from Slough, my dad and I discussed the race, and I came to appreciate that it hadn't all been down to bad luck; that I wasn't necessarily a victim of outrageous misfortune. The main reason my foot had come off the pedal was because I could see the finishing line, and thought I was home and dry. I allowed myself to be distracted, my technique fell apart for a split second, and the error followed; a bit like dropping a pass in rugby due to taking your eye off the ball.

I was 10, so none of this offered too much consolation at the time – and it didn't stop me torturing myself by repeatedly watching the video of the race once I got home. However, I can see now that my dad helped me to analyse things rationally and logically, rather than seeing myself as the victim of a terrible injustice. It was about taking responsibility, I suppose, which starts with taking responsibility for yourself, and not looking for someone or something else to blame – opponents, team-mates, the pitch, track, referee, ball, weather, misplacing your lucky socks – when things went wrong.

One of the other dads who helped run the team I was in, Scotia BMX, has said that I stood out from a lot of the other kids for being quite rational rather than emotional; and for analysing races in a rational way, rather than kicking and screaming and throwing my toys out of the pram. Well, yes and no. I would say I was – and still am – very emotional. But

I also think that I appreciated fairly early in my sporting career that your own performance is all that counts, and that winning isn't the be-all and end-all, because there's sod all you can do about your opponent. If you do the best ride of your life and come fifth ... there's no point being unhappy with that, is there?

As well as being my (more than willing) mechanic, my dad and the other dad I've just mentioned, George Swanson, helped organize the Scotia club's training sessions. My dad thought a lot about training, and about ways we could replicate race efforts in practice. He and George used to take us to the closest beach to Edinburgh, Portobello. It wasn't exactly the Côte d'Azur, but it was fringed by a long, wide footpath, which was excellent for training. They would line us up, six abreast, and have us race each other for 200 metres, before handing over to someone else, like a relay race. You'd rest a bit and go again – flat out. We'd be on our knees by the end of it, thanks mainly to there being a serious competitive dimension to this training, but it was a great way of raising our pain threshold, making these maximum efforts with nothing at stake but childhood pride.

Yet perhaps the most valuable lesson I learned from BMX-ing came from never being the best. Even as I progressed, there was always someone better than me – a target for me to aim at. I saw a lot of kids who would just sling their leg over a bike and win. Often it was because they had simply grown faster than the rest of us, but in some cases it was because they had outstanding natural talent, which owed nothing at all to training, or hours of hard work.

It was the same in rugby. I remember that one of the rival Edinburgh schools (who on one occasion beat us 54–0) had a winger with astonishing speed, and the ability to execute a deadly sidestep. This guy was the most naturally gifted player I ever shared a rugby pitch with ... and I think he packed it in at 15. I had been convinced he'd be a Scotland star of the future, but he disappeared and I never heard of him again.

I imagine that he, like other prodigies I have come across, lost interest because it all came too easily. They had so much natural talent that there was never any correlation, for them, between hard work and achievement. Often, such talent is all you need as a youngster – but as you get older, and the competition gets stiffer, talent will only take you so far. At some point, you have to start working, and as people catch up, you have to work harder. Which can be hard to accept if you've never made the link between hard work and success.

For this reason I think that 'talent' is vastly overrated in sport. I am thinking especially of power and endurance sports, but the idea that even tennis players and golfers such as Roger Federer or Tiger Woods are the best in the world simply because they are the most talented is ludicrous; they have talent, of course, but they have maximized it by hard work. It's why, particularly when it comes to young athletes, I think the term 'potential' has far greater relevance and value than 'talent'. Talent, as far as I am concerned, can in some cases be a nebulous, even damaging, notion; it can be a hindrance rather than a help.

Winning – and I did win from time to time – is a buzz, no doubt about it. But I got almost the same buzz from imagining how hard work might translate into success in the future. Even back then, I saw sport as a process, with the rewards coming at the end of it. It was my potential, rather than my talent, that excited and inspired me, driving me on.

The year after Slough, 1987, was another big one for me. I was fifth in the European championships in Genk, Belgium – the best ride of my BMX career, I'd say. But I had a bit of a disaster at the world championships in Orlando, going out at the quarter-final stage in the under-12 age group.

*   *   *

Genk, Orlando ... Slough – international travel was one of the aspects of BMXing that I most enjoyed; these trips could be eye-opening and even educational. Many of them were undertaken by car, sometimes just my dad and me in his old Citroen BX with its hydraulic suspension, and a mattress in the back of the car for me to sleep on.

We had some unforgettable experiences away from the BMX track. I remember driving to the World Games in Karlsruhe in Germany, and stopping en route at the Berlin Wall. My dad explained what it was, and what it stood for, and I stood and stared and struggled to comprehend that there were people on the other side who were trapped there, like animals in a cage, and shot dead if they tried to escape. The Berlin Wall came down about six months later, news which I could relate to and understand far better than if it had just been pictures on TV or in newspapers.

I also raced at Aalborg, in Denmark, at Perpignan, in France, and at an amusement park in Holland with the very Dutch-sounding name of Slagharen. Slagharen, which was like a Dutch Butlins, had an amazing track, probably the best in Europe. What I remember most about Slagharen, though, is the chalets we stayed in, which had paper-thin walls. And I remember this detail so vividly because of an incident involving a slightly older guy in our club, a 19-year-old student known to all of us as 'Voucher Man', because he seemed to have money-off vouchers for everything. He was a very nice guy, but I suppose you could say he was the archetypal stingy Scot; he was always dictating that we had to go to a certain place because he could get 2 per cent off, or a free medium drink if you bought four main courses, or something. You get the idea.

One night in Slagharen, Voucher Man announced he was going to eat in, while gently mocking us for choosing to waste our money in a costly restaurant. He had all the ingredients to make chilli, he said. So we went out and left him to it, returning a couple of hours later to retire to our beds and go to sleep.

We didn't sleep for long. Within an hour the chalet, with its paper-thin walls, reverberated to the unmistakable sound of Voucher Man's bowels emptying, in a hurried fashion; it sounded like a flock of pigeons were taking off in there. He spent the night shitting into a bucket, while the rest of us pissed ourselves laughing.

The other thing about Slagharen, which hosted the European championships, was that it had a freestyle area, with two half-pipes. I was desperate to play on these ramps, but Dad advised me not to. 'You're here to race,' he said. 'You don't want to tire yourself out on those things; they're dangerous, and you're not a freestyler ...'

I wasn't an especially rebellious child, but on this occasion I ignored him. Well, all my mates were having a go. And it did look like good fun. As long as you knew what you were doing, and had the skills to pull off such stunts ...

Which, as it happens, I didn't. But up the ramp I went, before swooping down, and back up, preparing for an aerial manoeuvre; into the air I soared, turning my bike and preparing to re-enter the ramp ... or not. I overshot it, missing the ramp altogether and finding myself briefly suspended in mid-air – a bit like the moment when Wile E. Coyote, in the *Roadrunner* cartoons, realizes he has run straight off the edge of the cliff, and, with his legs still going through the motions, waits for gravity to kick in.

I didn't have the proper kit on for freestyling – I didn't even have a helmet on. So when I hit the ground, with a thud, I ... well, actually I felt nothing, because I was knocked out. As I came to, I realized that my face had taken the brunt of it, the left side covered in a livid red graze. But my main concern was what my dad was going to say.

To make matters worse, I had hardly any time to prepare for gate practice, as you were allocated only limited time to practise on the track ahead of the next day's races. I met up again with my dad, whose reaction – apparently – was mild; taking one look at my damaged face, he probably figured that I'd learnt my lesson without him having to reinforce it. Meanwhile, I apologized profusely – much later he said that I had spent about half an hour 'havering', which is a Scottish expression for talking nonsense – and got on with my gate practice. I must still have been quite badly concussed at this point, though, because when I returned to the track the next day I couldn't remember anything about the course. It was the strangest thing: I had no recollection at all of the previous day. Sitting in the gate, waiting for the start, I might as well have been looking at the surface of the moon for all that I could remember about the previous day's practice session.

I have a picture of that race – there's a great view of the scab forming on my face – which was won, as many were, by a Dutch rider known as 'The Beast'. We were 11 at the time, but he was about six foot two and had a full moustache, having hit puberty when he was nine. I exaggerate, but only a little.

At 14, having committed seven years to BMX, I retired. The realization that I wasn't really enjoying it any more crept up on me gradually, and had much to do, I suspect, with the fact that many of my peers were also drifting away. It was 1990, and the bottom was about to fall out of the sport, in Europe at least. There remained a healthy scene in the United States, and that continues to this day, but by my mid-teens BMXing seemed passé, a – ahem – young man's game, and about as cool as Bucks Fizz.

It was time to get out. But I look back now with great fondness on my BMX days, even if the sport that provided my introduction to cycling would inadvertently, 15 years later, cause me great heartache.

These days, thanks to its inclusion in the Olympic programme, which came into effect in Beijing, BMX is enjoying something of a renaissance. The heartache I mentioned above owes to the fact that the inclusion of BMX in 2005 meant the axing of another discipline – my event, the kilometre. But there are no hard feelings: I maintain that it is the perfect sport for kids, and the perfect introduction to cycling, especially at a time when the roads are becoming more dangerous. It is also a great sport for adults – and the top BMXers are incredible athletes.

Former BMX riders now excel in all cycling disciplines, from my GB team-mate Jamie Staff on the track to Robbie McEwen, the Tour de France cyclist, on the road. What all of us former BMXers have in common is confidence in our ability to handle a bike – watch Robbie McEwen pull a wheelie, as he usually does at the top of the final mountain pass of the Tour, and you will see what I mean.

I'm pretty sure the boom days of the 1980s will never be repeated. But I am glad the BMX hasn't gone the way of those other great inventions of the eighties, the ZX Spectrum and Sinclair C5, and disappeared without trace.

CHAPTER 4

'That Can't Be Good for You'

I started getting a bit of stick from my mates at school. Nothing malicious: just low-level, good-natured mickey-taking. I remember an art class in first year of secondary school where I was relentlessly slagged off for being a 'BMX bandit'.

I like to think that things have changed a little now, with cycling more mainstream and not perceived as being too weird a pastime, but traditionally the sport has attracted a lot of individualistic characters. As a kid, you would generally follow your mates into team sports – football and rugby. I did these too, but the fact that I was a cyclist singled me out a little from many of my schoolmates. I remember Graeme Obree, the former world record holder and champion, talking in his autobiography about cycling as a form of escapism, because he was bullied at school. I think that for him cycling was a way of justifying why he wasn't out kicking a ball with his mates, or hanging around a shopping mall. Saying 'I'm going out on my bike' is a bit like getting the first punch in; it's a good excuse for being by yourself.

Fortunately I didn't have the kind of negative experiences that Graeme had; I certainly wasn't forced into cycling because of bullying, and I wasn't bullied on account of the fact that I was a cyclist. All the same, by the time I got to secondary school, BMX had had its day. It was seen by most people as a kids' sport – and there was nothing worse than that as you embarked on life in secondary school. One former classmate – Murdo, who is still a friend – has since claimed that any success I've had on a bike is all down to him, since he 'convinced' me to give up BMXing. He wasn't the only one who applied peer pressure. The truth was, however, that it wasn't anyone else's opinions that mattered; I had just had enough of BMX racing and wasn't enjoying it like I used to.

I still loved bikes, so I transferred my allegiance to the knobbly-tyred older brother of the BMX: the mountain bike. Mountain bikes were new, and although perhaps not 'cool' in the eyes of *all* my classmates, they were a bit cool, or at least grown up. And in Edinburgh we had a huge natural asset in the Pentland Hills, more or less on my doorstep. My first mountain bike outings – they felt more like expeditions at that age – were into those hills, and they have left me with some fabulous memories. In the early 1990s, when I first tried it, I would often head up there with my dad, who was quite fit, though I always managed to drop him on the climbs. It was part sport, part exploration, but what I loved most were the descents, which felt like the reward for all the hard work of climbing – it was as though you had to earn your fun. When I got home, there was another reward, which was eating. I developed a ravenous hunger when mountain biking, and devoured mountains of food after rides.

These days, when I'm travelling between Manchester and Edinburgh, as I frequently do, I pass the Pentlands as I drive into, or out of, my home city. It can prompt me to gaze a little dreamily at them (while keeping my eyes on the road, I should add, to reassure my mum, as well as any traffic police operating in the area). From the road they are just benign-

looking lumps; the kind of rolling, rounded hills that are typical of southern Scotland. Further to the north, especially in
the Highlands, the mountains are more rocky and jagged,
often looking like mini-Alps. But don't let the apparently
gentle slopes of the Pentlands fool you: they are steep and
rugged in places, and contain a labyrinth of hidden glens,
meandering and often quite gnarly paths, and trickling burns
(Scottish for small rivers).

It's a paradise for mountain biking, and I loved it. Unfortunately, it's also pretty incompatible with my career in track
cycling, because of the risk of injury. On a mountain bike, if
you don't crash on a fairly regular basis then you have to ask
yourself if you're trying hard enough ... so it's difficult to do
now, though it is something I intend taking up again when I
retire from track cycling. But I won't be racing. Definitely not
racing.

When I was getting into mountain biking, in my early to
mid teens, a series of cross-country races were staged in the
Pentlands. They were gruelling tests of endurance and
strength on courses that often got churned up; you'd finish
looking as though you'd been down a coal mine. They were
tough races, and they pushed me to levels I didn't know I
could reach. The contrast to BMX races, those 30-second
blasts, could hardly have been greater.

I think I realized, pretty early on in my mountain bike
career, that I'd never be brilliant at this sport. But I did win
one race. And it was an uphill race, bizarrely enough. It was at
Innerleithen, about 30 miles south of Edinburgh: a mass-start
event that went straight up a hill like a ramp and seemed to
get steeper and steeper. Clearly organized by sadists.

Not surprisingly, the front group was rapidly whittled
down. This was the kind of race where the action is at the
back rather than the front, with people hanging on for dear
life, until they can hang on no more. The mental battle is a

big part of it – when your legs are screaming, your lungs burning, your brain telling you to stop, and you have to dig deeper and deeper. With such efforts, the physical limits lie somewhere beyond the mental limits.

Eventually there were only five of us left, at which point one guy attacked, jumping clear as though going for the finish. Nobody was mad enough to try to match his pace, preferring instead to watch him gradually slowing down in the distance and then 'blowing up' altogether. The words they use in cycling to denote that moment when you hit the wall – 'blow up' and 'die' being the most common – say it all, really. There is no return, especially on a hill. When this guy ran out of gas on the hill he became almost stationary – we had to avoid him as we went past, as if he was a bollard in the road.

Then I attacked. I attacked! And nobody came with me. As ever, the effort started to really hurt after about 15 seconds, but I managed to keep a bit in reserve and avoid the fate of the earlier attacker. I won on my own, which, looking back now, seems hard to believe. Let me write that again: I won a hill climb. This, appropriately enough, represented the summit of my achievements as a mountain biker. I'd rather not dwell on other races, typically longer races, following which – as my dad likes to tell everyone – he would be waiting in the car park, thinking I must have suffered some mechanical or other disaster, only to see me finally haul my exhausted body to the finish, well after everyone else had packed up and gone home.

At around the same time, there was another sport that was beginning to exercise me, in every sense of the word. Rowing. I still enjoyed rugby, but the increasing number of injuries I was suffering persuaded me eventually to give it up, and rowing was the sport that replaced it at school – cycling, unfortunately, not being part of the curriculum.

One of my best mates at school, Grant Florence, had started rowing, but there weren't many guys who did it. For some reason it was seen at my school as a girls' sport; male crews weren't really encouraged. Obviously, for us male rowers, this wasn't an entirely undesirable situation. But that isn't why I was attracted to it, honest.

Seriously, it isn't. If it had simply been a ruse to spend time splashing about on the water with the girls, then I wouldn't have lasted very long, because this was a brutal sport. It was rowing rather than cycling, in fact, that opened my eyes to how hard it is possible to work at something. There was also a bit of family history in rowing. My uncle, John Poole, who's married to my dad's elder sister Joan, rowed in the 'B' crew for Oxford in the Oxford–Cambridge Boat Race in the 1950s. At 6ft 8in he's a good build for it.

Where we trained, the Union Canal, is a seriously thin strip of water. In places it is not much wider – or less narrow – than the boat. A fractional misjudgement can cause the oar to hit the towpath, perhaps taking a runner's legs from under him, or swiping an unsuspecting cyclist from their bike. Not that this has ever happened, to the best of my knowledge, but you feel it might. The Union Canal runs through the centre of Edinburgh and is a popular spot most days with crews of rowers.

In terms of location the canal was ideal for us, the boathouse being just a stone's throw from the school. There were other advantages, too. Apart from when it iced over, the canal wasn't much affected by the weather. Whereas the big rivers might arguably have offered more in the way of 'proper' rowing, and more room to manoeuvre, they were too choppy to row on when it was wild and windy, as it often can be in Scotland. Plus, on those big tidal rivers there were only certain times when you could row, and I heard, without feeling any envy, stories of other crews having to be out on the river as early as 6 a.m. At least we could row at any time.

We were out on the canal in all conditions. And I loved the whole scene, the social aspect, the camaraderie and the sense of being part of a committed team. You'd go down to the boat club before training and hang around, chatting to the boat manager, who happened to be Grant, the friend who got me into rowing in the first place. That was another thing: you were given responsibilities and jobs; I became club treasurer. George, who was in overall charge of the boathouse, tried to suss you out, I think, and if you passed the test you were trusted with the keys, given jobs to do, that kind of thing. Boat club treasurer was 'a thankless task', as was noted in a school report card at the time by one of my teachers, who added: 'So I thank him now – on paper!'

The teachers were less impressed by one incident, for which I must hold my hands up. We were driving back to Edinburgh after a day's training at Strathclyde Park when I found myself in possession of a super-soaker pump-action water machine-gun; a real beast of a weapon, which could fire jets of water up to about 30 feet. It was a hot summer's day, we were hanging out of the windows of our minibus, and as we approached Edinburgh, and slowed down for a roundabout, we began to draw alongside a sports car with its roof down. It was irresistible.

My weapon was loaded and I gave it both barrels: not just a squirt of water, but a proper skoosh. OK, it was immature and it can't have been pleasant for the driver, but all I can offer in my defence is that there is something in the Scottish psyche that disapproves of ostentatious displays of wealth, or flashiness. Soft-top cars fall into that category.

Monday morning came, however, and there was a letter waiting for me in registration. The head teacher was away, but I was to go and see his deputy, Mr Cowan. I knew it was about the water pistol incident. I had had a phone call the previous evening from George, the rowing man, who'd heard that the driver had complained to the school – well, we weren't exactly hard to identify, given that the minibus was emblazoned with our school's name. 'I'm so disappointed,' George had said. 'I don't know who it was.'

'It was me, George,' I said.

'I'm so disappointed, Chris. I don't know why you did it – you'll have to face the music.'

So on Monday morning I faced the music. 'I've had this letter,' said Mr Cowan. 'It seems that someone has used a water pistol on a member of the public. This is clearly a serious offence,' and as he said this, I thought I could detect a little smile. Still, he sentenced me to half an hour of picking up litter. On balance, I think it was worth it.

The training for rowing was more serious – and perhaps explains this frivolous diversion. In fact, thinking about the training we did back then can still induce a cold sweat – it really was brutal. At the end of my first year as a fully-fledged rower I was in the 'A' crew. Our coach was a student from Edinburgh University. He had some interesting ideas, this guy. Somehow he'd got his hands on some old East German Olympic rowing squad training programmes from the 1980s. He modified them very slightly for us. But only very slightly.

He was certainly committed. We had to be, too, or we'd be out. We trained before and after school, often five or six days a week, and through the summer holidays. It was highly structured, regimented even, but he put a lot into it, and so did we.

Our coach had some good ideas, but he was inflexible. His training ethos could be summed up in three words: push, push and push. To elaborate: keep working harder, don't listen to your body. We were pushing ourselves to the limit and beyond, and at least one of us was always ill with a cold, a chest infection, or run down. I remember one session when two of us were throwing up over the side of the boat, not through exertion but because we were ill. From the towpath, we heard our coach shout: 'OK, you back to normal now? Off you go again.' And it was about three degrees Celsius. As I say, brutal.

Now, you may well be putting the words 'East', 'German', 'Olympic' and '1980s' together, and coming to some fairly alarming conclusions. And yes, as we would all subsequently find out, many East German Olympic athletes were subject to state-organized doping programmes. While not wishing to condemn the East German rowers of the 1980s as doping cheats – I don't know if they were; and many of them, in any case, were apparently oblivious to what they were given – this information could possibly shed some interesting new light on the training programme we were attempting to follow in our rowing days. Quite apart from the fact that they might or might not have been on drugs, they were grown men. We were 16-year-old boys. But the real problem for me was not so much the rowing training programme; it was doing the rowing training *plus* my cycling training; *plus* the fact that we all still had seven hours' school, five days a week. I remember one Sunday when I took part in an 80-mile road race in the morning, then went, still in my cycling kit, straight to rowing training. Since rowing was a team sport, the schedule was sacrosanct – if you couldn't make the session, you weren't in the team.

Despite my misgivings about the severity of the programme – on top of my cycling training – the discipline of doing this training, of being part of such a committed team (rowers and coach alike), and the routine and suffering, were all, I think, good for me in the long run. What doesn't kill you makes you stronger, and all that. And there were certainly times when I felt that it might kill me.

It was as a pair with Grant, my best mate, that I enjoyed the highlight of my rowing career: winning a silver medal in the British schools' championship, held in Strathclyde Park, near Glasgow. In 1993 I also won two Scottish gold medals, in the coxless pairs and coxed fours, and I represented Scotland in the Home Countries International.

But in some ways a more memorable race saw me form part of an eight, when we took on our rival Edinburgh school, Heriot's. The eight was made up of our top four (our only four, in fact), plus their 'C' crew, who were happy to join us. They felt they were as good if not better than their peers in the 'A' and 'B' crews, and were only too delighted to have a chance to prove it. Their 'A' and 'B' crews joined forces, meanwhile, to make up the other eight. There were a lot of personal niggles, little battles to be decided and scores to be settled on that day, partly because our boat clubs sat side by side on the Union Canal, and partly because of the historic rivalry between the two schools. I was pretty oblivious to this, to be honest, but there were some guys who virtually lived at the boathouse, with lots of time, and ample opportunity, for feuds to form and fester. It all gave the contest an unmistakable edge.

As the race got under way they immediately, and with worrying ease, pulled a length ahead. They had been heavily fancied, not least by themselves ... but then, with about 750 metres to go, we began pulling them back. In rowing you find that crews can build up incredible momentum; or hit reverse gear. When the tide turned, so to speak, we kept pulling them back, pulling them back, pulling them back, and eventually rowed through them – as the rowing parlance goes – as we came to the finish. We celebrated as if it had been the Oxford and Cambridge Boat Race. That was in 1994, and it proved to be my final outing in a boat. But what a way to bow out!

I rowed for about three years, finally packing it in because my cycling was getting more serious. Having also moved on from mountain biking, I had now 'retired' from five sports, which is not bad for an 18-year-old. It either shows my versatility and willingness to try new things, or suggests that I was very fickle. I loved sport, but I suppose I was still playing the field, looking for 'the one' I would be happy to settle down with ... but enough of the romantic analogies.

I loved keeping busy, always being on the go – it had been a way of life from when I was seven, and riding BMX races – although some of my teachers were concerned about how my out-of-school interests would fit in with my work, and exams. One report card from 1993 says: 'I hope he will heed his tutor's comments and not neglect academic work in favour of all the other demands on his time.' One of my teachers had said: 'It is important that Chris does not spread himself too thin, i.e. that he balances the demands of his extracurricular interests with the academic demands of his school subjects.'

By now, my cycling 'career' had taken me away from the hills of the Pentlands and down two more conventional paths, one covered in tarmac, the other in wood: road racing – encompassing time trials and mass-start road races – and track racing.

I was a member of the Dunedin Cycling Club, a long-established Edinburgh club whose colours were (I thought at the time) a stylish, eye-catching combination of bright red and garish yellow. It was a club that catered for everyone, from dedicated club cyclists to aspiring racers. At the helm was Ray Harris, the club coach, and his wife Doreen, who did as much as Ray to help the club run smoothly. Together they would officiate at club 10- and 25-mile time trials, their stopwatches around their necks, clipboards in hand, but Ray's speciality was coaching, in which he was way ahead of his time. Ray was into 'numbers' and tests, whereas many others were decidedly old school, still basing all their thoughts on tried and tested principles.

On the road – which was by far the biggest area of the sport – that meant miles, miles and more miles. Typically, winters would be spent doing 'club runs' on a Saturday and Sunday; maybe 50 miles with a group of anything from a few to 20-plus on the Saturday, then around 70 miles on the Sunday, traditionally with a café stop. These rides would maybe average around 18–20mph, interspersed with a couple of sprints using 30mph road signs as imaginary finish lines. Midweek, club riders would do what they could, fitting their training around work, university or school. Most would do sessions on a 'turbo trainer', a contraption to which you attached your bike, having first removed the front wheel. The back wheel sits on a roller connected to a flywheel, meaning that as you pedal harder, the resistance increases. These lent themselves to shorter, more intense training – mainly because of the boredom of not going anywhere. To alleviate that, I used to listen to music. There were stories of others setting their turbo trainers up in front of a TV, and watching old videos of the Tour de France, or something similarly inspirational, as they pedalled away, going nowhere.

It could have been my winter turbo sessions that did as much as anything to convey to my family how serious I was becoming about my cycling training. Though my dad understood it, having accompanied me to BMX and mountain bike races for the best part of 10 years, my mum, though always very supportive, appeared quite bemused by it at times. As I have said, she was a nurse at the Edinburgh Royal Infirmary, working night shifts in the world-renowned sleep medicine department, and she would frequently pass me on her way out in the evenings. Invariably I'd be sweating and wheezing, and in a generally pretty horrendous state.

The reason for these encounters was that I would set my turbo trainer up in the stairwell, the half-way point between our flat, on the first floor of the house, and the freezing cold outside. I'd have the window open, an attempt to cool myself down, and Mum would have to squeeze past me and my turbo trainer on her way to work. I'd be between sets of intervals (short, sprint-like efforts), and I remember her looking at me with an expression that combined bemusement, affectionate amusement and mild concern.

'That can't be good for you,' she'd say.

To which I'd reply: '   '.

In other words, I'd be slumped over my handlebars in between sprint efforts, gasping for air, and incapable of conversation. Not that my silence ever stopped her shaking her head and remarking, on the way out of the door, 'That can't be good for you.'

Had I been able to reply, I might have said: 'Well, actually, Mum, it *is* good for me. That's the point.' Because this kind of high-intensity interval training, which really only came more widely into vogue in the late 1980s and early 1990s, was considered essential for any racing cyclist, even if it ran against the grain of the old 'miles, miles and more miles' school of training.

You didn't really need to be a genius to work this out. In fact, the 'old school' methods of training made no sense at all. What would happen was that the bedrock of the amateur cyclist's winter training would be the weekend club run. And in March he would start racing. The trouble is that races don't tend to be run off at 18mph. And they don't include a café stop. The saving grace, for many, might have been that most of their competitors were spending their winters doing exactly the same, accumulating lots of steady (a euphemism for slow) miles. As the season progressed everyone would get fitter – and faster – simply by racing.

Ray was different. He ran tests on his fabled 'Kingcycle' machine, which resembled a modified turbo trainer. This measured power output, a measurement cyclists were hardly even aware of until about 1990, which is strange, given that it is arguably the single most important factor in performance. However, until the Kingcycle, and later 'power cranks', there was no accurate way of measuring the watts you were generating through the pedals.

Incidentally, I say power is only 'arguably' the most important factor because there are others, such as pain threshold and mental toughness, and also because some riders who've gone on to have successful careers – the Tour de France cyclist Mark Cavendish being one example – have 'failed' lab tests intended to determine their potential based on their power output. As Mark, whose lab tests weren't exceptional, has shown, there are other significant factors, in his case ambition, determination, guts, doggedness, a healthy level of cockiness and self-belief … and a loathing of lab tests. The converse is also true: you get 'lab rats' who perform outstandingly in tests, and less well in actual races.

When I joined the Dunedin, my introduction to mainstream cycling – as opposed to BMX and mountain biking, both of which were regarded with some suspicion, or outright disdain, by cycling purists – consisted mainly of road cycling. But the club was more progressive and open-minded than some traditional clubs, embracing mountain biking, going on rides in the Pentlands and organizing races. This can be explained, I think, by two things – the fact that the membership was quite young, and that in our coach, Ray, we had someone who, though in his fifties, was young at heart and in his ideas. Now in his seventies, Ray still has his youthful enthusiasm – he is always one of the first people I hear from whenever I have any success, usually in email form, and with an exuberant message that is unmistakably Ray.

Despite our mountain bike outings – on which we were usually joined by Ray – the bulk of the club's activity centred on the road, and it was inevitable that I'd gravitate there as I moved away from mountain biking. Road cycling is quite diverse – time trials over any distance or duration from 10 miles to 24 hours; road races of up to 65 miles for juniors, 100-plus for seniors; hour-long criteriums, or circuit races. Theoretically there is something for everyone, and my early road career suggested my strengths lay in sprint finishes and short-distance time trials – I won the short 'prologue' time trial to the Forres Two-Day race, a race for seniors, though I was still a junior, then punctured, wearing the yellow jersey of leader, about 50 metres after the start of the first road stage.

By 1994 I had started riding on the track – I'll come to that in the next chapter – but I was persisting with the road, too, and in August I was selected to represent Scotland in the biggest event I'd ever ride on the road, the nine-day Junior Tour of Ireland. It was an eye-opening, and in many ways a chastening, experience. And, as with my rowing training, it can be summed up in one word. Brutal.

Before the Ireland trip I had a busy summer, with a bit of rowing thrown into the mix, and a job as well. I had moved on from my shifts at the local garage – scene of my encounter with my childhood hero, the footballer John Robertson – to a famous Edinburgh bookshop, James Thin's, before landing the plum job: in a bike shop.

In fact, there was nothing very 'plum' about the work I did in Recycling, a shop located on a side street off Leith Walk, the well-known thoroughfare that runs for about two miles from Edinburgh city centre to the neighbouring port of Leith. Now I think about it, the name Leith Walk conjures up an image of an idyllic, meandering path, which couldn't be more at odds with reality. Leith Walk is big, bustling, frenetic and fairly manic, and it's no accident that it and some of its pubs provide the backdrop to much of the action in Irvine Welsh's *Trainspotting*, the novel that exposes a different Edinburgh to the one you might see in the tourist brochures. I always liked Leith Walk, though, and ended up living in a flat there from 2000 to 2002.

My job in the bike shop was pretty unglamorous and definitely belonged more to the Edinburgh of *Trainspotting* than the posh Edinburgh. As the name of the shop suggests, its main business was recycling old bikes, scrubbing them up and making them roadworthy, then selling them on. There were some crappy jobs, and, as the most junior member of the team, I was given the crappiest ones. I'd get the real rust buckets, and have to go at them with the steel wool and T-Cut, scrubbing all the muck off, or as much as I could, then sticking on new tyres, and making sure the gears and brakes worked. I loved it, absolutely loved it – the banter, the oily smell of the place, being surrounded all day by bikes – but it was hard work. And, given my fondness at school for maths and other logical subjects, I had moments when I contemplated the economics of it. The owner of the shop paid about £20 for the old bikes, then sold them on – sometimes just a few hours later, after I'd worn my knuckles to the bone – for about £50. For my labour I was paid £2 an hour. It didn't really add up. And to make it worse, and on account of my considerable appetite, I spent approximately half my day's earnings in the 'deli' around the corner.

I loved working there, because I was mad about bikes. But I wasn't daft. I didn't like the idea of being taken advantage of, and so I decided that if I went back the following summer, I would ask for a raise. When the call came, I was ready. Sort of.

'I might have a vacancy in the summer,' said Mr Recycling when he phoned in the spring, 'if you're looking for a job.'

'Possibly,' I said.

'Great,' he said, 'you'll still be on £2 an hour.'

'I'll think about it,' I said, 'and get back to you.'

There was another bike shop on the other side of town, called The New Bike Shop, owned by Chris Hill, who had been helping me out with a little bit of sponsorship. I knew Chris, but I didn't speak to him about a job. Yet for some unfathomable reason, when I called Recycling back, I said: 'I've been offered a job in a different bike shop at £3 an hour. Could you maybe match that?'

'Oh yeah?' said Mr Recycling. 'Who's that with?'

'Er ... it's The New Bike Shop,' I said, mentioning the first bike shop that came to mind.

It was his turn now to say he'd have a think about it and get back to me. Our game of poker was reaching its final stages, but I had just played a duff hand. When he phoned me back, he said: 'It's strange, Chris, because I spoke to the owner of The New Bike Shop, and he said he didn't know anything about the job he's offered you ...'

The only consolation was that this conversation was taking place over the phone, because my face turned bright red. I spluttered something in response, but Mr Recycling just laughed and said: 'Don't worry, I'll give you £3 an hour.' I think he was quite impressed that I was sticking up for myself, even if my negotiating technique had been a little dubious.

I didn't waste a minute of that summer in 1994. I would work all day at the bike shop, and in the evenings I would be picked up to go rowing, or else went training on my bike, either on the road or at the nearby Meadowbank Velodrome. At the end of the summer I travelled to Leicester for the national track championships, and from there went straight to Ireland for the Junior Tour.

Leaving Leicester, with my dad at the wheel, we were late getting to Stranraer for the ferry, which meant catching a later one and arriving at the race HQ, a school hall in a village, at around four in the morning. It wasn't a disaster – I slept in the car, which is something I'd got down to a fine art 10 years previously on our travels through Europe for the BMX races – but the race started at 9 a.m. the next morning, which was far from ideal.

The Junior Tour of Ireland is one of the most famous, and toughest, stage races for juniors, and it has proved a breeding ground for some top road riders, including the great Irishmen Sean Kelly and Stephen Roche. Not only did it last nine days, with stages as long as 65 miles each day, but the roads in Ireland were renowned for being tough – they were rarely flat, always undulating, and the surfaces in many places left much to be desired. I had never attempted anything like it before, but I felt reasonably confident I could hang on during the flat stages and then have a chance whenever a stage was decided by a mass bunch sprint.

As we got under way, though, I remember feeling great relief. The *peloton* of around 120 eager juniors showed very little urgency, and ambled along. True, the roads were a little bit rougher than the wooden boards I'd been riding all week at the velodrome in Leicester – and in places bore a closer resemblance to the tracks I'd tackled on my mountain bike – but I could handle the pace. It was as if the riders had agreed a pact; that the race was so long, and so hard, that it would start in civilized fashion.

I'd overlooked one thing: the race hadn't started. Here I was, riding along thinking, 'Phew, this is OK; I think I can handle this,' totally oblivious to the fact that the flag hadn't yet dropped.

To my surprise, after about an hour we stopped en masse. Most riders peeled off to the side of the road to answer the call of nature, while I wondered what was going on, and how everyone except me seemed to be in the know. I soon found out. When the calls of nature had all been answered, we lined up again. This time a flag appeared, and someone shouted 'Go!' The race was on.

And it really was on: it was flat out from there to the finish, 65 miles away. That first hour, I discovered, had been the neutralized zone, which would be another less than welcome feature of the Junior Tour of Ireland. In order to get around the rule that juniors could only race for a maximum of 65 miles in a day, they had these huge 'neutralized zones' – sometimes as long as 25 miles – taking the total distance for the day up to around 90 miles.

When the stages started, the entire field would be strung out in a long line for most of the day, a sign that the bunch was going flat out. It was aggressive racing, too, with the Irish riders the main protagonists, and all eager to leave their mark on their national tour. It was a struggle to hold your place in the field, not least because of another rule that applied to juniors – the fact we were only allowed a maximum gear of 93 inches, which corresponded to a 52-tooth chainring at the front, and a 15-tooth sprocket at the back.

The purpose of this rule was to encourage younger riders to spin small gears rather than push big ones; it was designed to protect joints and improve suppleness. A fine principle, and it shouldn't have been a handicap in Ireland – after all, we were all using the same gear, so we were all in the same boat …

Weren't we?

I started to wonder. Especially when I saw some of the Irish riders driving on the front all day, their legs seemingly turning a lot slower than mine, which were almost spinning off just trying to keep up. There were gear checks at the end of each stage, and at one of the gear checks the Irish got pulled over. A couple of guys had blocked off their gears, meaning that they had bigger gears on their bike, but couldn't access them. That wasn't allowed, but they weren't disqualified – they were relegated to last on the stage, and allowed to carry on.

After a few days of the Junior Tour I was on my knees. I was the Scotland team's sprinter, expected to be up there at the finish, but I woke up each morning wondering how I'd make the start, never mind the finish. There were other challenges, too. The diet was decidedly 'old school', with our team manager insisting that we start each day with an enormous plate of pasta and beans. 'Get it down you, boys,' he would say, and it was interpreted as a sign of weakness if you couldn't manage it all. Loss of appetite is one of the signs, on a stage race, that someone has gone beyond their limit. But the reality was that the pasta and beans combination was so disgusting, especially first thing in the morning, that it was a struggle to eat it no matter how hungry you were.

The Junior Tour of Ireland exposed me to other aspects of cycling culture. Put a team of 17-year-old boys together in a stage race and there will inevitably be some shenanigans, even if they are focused on what they're doing. One evening, about half-way through the race, our manager, who was also acting as soigneur (masseur), and whom we secretly christened 'Wee Nutter,' was addressed by one of the riders by this moniker. He flipped and it prompted a semi-light-hearted wrestling match between the two, which ended with our manager/soigneur hurting his thumb quite seriously. So seriously, in fact, that he couldn't give us massages for the remainder of the race, which was quite a drawback in terms of helping our recovery for the next day. Another feature of the Junior Tour – which we riders didn't experience – was the legendary 'night stages.' For many of the managers and mechanics these seemed more of a priority than the day stages – i.e. the races – and acted as an excuse for them to drain Ireland of its supplies of Guinness.

As for the racing, it was like groundhog day. The painful legs when you woke up; the ordeal of breakfast; the long neutralized section; and then balls to the wall racing for three hours. I remember one stage in particular – 60 miles long, and covered in not much more than two hours. Our average that day was 29.6mph – you don't get many stages of the Tour de France run off at that speed.

Despite all that, I did manage to force my way into the top 10 on three stages, my best placing being fifth in one bunch sprint. But on stages where there were hills I had no chance – having had a growth spurt in my late teens, I was bigger than most other road cyclists, who tended to be small and wiry – and it turned into a massive test of endurance and willpower just to finish. By the end there were three of us left in the Scottish team – the other two having abandoned – but I did finish, which gave me a lot of satisfaction. The 1994 Junior Tour of Ireland also gave me the answer to one question that had lurked at the back of my mind, as it does with any young cyclist.

Would I ever ride the world's most famous race, the Tour de France?

No. Definitely not.

CHAPTER 5

Going Round in Circles

It was with the Dunedin Cycling Club that I started riding at Meadowbank Velodrome, the track in Edinburgh that was built for the 1970 Commonwealth Games, and rebuilt for the 1986 Games.

I vividly remember my introduction to Meadowbank. But I'd imagine that most people remember their first visit, because it's so difficult to find. It's in a strange place, out on a limb from the rest of the Meadowbank Stadium and sports centre, which includes an athletics stadium and football pitches on a sprawling, campus-style complex. You enter the car park, with the main stadium on your left, and then drive to the furthest corner of the car park, where a narrow, pock-marked road runs parallel to the main Edinburgh–London rail line. After about 100 metres it opens out into another small car park, with a Portakabin – headquarters to the Scottish Cyclists' Union – on your left, and, straight ahead, a big, white, pebbledash building.

There is no clue that it is a velodrome, and no obvious entrance. You gain access to it by some steps that lead down into a dark tunnel, which tends to act as a repository for rainwater ... ah yes, rain: a subject I'll return to in a moment.

There are often a couple of puddles to avoid as you make your way through the tunnel, heading for the set of steps at the other end, taking you back up into daylight.

I remember emerging from the tunnel that first time, blinking, into the light, and being taken aback, and a little intimidated, by what I saw. For all that the place was clearly quite run down, and the entrance so unprepossessing, there is nothing that really prepares you for your first view, 'in the flesh', of a velodrome. Before me there stood what looked like a wooden wall of death: the corners really were like vast vertical walls rearing up from the ground. Though I had known what a velodrome was, I hadn't anticipated how steep its corners would be. And, funnily enough, that's usually the first thing most people say when they enter a velodrome for the first time.

Meadowbank's only failing – and one of the reasons for it looking so run down – is that it has never had a roof. Rain has always been the curse of the place, and many a scheduled session of racing or training has been destroyed over the years by rain, which renders the wooden boards unrideable by transforming them into an ice rink. But the problem goes beyond interruptions to the calendar. The constant exposure of the track to the elements has taken its toll, damaging the boards, and leaving them prone to splintering. As I write, the Meadowbank Velodrome still stands – just. I supported the 'Save Meadowbank' campaign in the run-up to the Beijing Olympics, and following the Games the track – and indeed the entire complex – was granted a reprieve by Edinburgh Council. It would be nice to think that this was in response to the campaign, but I suspect it also had rather a lot to do with the economic crisis and its effect on the value of the land that the track sits on. The site of the velodrome had been earmarked for luxury flats, but as the value of land plummeted, this scheme made less and less financial sense to the council. So, Edinburgh still has a cycling track, though for how long, no one really knows. It could certainly do with a new one – nothing fancy, just something beginners can have a shot on, and serious riders can train on, 12 months of the year. In other words, preferably with a roof.

Thinking back to my early outings on the track, there was no real Eureka! moment; nothing, initially, that indicated to me that I had finally found the sport to which I would dedicate the next 15 years – and counting – of my life. The first time I turned up was on a Friday evening for a Dunedin track night. I suspect that everyone has felt daunted before going out there, and I was no different. I was given a track bike belonging to the East of Scotland Cycling Association – a very basic, fairly old machine with no gears and no brakes, as is the norm with track bikes.

Track bikes have 'fixed wheels' – only one gear and no brakes – and so you slow down by easing the pressure on the pedals, which is a lot less effective than squeezing some brake levers with your fingers. As a consequence, you have less control on a track bike, and once you are up there on the boards, you are largely at their mercy. Or at least that's what it feels like at first.

As I wheeled my borrowed track bike over to the straight – where the gradient is more gentle – and swung my leg over, I was very nervous and a little bit excited. There was a group of riders lapping the 333-metre track, going at around 25 to 30mph, riding in a compact line, one tucked behind the other for maximum shelter. Riding in such close proximity to each other with no gears and no brakes looked as if it took skill and nerve in equal measure, and I wasn't sure when, or if, I'd be able to do that. My first thought was that I should keep out of their way.

Our club coach, Ray Harris, who was running the training session, gave me a few pointers. 'Keep your speed up – if you go into the banking too slowly, the tyres will lose their traction and you'll slide ... look where you want to go – straight in front of you ... use the lines on the track, especially the black one near the bottom, to keep your bearings ... overtake riders on the outside, not the inside ... and whatever you do, don't try to stop pedalling!' This is the biggest danger for the fixed wheel novice. If you make any kind of effort on the road you can freewheel for a bit to recover. If you try that on the track, with the 'fixed wheel' bikes, you'll do a good impression of a cowboy on an angry horse, and end up on your (soon to be splintered) backside. The pedals won't stop, so you can't just stop pedalling; you have to ease off gradually. Depending on how fast you're going, it can take a lap or two to come to a complete halt.

As I set off off along the home straight, Ray shouted after me, urging me to press harder on the pedals, and to increase my speed as I entered the banking – to commit to it. Commitment was the key; if I backed off at all I'd slither down the track. But it's counter-intuitive: your instinct is to back off, because if the banking seems steep from the centre, it appears even steeper as you ride into it. And it does appear, at first, as though you are riding *into* a wall rather than around a bend; it can induce a claustrophobic feeling, looming over you, almost swallowing you up and giving you nowhere to go. The bend curves to the left, but every instinct is telling you to lean to the right to try and correct that. It takes several laps just to begin to feel confident on the bends; to ride at speed, leaning, counter-intuitively, into them rather than trying, counter-productively, to lean out of them.

As I got up to speed on that first session I could feel my confidence growing, and my fear turning to exhilaration. By the end of my few laps I was enjoying it, though I didn't have the confidence, yet, to ride in a group – or go too close to other riders. That would take a few more outings. But I started heading down to the track – about a 20-minute bike ride from my house – on a regular basis. Our Dunedin track nights weren't formal training, as such, but more like a bit of fun. I worked up to riding in the group, and we'd do around 40 laps of 'through-and-off' – riding in a line, taking turns at the front before swinging up the banking, dropping back and latching on to the back of the string. If you've seen a team pursuit race, it's the same idea, but usually with anything from four to about 15 riders.

Did I have any talent? If I did, it was well hidden – though, as I have said already, I think the notion of 'talent' is over-rated. Counting against me, at this stage, was that I didn't specialize in one event: I did everything. I began taking part in the Meadowbank Track League on a Tuesday evening – when it wasn't rained off – where I would ride every race going. I was 16, still reasonably skinny – around 74 kilos, as opposed to the 93 I weigh now – and trying to be as lean as possible. If you look at most cyclists, they are as slender as jockeys, with large thighs, but sunken cheeks and protruding rib cages. The only cyclists who didn't conform to that stereo-type were track sprinters, but I was a long way from deciding that's what I wanted to be. I was still riding the road, and doing endurance events – the pursuit and bunch races – on the track.

By 1993 I was riding the track league most weeks, and my first full season of track cycling coincided with the sudden emergence on to the world stage of a Scottish superstar. Graeme Obree, mentioned at the start of the last chapter, had been winning time trials for years, while enjoying a close rivalry with Chris Boardman, the English rider who, the previous year, became the first British cyclist in 84 years to win an Olympic gold medal, claiming the pursuit at the Barcelona Games – another event that I found profoundly inspiring. Boardman's success seemed also to inspire Obree;

he could see his rival's career taking off and his name in lights and obviously thought, 'That could be me.'

But the question for Obree was, how? He set his sights on the prestigious world 'hour' record, which had been established in 1984 by the Italian Francesco Moser, beating the mark set in 1972 by the legendary Eddy Merckx. 'The hour' is an unusual race, measuring simply the distance you ride in 60 minutes, and it was seldom ridden – mainly, perhaps, because it was so brutally tough. After his record 'hour' Merckx reckoned it had taken five years off his life.

Boardman had announced that he would have a go at Moser's record in July, but Obree cheekily beat him to it, travelling to the Hamar track in Norway and bettering Moser's mark just a week before Boardman's planned assault. It was an audacious thing to do, but that was Obree all over. Though he had no real back-up or financial support, he lived by the credo of nothing is impossible – or 'impossible is nothing', as one of my sponsors puts it. Though Boardman beat his record a week later – only for Obree to claim it back the following year – Obree also won the world pursuit title that year, beating Boardman.

Obree became my cycling hero, as did Boardman. We weren't blessed, in Scotland or Britain, with an abundance of world-class riders we could aspire to emulate, but Obree and Boardman's rivalry sparked huge interest. Apart from them, the 'heroes' of the sport were, and had always tended to be, the continental road riders, or, on the track, the Australian and French sprinters. Boardman's victory in the 1992 Olympics was a big inspiration to me – I listened to it on the BBC's World Service on a family holiday in France – and Obree ticked every box as far as I was concerned – he was the best in the world, he was an original, he was inspirational ... and he was from Scotland.

Cycling Weekly was a good resource for the latest Obree news. But it was surreal that he was one of us, competing in my own backyard. Guys from my club would come home from time trials in the West of Scotland, having competed against him on the GD21 course, or whatever, and report back. The times he was doing were unbelievable: he'd go four minutes faster than me over a 10-mile time trial. He seemed superhuman.

I first saw him at the national championships in Leicester in 1993, a month after he broke the hour record. This was before the world championships, and he had to win the national title to be selected for the British team alongside the Olympic champion, Boardman, whose selection had been guaranteed. Obree reached the final, where he faced Bryan Steel, one of the country's most consistent pursuit riders. I was in the crowd watching, preparing to cheer on Obree, but my heart stopped as the race got under way and he pulled his foot out of the pedal.

He had been a strong favourite to beat Steel, having qualified fastest, but this mishap looked to have cost him the race, and his place at the world championships. Obree lost several seconds trying to get his foot back in – something that's not easy on a fixed wheel bike, with the pedals constantly in motion – and when he eventually began to get going, working hard to turn the huge gear he used, he was well down on Steel. I was caught up in the excitement of it and moved to the edge of the track, cheering him on. It was a classic pursuit race, and gradually Obree began to reel him in, eventually coming through to win. It was an amazing performance, and entirely typical of Obree, whose life story was far from straightforward, and involved overcoming – sometimes self-inflicted – hurdles and difficulties. Funnily enough, I recently watched a Graeme Obree DVD with footage of this race, and saw myself standing watching in the back straight – a skinny youth in a white cap.

Obree wasn't the only rider to pull his foot out of the pedal at those championships. I did, too. It was in qualifying for the junior pursuit, and I was using the old toe-clips and straps, which, ironically, were supposed to be more secure than the new clip-less pedals. Embarrassingly, and unlike Obree, I wasn't able to reattach my foot to my pedal – there are echoes here of my traumatic foot-pedal mishap at the BMX world championships in Slough seven years earlier – and so I rode the entire race, all three kilometres, with my foot resting on top of the pedal, rather than secured in it. Consequently, it took me roughly the same time to cover three kilometres as for Obree to do four. I didn't qualify.

And I didn't do much better in the sprint, scraping through qualification in seventeenth (eighteen went through), then dead-heating in the first-round 'repechage'. My campaign didn't last much longer, but the experience of riding those championships, at the end of a summer when I'd been doing more rowing than cycling (I had just come from the Home Countries rowing championships, which were also a disaster: we sank the boat) was an eye-opener. As far as track cycling went, I recognize now that I was really only playing at it, and my going to the British championships was the equivalent of a golfer whose experience is limited to the driving range playing a round with Tiger Woods.

Well, maybe that's a slight exaggeration, but I was certainly up against some serious opponents. Some of them had highly specialized, and very pricey, track bikes, whereas I used the same machine for sprint and pursuit, the only concession being to change the handlebars between races. I was competitive in terms of my attitude, but I wasn't under any illusions – I knew I didn't have the same experience, and hadn't put in the same work as some of the others.

Really, the highlight of my first national track championships didn't come in any of my races, but in briefly meeting Obree. He was so unassuming and approachable; no matter who you were (or weren't), he put you at ease, and you got the impression he'd happily spend all day signing autographs, posing for photographs and chatting. He just seemed so normal. But as far as performance was concerned, he occupied a different planet.

When I returned to Leicester for the national championships the following year, having ridden virtually a full season of track league – and more or less finished with rowing – several things had changed, including my club. Over the winter of 1993/94 I decided I wanted to focus more on track cycling, and I joined a club dedicated to the track, the City of Edinburgh Racing Club. This was an impressive set-up, the Manchester United of British track racing, since it didn't only sweep the board at the national championships, but it also tended to sign up all the best talent. I don't include myself in that category, incidentally, but it was a club that took racing seriously, and it had an aura about it. A bit like the British track cycling team now, it was a club where mediocrity was not accepted; when you went to the British championships, you went there to win medals. At that time in Scotland only a very elite group of people had ever won a medal in a British championship. It was a big deal. But that was the purpose of 'The City', as the club was known. When I joined, I didn't say I was going to do this or that, but I stated my goals, which were to win a medal at the British championships. That pressed the right buttons. British medals were the City of Edinburgh Racing Club's *raison d'être*.

But in 1994 I came up against my *bête noire* – to keep the French going – in a fellow junior sprinter, James Taylor. He had been riding for a few years and he brought all his experience to bear in match sprinting, which is the most tactical of races. I was quicker than him – I was actually fastest in the 200m qualifying time trial, which came as a major surprise as I hadn't trained for it. But, having exceeded all expectations by reaching the final of the junior sprint, against Taylor I had no idea what to do. I was naïve, and my tactics were dreadful. In the first race, he pinned me to the fence, at the top of the track; and from there he was in control. I knew I was faster than him; but I didn't have a clue how to beat him in a head-to-head scenario.

I came off after that first heat and received a bit of a dressing down from Brian Annable, who ran – and still runs – the City of Edinburgh club. He didn't enjoy seeing his boys beaten; and he certainly didn't enjoy seeing them humiliated. 'What did you do that for?' he asked, meaning: why did I allow Taylor to pin me to the fence? 'He made you look like an arse!' he added, just to make sure I got the message.

And it might have been true, but it didn't really help me going into the second heat, where, predictably enough, the same thing happened. Though I knew I was quicker than Taylor, he had guile and what we call 'track craft'. In a *mano a mano* contest he could dictate things – the mark of a skilful sprinter.

Still, a silver medal in the British championships, though it might not have pleased Brian Annable, was a fantastic result for me, especially as it got me a place on the British squad, which meant once-a-month sessions, under the watchful eye of the national track coach Marshall Thomas, at the brand new Manchester Velodrome. It vindicated my decision to join The City and to devote more energy to track racing. I was still growing, and beginning to fill out, which made me less suited to other cycling disciplines, and my enthusiasm was increasing at a similar rate. By now I'd usually be at Meadowbank twice a week, once for training, once for track league; I was really keen and motivated, and I felt that I could go somewhere. I was improving with every race, which was massively exciting. It felt as though I was embarking on a journey, and I didn't know where it would end; I didn't know what the limitations were, or even if there were any. But I was desperate for help, for guidance – and there wasn't much of that to be had.

I was also at another crossroads, a more important one. I was in my final year at school and considering my next move – a decision that wasn't really helped by the computer programme I completed at school, which was supposed to tell me what career my skills and interests were suited to. Other than being convinced that I should go to university, I didn't have a clue what I would do in the longer term, so I was curious to see what the careers advice would be. After feeding in all the relevant information – in response to questions as bizarre as 'Would you rather work in a blue room or a green room?' and 'What's your favourite month?' – I waited anxiously for the answer that could determine my future.

Or not. The computer said: Brewer. Or advocate.

At school, as I have said, I was more interested in the sciences. I quite liked English too, eventually graduating from my 'What I did at the weekend' essays about BMXing. But I preferred logic to ambiguity. For my Highers – the Scottish equivalent of 'A' levels – I did maths, English, physics, chemistry and biology, but I was disappointed with my results. Having got 'A's in the preliminary exams, I ended up with two 'B's and three 'C's in the actual exams.

There's an interesting parallel with sport here, I think. Academically, I never felt that I struggled. I got top marks in my Standard Grades, and progressed through school without ever really working – or feeling that I had to. When I got to fifth year, and the all-important Highers, I had that same mentality, and didn't really work for them. I was complacent, thinking that, since I'd always done OK in exams, I'd sail through.

Looking through some of my report cards – an embarrassing but necessary part of writing an autobiography – I spot a theme emerging around this time, one that is sometimes buried, though not too deeply, in the subtext. In one I'm described as 'a highly motivated pupil [but] I agree with [another teacher's] remarks about chatting. Perhaps this is just a sign of enthusiasm.' In physics, apparently I 'ask and answer questions frequently – usually about physics'. In French: 'I hope Chris will not spend too much time trying to be funny, which he undoubtedly is, but it must not be an end in itself.' I think he meant that I was funny in French, not English. I should have stuck at it.

But it was my English teacher, Christopher Rush – now the highly respected author of several acclaimed books – who identified my biggest shortcoming. 'Chris has performed ably on all fronts except one … the weak front? Failure to revise adequately for tests. The same must not happen when it comes to exams.' Alas, Mr Rush, it did.

I recognize now that I was complacent about my school work – that I never felt it necessary to work hard for exams. Yet in sport the converse was true. In each sport I took part in I recognized the need for hard work; I never felt that it came easily, because there were always people better than me. Nobody ever told me I was 'the next big thing' – as certain of my young rivals were told. (Subsequently, quite a few have told me, whenever I've had any success, that 'I always knew you'd do that …' though I don't remember them saying anything at the time.) In BMX, rugby, rowing and cycling, there was always at least one person better than me, meaning that I could never rest on my laurels. One thing I've realized about myself is that I can put 100 per cent into something, but only if I'm really motivated to. Maybe that's the case for most people, but I think that if sport had come easily to me – if I'd been top of the tree – I would probably have lost interest at an early stage.

After my silver medal at the 1994 British track championships I was satisfied, because it meant I had made progress, but there was absolutely no danger of me being complacent. I knew that if I were ever going to beat the James Taylors of this world I'd have to work very hard. And I'd have to combine it with my studies for a university degree. Despite my disappointing grades in the Highers, I got an unconditional offer from St Andrews University to study physics and maths. St Andrews was perfect: far enough away from Edinburgh to ensure that I wouldn't go running home at the first opportunity, but close enough to return if I wanted to.

CHAPTER 6

Craig and Jason

My first year at St Andrews University, which turned out to be my only year, was brilliant. I threw myself into student life, going out most nights, making new friends, eating rubbish and enjoying a drink or two, or three. It was great fun, if incompatible with the life of an athlete, though I had decided not to be an athlete that first term. At least I think I had decided, but maybe I didn't decide; maybe it just happened. And I was pretty sure I could get away with it, more or less. In those days track cycling was a summer sport – it switched to winter a few years ago – and the serious work wouldn't need to start until the New Year.

At home over the Christmas holidays I got back on my bike, and when I returned to St Andrews for the second term I scaled back on the social life. Easter brought an exotic racing trip to Trinidad and Barbados, which would set me up for a year of solid progress, though it started with a bang, following a crash, that ended with me sporting a neck brace.

The racing in the West Indies really has to be witnessed to be believed; it is like nowhere else, and should definitely feature on the 'must do' list for any track cyclist. It is strange, because, at international level, riders from this part of the world haven't had massive success; and yet to race there, in front of thousands of exuberant fans, you'd think it was the national sport. The meetings are like carnivals with an atmosphere similar, I would imagine, to the biggest cricket matches, with the fans singing, dancing and chucking ice cubes at you as you raced. Well, it is hot.

Riding our bikes into Bridgetown, the capital of Barbados, we were treated like heroes, but even that didn't prepare us for the atmosphere inside the velodrome, with its large, concrete, lumpy track, a running track around the inside, and stands absolutely jam-packed with people, probably around 5,000 of them. I was there with two fellow sprinters, Craig MacLean and Peter Jacques, and the endurance rider Martin Williamson, all City of Edinburgh club mates, and on the first night I lined up alongside eight other riders for a keirin. The others were from the islands, with some South Americans there too, including a couple of Cubans who quickly gained a reputation for their no-holds-barred style of racing.

There was some pretty rough riding, to be honest, with the rules sketchy, and an anything-goes approach, particularly when it came to 'primes'. These are special prizes awarded at the end of certain laps, announced the lap before with a blast of the 'commissaire' (referee)'s whistle. Some of these guys would run over their granny to win a prime – a prime, I should add, that carried prize money (we worked out) of approximately £3.50.

In the keirin, with the lumpy track and the jostling, it felt dangerous, and so it proved. I was 'hooked' by one of the Cubans, meaning he cut across my line, and down I went, like a tonne of bricks. I was in a bad way, with multiple cuts and road rash, but it was my neck that gave most cause for concern. As I lay on the track I was attended to by an official from the Barbados Cycling Federation, who took me to the local hospital, where I was examined and fitted with a neck brace.

I feared the worst, that my racing trip to the West Indies would be cut short after 24 hours of an intended three-and-a-half week odyssey, but, after a couple of days, I had recovered sufficiently to remove the neck brace, get back on my bike and resume racing. The rest of the trip included racing in Trinidad, where we stayed in a terrible hotel, occupied by an army of cockroaches, and competing in one of the most bizarre velodromes on the planet, involving a two-and-a-half hour journey by mini-bus into the middle of a jungle in Palesco. It was a 500-metre track but with bends as steep as a 250m track, which made it unbelievably dangerous, and meant you could hardly ride above the black (bottom) line on the banking. You'd have to ride single-file around the bends and then overtake on the long straights. I fell off there, too, in an incident that proved the point just made: a guy was riding above me on one of the bends, and, even though he was going at a decent speed, his tyres slipped, and he slid down the banking, taking me out. Fortunately I wasn't too badly hurt this time.

The other memorable incident in Barbados concerned one of my team-mates, Martin. While Craig and I had travelled straight there from a training camp in Majorca, and therefore had a bit of colour – meaning that our skin had turned from the usual Scottish pale blue to creamy white – Martin was as white as a sheet. When he was in the local supermarket he decided to do something about it. On the shelf he saw something called 'Melatonin', which he mistook for a natural remedy that he had heard was used by bodybuilders to make their skin turn darker more quickly (basically making their skin more photosensitive). He didn't realize melatonin was also a natural sleep-promoting remedy. When he looked at the packaging, it said to take one before bed time. 'Why bed time?' he asked, before stretching out under the sun for the remainder of the afternoon.

It was our first day, we were racing in the evening (when I would suffer my heavy crash), but, as we started to think about leaving, we noticed that Martin had crashed out. We tried to wake him, but he was completely zonked. After several coffees a very lethargic Martin started to come round. But he wasn't any browner.

Even after living the typical life of a fresher student in that first term at university, I found that, once I got my head down and resumed training, with the training camp in Majorca and racing trip to the West Indies both providing essential building blocks in my preparation for the season, I was still on an upward curve. At the British championships that summer I won my first gold medal, riding with City of Edinburgh in a new event, the three-man team sprint, and added a silver medal in the team pursuit.

As well as Graeme Obree there was another Scottish cyclist who proved a great influence, and an inspiration, at this time. Craig MacLean, one of my companions in the West Indies, was five years older than me. In fact, he still is.

Craig and I were Dunedin club-mates, and he too had dabbled in mountain biking and road racing, but by the mid-1990s he was committed to the track, and he was already enjoying some success. Like me, he did a bit of everything, but his main attribute was an incredible turn of pace. Whereas I was still relatively skinny, he was stockier and shorter – more the classic build of a sprinter. He was muscular, but as lean as a particularly lean piece of fillet steak. Craig was definitely going places, even if the City of Edinburgh Racing Club didn't see that at first. His application to join the club in 1995 was rejected, so he raced that season with the Moray Firth club, based up in the Highlands, which is where he comes from.

I had a long way to go to catch Craig up, although sometimes, if he was on his worst day and I was on my best, it would be close. I remember the first time I beat him. It was during that breakthrough season, 1995, at the Scottish 15km scratch race championship, in a bunch endurance race on the outdoor track at Caird Park in Dundee. This was a track in an even more decrepit state than Meadowbank, and concrete rather than wood, but on this occasion it hosted a great race – though I may be biased.

As we came to the finish, I led it out, with Craig on my wheel. I was going hard, full gas, and I was aware of Craig moving off my wheel, and beginning to claw me back, inching up towards my right shoulder, when I dug as deep as I possibly could, and broke him; he swung off up the track fairly melodramatically, settling for second. Already Craig was seen as the main man, the daddy, and I was regarded as his protégé, which led some to the natural assumption that he had gifted me the race. John McMillan, the race commissaire, came up to both of us afterwards and said: 'Craig, if you're going to give him the race, do it more subtly than that ...'

I was fuming! I knew I'd won it fair and square, but Craig didn't correct John – he just laughed. It was like that Billy Connolly sketch, where he mimics someone tripping up on the pavement and breaking into a run as if he had been about to do that all along. Craig was happy to maintain the illusion, because it saved his face. Competitive bugger.

And just to compound the insult, the annual Scottish Cyclists' Union handbook, which is the bible of Scottish racing, later listed Craig as the winner! He had won it the previous year, and he would go on to win it again the following year, but his name appears as the winner of the title three years in a row. It was my first senior title, and something I was very proud of. Imagine how I felt when I found that my name was missing from the record. I was gutted!

Returning to university after a summer that had yielded senior gold medals in the British and Scottish championships was difficult. St Andrews is picture-postcard beautiful: a seaside town surrounded by vast, golden beaches, as well as the most famous golf course in the world. But I was more interested in velodromes, and increasingly concerned about its isolation in relation to the nearest of them. Meadowbank was around an hour away, and Manchester, to which I was by now almost a weekly visitor, up to five hours.

My dilemma was made worse by the fact that I was less and less sure about the course to which I had committed four years of my life. Maths and physics had been the subjects I'd done OK in at school, but now, though I was passing the exams, and coping with the course work, I was no longer enjoying them. I was also beginning to wonder where they would take me and, more to the point, whether I really wanted to go there ...

I returned for my second year harbouring these doubts, and within a couple of weeks I realized they weren't going to disappear, but would grow worse. When I made the decision, I made it quickly. The degree I'd chosen wasn't for me, and there was no point in prolonging the uncertainty. I phoned my parents, told them my decision, and, though I'm sure they were concerned, they couldn't have been more supportive. Subsequently they have admitted to thinking 'What the hell is he doing?' and they weren't all that reassured by my new plans: to try and get on a sports science course. At the time, though, they didn't interrogate me too much. My dad came and collected me, and I returned home, where my parents made it clear that I couldn't 'sponge' off them, and that I would have to get a job – or sign on. I signed on, for one week, and then got a job once again at James Thin's, the bookshop.

And so I became a 'dropout' – a loaded phrase if ever there was one, conjuring up an image of a *Young Ones*-style waster.

Me, aged 2, and my Space Hopper in the garden of the family home in Edinburgh.

My sister Carrie (AKA Miss World) and me – our school uniforms were slightly unusual ... Sadly, my papier-mâché hat was destroyed by Coca-Cola at the fancy dress party we were en route to.

Left: My second bike, acquired from a neighbour, was actually a girls' bike, with a sloping down tube. Note the embroidered 'BMX' on my cap – thanks Mum.

Right: Florida, venue for the 1987 BMX world championships, and a day off at the Epcot theme park in classic eighties outfits.

Butter wouldn't melt. Primary seven: the rectangular badges were awarded for representing the school at sport. Mine were athletics, rugby, football, cross-country, basketball ... but not cycling.

Scottish national BMX championships, Nairn, 1988.

Above: On the podium with my closest rival, Matt Boyle, at the 1989 British championships.

Right: In the gear of my first sponsored team, GT, in 1989. The '1S' on my number plate means I'm number one in Scotland.

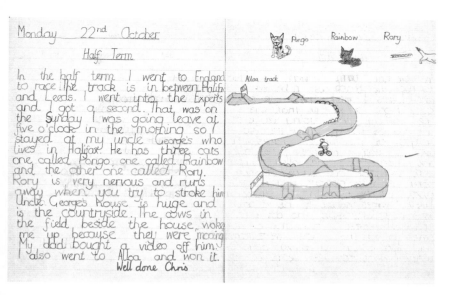

Monday 22nd October

Half Term

In the half term I went to England to race. The track is in between Halifax and Leeds. I went unto the Experts and I got a second. That was on the Sunday I was going to leave at five o'clock in the morning so I stayed at my uncle George's who lives in Halifax. He has three cats one called Pongo, one called Rainbow and the other one called Rory. Rory is very nervous and runs away when you try to stroke him. Uncle George's house is huge and is the countryside. The cows in the field beside the house, woke me up because they were mooing. My dad bought a video off him. I also went to Alloa and won it.

Well done Chris

Pongo   Rainbow   Rory

Alloa track

Early flowering of my literary talent and artistic skills.

Above: The year I won my first trophy, for finishing third in 1984 at a race in Southampton.

Above: Another race, another trophy...

Left: Junior Tour of Ireland 1994, making a break for glory on the final stage (it was doomed: I was caught).

Speeding to my first Olympic gold, and an
Olympic and sea level kilometre world record,
at the Athens Games, 2004.

With Craig MacLean and Jason Queally and our silver medals on the podium in Sydney, and I'm biting my bottom lip as if it holds the tears in. The truth is, I was more stunned than emotional.

My first individual title: the 2002 Commonwealth Games kilometre. Having just stepped off the podium, I can't believe that I've won.

'And the gold medal, and Olympic champion, Chris Hoy...' the announcer has just said, in Athens 2004.

'Yesssssss!' – one of about five celebration laps after winning team sprint gold at the 2006 Commonwealth Games.

Matt Crampton, Jason Queally, Jamie Staff, me, Ross Edgar, Craig MacLean, Shane Kelly, Ryan Bayley and Shane Perkins (left to right). Team sprint gold for Scotland at the 2006 Commonwealth Games in Melbourne – a big relief after the disappointment of my bronze in the kilo.

One of my favourite pics: celebrating winning the keirin at the 2007 world championships in Palma. Like my 2002 Commonwealth Games success, it felt like the start of something. Teun Mulder, one of two Dutchmen in the final, is behind me.

That wasn't quite the life I had in mind. There was a feeling of failure, I suppose, but I knew that I couldn't keep going with the degree, because I wasn't enjoying the course. I had a great social life in St Andrews, a really good group of friends, but that wasn't enough to keep me committed, and motivated, for another three years. As for losing face, I wasn't too worried about that, to be honest; the fact I had an alternative plan made it a justifiable decision, I reckoned.

Still, when people asked, 'So, you've packed in physics – what are you going to do?' and I said, 'Sports science', the typical response would be: 'Er … oh, OK'. What they were probably thinking was 'Mickey Mouse', because sports science degrees were fairly new back then, and there was a general lack of understanding about what they involved.

Craig was another reason for wanting to be in Edinburgh. We had become good friends – we shared the same sense of humour and spent so much time together that we were practically finishing each other's sentences. We also had lots in common, not least our enthusiasm for our sport, and, more importantly I think, our curiosity. Although Craig's second application to join The City for 1996 was accepted, it was clear that we were, to all intents and purposes, on our own. If we wanted to succeed we'd have to do it together – there was a dearth of coaching expertise, or any practical support in terms of sponsorship and funding. The City was an ambitious club, and great to be part of, but it had few resources and minimal funding.

But The City was as good as it got in the UK. Quite simply, there was practically zero sponsorship in track cycling, and it was ludicrous to think that it could ever be a career. It was a passion, a hobby, and for me it was coming close to being an obsession. It was all I thought about, all I wanted to do, and if that is the definition of 'obsession', then I suppose I'd have to admit it. But at the back of my mind – and occasionally venturing to the forefront – was one of life's golden rules, instilled in me by my parents: that I needed, in the classic parents' phrase, 'something to fall back on'. In other words, a degree or qualification that would enable me to find a job when, inevitably, the day came to enter the real world.

Craig already had something to fall back on, having qualified as a piano tuner. But now, as we prepared for the 1996 season, he was fully committed to cycling – and just as obsessed as I was.

Looking back, I recognize the years 1995 and 1996 as key ones. My gold medals in the British and Scottish championships in 1995 acted as a catalyst for me to think that I could enjoy some success in this sport, if I worked hard at it. I mentioned in the Introduction that I was more interested in the question of 'how' than in that of 'why' some people decide to commit themselves so fully to something, to the extent that it does come close to being an obsession.

But now, when I think of this period, when there was no real sponsorship, no lottery funding, few positive role models in the sport – at least few who actually made a living from it – and general uncertainty, I do ask myself: why? It's hard to explain what kept me going. I certainly got huge satisfaction from achieving success, and winning races, but there was something far more powerful than that driving me on. For me the most potent motivational fuel was not ambition, I think, but curiosity. I wanted to see how far I could go.

As I said earlier, it felt as if I were embarking on a journey, with the destination – and indeed the stop-off points – unknown. But that was the most thrilling thing about it: I could dream about where it might take me. The Commonwealth Games in Kuala Lumpur in 1998 was an obvious goal, the Olympics in Sydney in 2000 a long shot, but that's all these thoughts were at this point: dreams.

Some people take a gap year, and buy a round-the-world ticket, setting off with no fixed itinerary, only vague ideas of where they might go and what they might find. I suppose I was doing something broadly similar, but for no fixed period, and with Craig as my travel partner, even if our 'travel' usually entailed nothing more exotic than repeated visits to a secluded road by Edinburgh airport – but more on that in a moment.

Craig was approaching his mid-20s, and I think he was very conscious of it being his time. Like me, he was also on a steadily upward curve of improvement, and he didn't know when that would end, but he was probably in more of a hurry than me. I was his sparring partner but I was also like his mini-me, in his shadow. I was working in the bookshop and had applied to start sports science at Heriot-Watt University. Craig was unemployed, scraping by and no more, and it wasn't easy for him. Then again, we had a friend the same age as Craig, who we'd cycled with before he gave up and got a 'normal' job. He was already earning a lot of money, but I remember him saying he'd give up what he was doing to have the opportunity to do what we were doing. 'Living the dream' was how he put it. And I don't recall noticing that his tongue was in his cheek.

Craig was no 'workshy fop', to quote Vic Reeves. He considered cycling his full-time job, even if there was no money in it. We became virtually inseparable, training together, and, when we weren't training, poring over training manuals. Craig was a voracious reader of books, at least a voracious skimmer of books and borrower of library books. He trawled libraries in Edinburgh, taking out books about training, fitness, physiology, muscle power – anything that might yield even the tiniest nugget of useful information or advice.

Some of this information influenced our training, which was experimental, to say the least. We became fascinated by the 'big gear principle' in training. Craig had watched Graham Sharman, an Australian sprinter, using very big gears, and it made sense to him. It could improve strength, and specifically cycling strength; it was like doing weights, but on a bike. We decided that this was important; that it should be a central plank of our training, pushing a huge gear, no matter how slowly you were going. We'd find hills and grind our way up them.

And we found that quiet little road by Edinburgh airport, which was perfect. Traffic was virtually non-existent, it was over a mile long, and it was dead straight.

It was just as well there was no traffic, because we might have caused an accident with drivers craning their necks as they went past, trying to work out what the hell we were doing. Picture the scene: two racing cyclists in full gear, pedalling very slowly, clearly making big, vein-popping efforts, but moving at a snail's pace. Had anyone been out for a stroll, they would have overtaken us.

The explanation was that this was the latest method of strength training we'd hit upon: riding with the brakes on. The harder we pushed the pedals, the more we squeezed the brakes, easing the pressure only enough to avoid coming to a standstill and toppling over. It was crazy. At the time we thought it was genius.

Now I think it fell somewhere between madness and genius. As on-the-bike strength training, it was not bad. It was very specific. But, as with most of our training ideas, it was only half right. We were missing vital elements, such as the requirement not only for muscle strength, but for speed of contraction. Craig did other crazy/genius things, such as filling the tubes of his bike with lead shot, making it almost impossible to lift, but again good for strength work. He also attached panniers and filled them with disc weights, which was less sensible – it made the bike completely unbalanced, and almost impossible to handle. At one point, his training bike weighed 50 kilos!

Craig was always coming up with ideas like this, and in this sense he was similar to Graeme Obree, who was renowned for thinking 'outside the box'. Craig was almost like the sprint version of Obree; he recognized there was no blueprint for success for sprinters in the UK, which encouraged him to be as innovative as possible.

By this time, when we weren't doing our slow-motion training by the airport, Craig and I were travelling to Manchester, and the country's only indoor velodrome, on a regular basis. Most weekends, in fact. We had British squad sessions with Marshall Thomas, the only coach employed full time by the British Cycling Federation, but these sessions, like those involving just Craig and me, though well-intentioned, were often ill-conceived. Because our track time was so limited, we felt we had to take maximum advantage of our trips down there. But that didn't necessarily mean doing quality training. It meant simply doing *as much* training as physically possible.

I trained like a lunatic on those weekends. The number of flat-out efforts I would do in a 48-hour period would be crazy, and I would come home absolutely knackered: it would take me all week to recover. But at least you felt that you'd made the most of it. Going to Manchester also meant that we met, and got to know, the other British riders, though they were in the dark about training, too. We heard rumours about what kind of training programmes the nations at the top – the Australians, French and Germans – were following, but there seemed to be a huge gulf between us and them.

It was in 1996 that I had my first encounter with Jason Queally. Jason would go on to be as big an influence as Craig, but our first meeting was memorable for all the wrong reasons. It was the City of Edinburgh Grand Prix meeting at

Meadowbank Velodrome, where Craig, Jason and I all rode a bunch scratch race that ended in a massive pile-up. Craig was leading it out towards the finish, but he flicked out and I caught his wheel, crashing and bringing down half of those behind me, including Jason.

Jason, who was a year older than Craig, and six years older than me, was a big, broad-shouldered former water polo international, and as strong as an ox. I learnt later that his introduction to cycling, only a year previously, had been through riding to and from university in Lancaster. Since he was clocking up quite a few miles on his bike, someone suggested he try a triathlon. And so to test himself out as a cyclist he went to a local circuit race, which began with a timed lap. The course was a kilometre, he was told, and he won it, beating all the established riders, with a time that raised their eyebrows.

Once they'd digested his performance, they told him he'd gone obscenely fast. Jason was sceptical. But he checked his time against the times for the kilometre time trial at the national track championships, and saw he was only a couple of seconds down on the winner on a (much faster) velo-drome. That can't be right, he thought, so he measured the circuit, thinking a mistake must have been made: that it couldn't be a kilometre. But it was. Next, he went to Manchester, rode the track league, and, on one of his first outings, broke the regional track league record for 200 metres.

Less than a year later, he was unfortunate enough to be glued to my back wheel as this bunch race at Meadowbank neared its finale. It was as we rounded the final bend, with a train of four or five City of Edinburgh riders having led the race out, and with Craig now on the front, that I came out of his slipstream to begin trying to move up alongside him. But, as I did, he flicked slightly to the side, not intentionally, but just enough for my front wheel to collide with his back one, and for me to lose my balance. We must have been travelling at about 35mph when I crashed, and took Jason out, but it wasn't the speed that did for him, it was the splinter that lodged in his back, which I could clearly see as I looked across at him from my own prostrate position. It was more like a fence post than a splinter, to be fair, and Jason's scream of 'I've got half the fucking track in my back!' was not unreasonable in the circumstances. And neither was the fact that my own mother, on first aid duty, attended to him rather than to me.

It was my mum who took Jason to hospital, where he was told by doctors that the splinter could have killed him; that the strong chest muscles he developed through swimming might well have saved his life by preventing it from piercing his chest cavity. He made a full recovery, but the accident altered the course of Jason's cycling career. He vowed never to ride a bunch race again. And he never did. As a sprinter, that meant the events he would focus on would be the kilometre, a timed solo effort against the clock, and the team sprint, which, though it meant riding in close proximity to two team-mates, was controlled, and therefore relatively safe.

Despite Jason's crash, he and Craig were emerging as the most promising sprint cyclists in the country, with a few of us – myself, Craig Percival, Alwyn McMath and Peter Jacques – vying for the third spot in the team sprint. This was still a new event, in which we had won gold as a club at the 1995 British championships, and it would feature in the world championships in 1996. These would be staged, for the first time, at the facility that was still barely two years old: the Manchester Velodrome.

I knew that the team sprint represented a possible opportunity for me to gain a foothold in the senior British team, and I began to focus my efforts on being the fastest man for the opening lap. The way the team sprint works is that the three riders line up side by side, with one leading the other two for the first lap, then swinging up the banking, his job done. Man two takes over before doing likewise next time around, leaving the third man, the anchor, to ride the third lap and finish the job.

Craig, Jason and I would train together during sessions at Manchester, but with little formal advice. We were self-coached, really – all acting as coaches for each other. And so you'd have a situation where I'd do an effort, with Craig and Jason watching and then feeding back. Watching from the sidelines, they could watch your technique and critically analyse it.

Like Craig, Jason had very clear ideas about training – which was remarkable given how new he was to the sport. One of his principal beliefs was to do with rest. Jason was a big fan of resting, which doesn't mean he was lazy. He trained bloody hard, but when it was time to rest, boy, did he rest. On one later training camp in Perth, Australia, I remember our then coach, Shane Sutton, phoning British Cycling's head-quarters in Manchester and expressing his bafflement – and no little concern – at the amount of time Jason spent doing … well, nothing. 'Someone's gonna have to come out here and surgically remove the sofa from his arse,' said Shane, only half joking.

Craig wasn't quite so preoccupied by getting such 'quality rest' in between sessions, but he and Jason were similar in so many respects – both being very curious and fascinated by the process of training, while, paradoxically, also having some very fixed ideas about certain aspects. It could have been this unwillingness to compromise in some of their ideas, as well as the similarities between the two of them, that contributed to the clashes they would have further down the line.

But back then there was an innocence and naïvety about our approach, though already Jason and Craig, perhaps because they were a bit older than me, were not afraid to raise their heads above the parapet and argue for more support. Jason doesn't suffer fools gladly (who does?), but he has no ego at all, and so the frustration that would sometimes spill out was not because he felt hard done by or considered himself special. He was 100 per cent focused on fulfilling his potential as a cyclist, and all he wanted was the support to match his own commitment – support that, back then, was completely lacking.

Since the 2008 Olympics much has been written and said about the success of the British cycling team, and the importance of the programme that was established, with lottery funding, in 1997 – which I'll go into in the next chapter. And it's only right and proper that, more than a decade on, it is hailed as a phenomenal success. But that doesn't mean it was plain sailing from day one ... far from it. There were healthy discussions, 'robust debates', arguments, the odd tantrum; but I believe that without Jason and Craig, Team GB would not have enjoyed the success it had in the sprint events in Beijing, with all five sprinters in the team returning home with at least one medal, and a combined total of six from the four men's and one women's events.

Remarkably, both Craig and Jason, at 37 and 38 respectively, were in contention to make the team for Beijing until just a few weeks before the Olympics started. They missed out, by the narrowest of margins, but I would argue that this is immaterial, and that the team's collection of medals – the great haul of China – should be seen as their legacy.

None of us would have been in such great shape had Craig and Jason not been pushing us all the way, nipping at our heels, almost until the moment we boarded the plane for Beijing. We have much to be grateful to them for.

CHAPTER 7

Holding Your Hand in the Fire

1996 was an Olympic year, but I was miles away – literally and metaphorically – from Atlanta, where the Games were held. Marginally closer, though still not even on the same continent, were Jason Queally and Craig MacLean, but not a single sprint cyclist was even selected for the British team, which comprised only a handful of riders, including Chris Boardman and Graeme Obree.

Boardman, the gold medallist in the pursuit in Barcelona four years previously, took bronze in the road time trial, but Obree had one of his periodic dips in performance, because of a recent illness, and failed to medal in the pursuit. It was a sad beginning and end to Obree's Olympic career: the Atlanta Games would prove to be his only chance to crown his career with the ultimate prize.

In 1997 he was attempting to come back from that disappointment, but with limited success. That was the year I made my World Cup debut for Great Britain, which, rather strangely, came *after* my first appearance in a world championship, in 1996. That took place in Manchester, which meant a big British contingent, and I got the nod in the team sprint, together with Craig MacLean and Jason

Queally, who had recovered from his terrible crash at Meadowbank.

It wasn't my first world championships, of course – who could forget Slough in 1986? With all respect to Slough, the senior track cycling world championships were a huge deal, but there were uncanny echoes of 1986 when, once more, a foot went astray from a pedal at an inopportune moment. This time it wasn't me but Jason who pulled his foot out with his starting effort. It meant that our challenge for world championship glory was snuffed out in the blink of an eye, or slip of a foot. Craig was raging. I was frustrated, but I tried to be pragmatic: I felt sure we'd have other chances, and I was grateful to experience the atmosphere and pressure of a world championship so early in my career.

By 1997 the long-anticipated lottery funding was, so the rumour mill informed us, moving closer to becoming a reality. It was a hugely exciting, perhaps life-altering, possibility. Nobody knew how much money would be going into cycling, but they knew one thing: it would be more than before.

Yet I can honestly say that the possibility of funding wasn't the biggest factor in me committing more and more of my life to cycling. I was motivated by my curiosity, still, and by the thrill of embarking on a journey that felt like a magical mystery tour. My sports science course at Edinburgh University (the course transferred from Heriot-Watt to Edinburgh University while I was there) was great, and it perfectly complemented training and racing. I was interested – and indeed had a vested interest – in the subject, since I could relate a lot of it to my own training and racing. I was hungry to learn, still having no coach, or anyone who could provide me with answers to the questions I had. Added to that, the demands of the course weren't horrendous, and my fellow students were an interesting bunch, including the rugby player Tony Stanger, a mature student who had been one of my schoolboy heroes for his role in Scotland's famous 1990 Grand Slam-winning team. Tony of course was the man who scored the winning try against England at Murrayfield: credentials that make him a *bona fide* legend in any Scotsman's eyes.

As I mentioned, I didn't ride my first World Cup until that 1997 season, and my debut came in Milan. The series – usually over four or five rounds in all corners of the globe – was introduced in 1995 as part of the International Cycling Union (UCI)'s efforts to promote track cycling worldwide and to give the season some kind of structure. Unlike road cycling, which for over 100 years has had a calendar that is all but set in stone – early-season stage races, spring classics, summer major tours – this was lacking in track cycling. The World Cup series, which is now held over the winter and builds towards the season-ending world championships, has helped establish a structure and a calendar that people can understand.

In Milan I had an unexpected World Cup baptism when a health scare forced Rob Hayles, one of the team pursuiters, to withdraw from the meeting. He had a suspected problem with his heart, but luckily it proved to be nothing serious and Rob has gone on to have a long and successful career.

They had no reserve for the team pursuit, so up I stepped to join the hugely experienced trio of Bryan Steel, Johnny Clay and Matt Illingworth. It was a daunting proposition for a 21-year-old who still felt that he was finding his feet as an international track rider, and as a sprinter at that, but I contributed what I could, drawing heavily on the team pursuit experience I'd had with the City of Edinburgh club, in particular my British gold medal from two years earlier. My job was basically to survive for the first three kilometres, since only three riders need to finish – and we actually did well, finishing fourth. But it was hard, on a big outdoor track with nowhere to hide, and no let-up at all. On an indoor wooden track, sheltered from the elements, you can at least cruise a little when following in the slipstream of the rider in front.

My event was the team sprint, and in Milan I joined Craig MacLean and Craig Percival, to place a stunning – in the sense of it being completely surprising – second. Poland won, but we hardly noticed that – we were preoccupied with trying to get over the shock of a World Cup medal: Great Britain's first ever World Cup medal in a sprint event. It also meant that after my first World Cup I had scored world ranking points as both an endurance rider and a sprinter, which is something I've never achieved since.

The journey had well and truly started, but we had no illusions that this meant we'd start winning medals at world championships. In Milan, for all that we were delighted with silver, we knew we'd been up against relatively weak opposition. We understood that most countries saved their top guns for the world championships; against the very best that the world had to offer, we thought we could be in the top ten, which would still have represented encouraging progress.

At the world championships in Perth in 1997 I had more than just the competition to contend with. I also found myself not only on the same team, but *sharing a room*, with one of my heroes.

There is something very strange about getting to know your heroes – or getting to know them as people, rather than as images on the posters on your wall, or figures on the TV. For example, I found it very surreal, at the Commonwealth Games in 2006, to be asked for my autograph by Gavin Hastings's two children.

In Perth I was in the reception area of the hotel when they were going through the room list, handing out keys, and our coach, Doug Dailey, said: 'Graeme, you're with Chris ...' I was thinking 'Yesssss!' I tried to play it cool on the outside, but I was well chuffed. And so I got to know Graeme Obree as rather more – a whole lot more – than a 2-D image. It was quite an experience.

After the viral infection that wiped out his 1996 season Graeme was attempting to return to his previous level in 1997, but it just wasn't happening for him. Apart from the illness, he'd had problems with the authorities. Two riding positions he had pioneered, both the original Obree position and the later 'Superman' position – hands forward, arms outstretched, using handlebar extensions – had been banned by the UCI. He was selected for Perth as a reserve for the team pursuit, coach Doug Dailey probably reckoning that to be involved could give him the motivation he needed to keep going for the Sydney Olympics three years later. That's my reading, anyway. Doug was a great Obree supporter, through thick and thin – and when it was 'thin' with Graeme it could be thinner than a slice of Parma ham.

Doug was a real stalwart of the British team, having served as coach, sometimes on a voluntary basis, since the dawn of time. Or so it seemed. In football they talk in glowing terms of people like Sir Alex Ferguson as 'a great football man'. Doug is 'a great cycling man', with all that implies – he lives and breathes the sport, he knows and loves it as well as Sir Alex knows and loves football, and it is significant that, through all the changes in the sport over the past decade or so, he is still involved.

So Doug's strategy with Obree was sensible, I thought. He wanted to keep this maverick involved, keep him part of things, to show that he was supported. But Doug – in fact none of us – knew the extent of Graeme's problems, and we wouldn't find out for several more years, when his book, *The Flying Scotsman*, revealed, in harrowing detail, the battle Graeme fought with mental illness.

Clearly he was having problems of this nature in Perth, though I – perhaps naïvely – was oblivious. Sharing a room together, we had some amazing conversations; truly amazing, the like of which I can honestly say I've never had with anyone else. We'd sometimes chat till 2 a.m., though often it wouldn't be so much a two-way conversation, more a simple case of me sitting listening to him. A lot of it was his life story, basically, and I told him he had to write a book. I said it would make an incredible film – not that I'm claiming any credit for the fact that a film, also called *The Flying Scotsman*, was eventually made. Anyone listening to Graeme talk about his life would have come to the same conclusion.

He was, simply, an incredible person to spend time with. There were occasions when it would be getting late, maybe one or two in the morning, and I'd be starting to think that I really should get some sleep, because I'd have to get up early the next day. At the same time, I honestly didn't want him to stop talking.

His life story was fascinating enough, but I was equally interested in what he had to say about his sporting career, and how he'd achieved the seemingly impossible: training himself, alone and unsupported, to break one of the most prestigious world records in the sport. I knew how unsupported he'd been, thanks to a 1994 TV documentary, *Battle of the Bikes*, which depicted his rivalry with Chris Boardman, juxtaposing the two of them tellingly. It showed Chris discussing his attempt with his coaches and advisers, and wheeling out his state-of-the-art bike, and then cut to Graeme, training on his own on a turbo trainer in the tiny and cluttered backyard of his house in Ayrshire, on a complete rust-bucket of a bike.

In Perth, Graeme talked to me passionately, and utterly convincingly, about wanting something so badly that you can *will* it to happen. And I honestly think that on that trip he helped instil in me that belief: that if you want something enough, and work unbelievably hard at it, you can get it. Listening to where Graeme had come from, and what he had done to reach the heights he'd reached, was all the proof I needed – or that was certainly the impression I was left with as our late-night discussions wound on into the early morning.

Graeme thought he was nothing special – something I, and thousands of others, would disagree passionately with – but his main point made sense to me: that determination, desire, dedication, and a steadfast refusal to accept the expectations that other people might have of you, are infinitely more important than natural talent, whatever that might be. And these, as he said, are things you can largely control.

He told me that he thought about racing as a problem-solving exercise. He looked on his career as a series of tiny steps, all leading to the ultimate goal. For years, he said, he kept quiet about that goal, because he feared what people would say – that in Britain there'd be a negative, perhaps even mocking, reaction to someone saying they were going to break a world record. I know that Graeme was badly bullied at school, and his fear of what other people might say perhaps owed something to those experiences.

With Graeme, there was also his trademark ability to push himself beyond any normal limits of pain. He described, in mesmerizing detail, what he went through at the 1995 world championships, held at high altitude in Bogota, Colombia, where he reached the pursuit final and faced the Italian, Andrea Collinelli. I remember so clearly watching it on *Eurosport*, because it was an epic. No offence to pursuiters, but watching a pursuit race – in which two riders start on opposite sides of the track and race over 4 kilometres, or until one catches the other – can be about as thrilling as watching paint dry. But the 1995 final between Obree and Collinelli must go down as one of the most exciting in history.

The lead changed about nine times; they were so evenly matched that there'd be no more than a hair's breadth between them at the end of each lap: Obree, Collinelli, Obree, Collinelli, Obree, Collinelli … it was a war of attrition, in the end coming down to who wanted it the most, though that doesn't adequately convey it; it makes it sound as if it were a simple question of desire, of who most fancied being world champion. This race went beyond that: it was a question of who was willing to put themselves through hell to win that world title. And given the oxygen-starved air of Bogota it really would feel like hell for both of them. Having now competed at high altitude myself, I appreciate how tough it must have been.

Sitting in our room in Perth, Graeme re-lived that final, and by the end of the story I was under no illusions about what it had taken to win it. I'm sure I had tears in my eyes as I listened. He said he'd rather die than finish with an ounce of effort left in his body; he raced while consciously trying to empty his body of everything it had. That way, he said, he reckoned that he was either going to win it or kill himself trying. That's how much he said he wanted it.

His description of that race had a huge impact on me. It was extreme, of course, but that's Graeme. He doesn't do – one of his favourite terms of non-endearment – 'wishy-washy'. But there was one thing he said that resonated more than anything else, and which stuck with me. 'You always think you're at your limit,' he said, 'and that you can't go any harder – but just when you think that, push a bit harder.' It might sound obvious or simple, but I knew exactly what he meant, and I knew that it could make a significant difference. It applied not only to racing, but – perhaps even more crucially – to training.

It rings especially true in the event I would later dedicate myself to: the kilometre. The important point is this: that only *you* know. When it comes to that crunch point, usually on the final lap, or in the final few seconds of a race or training session, when your body's screaming at you to stop, all you've got to do is throttle back half of one per cent to make it bearable, or tolerable. It's a minuscule drop-off in effort; and nobody would know – not even the coaches studying you from the centre of the track.

I know, because I've done it myself. You come off the track and your coach says, 'Good effort, well done.' But inside you know otherwise. A little voice is saying: 'Nah, you know you backed off.' In this respect, perhaps, Graeme had an unexpected and unconventional competitive edge: he didn't have coaches to answer to, only himself. You can kid other people, but you can never kid yourself.

He said that he won that race in Colombia because he committed to it 100 per cent. He didn't think he was a better athlete than Collinelli, but he wanted it more. 'It's like holding your hand in the fire,' he said. 'It's a case of who can deal with the pain the longest.' As I said, Graeme is an extreme character, and his analogies can be pretty horrifying, but if he hadn't believed extreme things, and trained in such an extreme way, he wouldn't have achieved what he did.

He is also eccentric, though. In Perth he had a cell biology textbook with him: that was his reading material. It was as research for his next project: discovering a cure for cancer. Seriously.

On the flight home, having not raced in Perth, Graeme had a few beers. But he kept reading this book, in the inimitable Obree style: holding the book in one hand, a beer in the other, his arm tilted at an impossible angle, a look of rapt concentration on his face. Everyone else was asleep, but Graeme kept on studying the book, his reading light the only one to illuminate the cabin. Suddenly he shouted: 'Fuck! Fuck!' No doubt he'd reached a conclusion of some kind. But at the time I was worried that, rather than having found a cure for cancer, possibly the explanation was that he'd simply overdone it on the beers. And so when we stopped in Singapore, and the pilot announced that a passenger was going to be removed for being drunk, I feared the worst. It came as something of a relief to see the air stewards walking straight past Graeme and heading for one of the Russian cyclists, who was then unceremoniously hauled off the plane, his feet dragging along the ground, completely out for the count. Graeme kept a low profile after that.

As for my own world championships, well, it was great to have qualified in the team sprint, which we'd achieved by virtue of our second place to Poland at the World Cup in Milan, and fifth and third respectively at the World Cups in Sardinia and Athens. In Perth, though, we knew that everyone would be at their best, and that the competition there would give us a clearer indication of where we really stood in the world. The team was Craig MacLean, Craig Percival and me, with me still the lead-out man, my job being to blast through the first lap before handing the baton, so to speak, to Craig Mac. We finished sixth, which was very satisfying. We'd have been happy, I think, with anything in the top ten, and so we reckoned we were making good progress, advancing steadily in the direction of the podium. The winners were the French, who seemed unbeatable, but the scary thing was that they had a newcomer in their team, an 18-year-old called Arnaud Tournant. I'd raced him the previous year at the European under-23 championships in Moscow, where I competed with my arm in plaster after an unfortunate incident at the Manchester Velodrome. Tournant won the kilometre in Moscow, while I, with plaster modified to allow my hand to grip the bars, recorded one minute, six seconds – a personal best by a substantial margin – to finish 12th of the 25 starters. I was blown away by Tournant, though. Then just

17, he beat me by three seconds, and here he was, a year later, winning a senior gold medal. He was 18, I was 21 – he was a phenomenon and there seemed an incredible, un-bridgeable, gulf between us. Of course if I'd told Graeme I thought that, he'd probably have slapped me and said: 'Don't be so wishy-washy.'

When I returned to Edinburgh from Perth there was a letter waiting for me. It was from the British Cycling Federation, and it contained the kind of news that you fantasize about. I'd won the lottery, sort of. The long-rumoured lottery funding was about to become a reality, and I was to receive an annual grant of £10,000.

It was the stuff of dreams. Craig and I – he received the same – were going to fulfil one ambition: we'd be able to devote ourselves full time to cycling. In essence we'd been doing that anyway for a couple of years (albeit I was also fitting in my university studies, just), but with money coming in, it wasn't so difficult to justify the sacrifices we were making. But it wasn't a case of simply receiving a cheque for £10,000; there were catches, and certain hoops you had to jump through. For one thing, a substantial chunk of the money had to be spent on training, racing and associated expenses. Training camps, equipment, travel costs – that kind of thing. And we had to pay for this up front, then claim it back. But still, I was delighted; it meant that when I finished university – I still had 18 months to go at this point – I wouldn't have to look for a job, which meant I could train and, almost as importantly, recover from training by properly resting. Not Jason Queally-style resting, just enough to recover from one session before embarking on the next one.

Trips to Manchester became even more frequent over that winter. I was clocking an incredible number of miles driving from Edinburgh to Manchester and back, often more than once a week, and always in my faithful Citroen Xantia. I say faithful ... I don't know why. My dad's old car had two wheels in the scrapyard, and might have been headed there after I racked up 70,000 miles in not much more than a year. It was an old diesel, with the Citroen suspension system, which kept breaking. It would typically break mid-journey, on the most remote stretch of motorway, as you cross the moors from Scotland to England. It would just go, and I'd bottom out, bouncing along the ground. At 70mph – always observing the speed limit, naturally – I'd have to pump it back up with the lever, jacking it up on the move. Every journey I'd be thinking, 'This is the one where I'm not going to make it,' waiting for it to go completely – and this being in the dim and distant past, in the days before mobile phones, my big fear was that I'd be stranded in the middle of nowhere. I drove with my fingers crossed, and, in between journeys, took it to the garage to get patched up.

Still, it didn't let me down, and I was able to train regularly at the velodrome as I prepared for 1998, which promised to be a big year, with my first ever multi-sport games, the Commonwealth Games in Kuala Lumpur.

As often happens in sport, though, I didn't make the progress in 1998 that I had thought I would. After 1997 my expectations were high, and they weren't fulfilled. By the time I got to Kuala Lumpur I wasn't at my best. It had been a long season, with some decent performances: third in the team sprint at the European championships; fifth in the kilo at the European under-23 championships; third in the team sprint at a World Cup in Hyères, France; gold in the team sprint at the British championships, and two bronzes at the same championships in the kilo and sprint. But the biggest let-down came at the world championships in Bordeaux, when our second man, Craig Percival, misjudged his start, allowing me, as lead-out man, to race into a ridiculous solo lead while Craig P was stranded in no man's land, with Craig

MacLean sitting helplessly behind him. After sixth in Perth the previous year, we slipped to tenth, which was gutting.

I arrived in Kuala Lumpur in September with that disappointment still raw, and feeling pretty jaded physically. Which was a great shame, because the Commonwealth Games meant – and still mean – a great deal to me. These games have their critics, though I suspect that they are generally people who haven't experienced them first hand. It is worth emphasizing that it is athletes who give sporting competitions meaning; if it means a lot to the athletes, you can be guaranteed dramatic and entertaining sport. And the Commonwealth Games do mean a lot to the athletes, at least the ones I've spoken to, whether they come from the major powerhouse that is Australia – *especially* if they come from Australia – or from the smaller countries, like Scotland. For me, it's the only opportunity I have to compete for Scotland, which makes the Commonwealth Games a unique and special event.

But in KL I was disappointed with my performances, and Craig was no happier with his. With no team sprint on the programme we entered the individual events, the sprint and kilo, and I finished ninth in both. I'm not sure if I was ever officially awarded a higher position in the sprint, after the rider who knocked me out in the second round, Stephen Alfred, subsequently tested positive for performance-enhancing drugs. He finished just behind Craig, who was fifth. Craig was also fifth in the kilo, while Jason Queally won the silver medal behind an Australian, Shane Kelly. That was the story of the KL Games: Australian dominance. They qualified first, second and third in the qualifying time trial for the sprint, and ended up with gold and silver; they won the men's scratch race; took gold and silver in the women's pursuit; gold and silver in the men's pursuit; gold and bronze in the kilo; gold in the team pursuit; and gold in the women's points race. No major games would see such dominance by one nation until ... well, we'll come to that in due course.

The only bright spot for us was Jason, who separated the Australian riders Shane Kelly and Joshua Kersten in the kilo, proving they weren't on a different planet altogether – or not all of them. Jason's performance gave Craig and me encouragement. We trained together all the time, and knew what Jason did, so now we also knew that there wasn't some secret that the rest of the world was in on, of which we Brits were oblivious. Then again, there is only so much consolation you can take from someone else's performance; it is your own that you worry about. And there wasn't much satisfaction to be taken from mine.

But the experience of being at a multi-sport games was interesting; it gave me a taste of what to expect if I could make the British team for the Olympics in Sydney in two years' time. But first we needed a big performance in 1999. We had to prove that 1998 had only been a blip, and that we were still improving as a trio, still moving steadily in the direction of the podium.

And we did.

Cut to the Berlin Velodrome, the venue for the 1999 world championships, and me – the lead-out man – with Craig by my side, Jason by his side, the three of us awaiting the start of the team sprint. But not just any team sprint – this, unbelievably, was the final. Having qualified fourth, we beat Greece in the second round, recording the second fastest time to qualify for the final and meet – you guessed it – the fastest qualifiers, France. I burst from that start gate with all I had. We were guaranteed a medal; some of the pressure was off, and I was determined, as Graeme Obree might have put it, to empty my body of every last micro-ounce of effort it contained. And I think I did: 18.01 seconds was my fastest ever time, it put us up on the French, and it set up Craig for lap two, who in turn catapulted Jason into lap three, just down on the French at that point, with everything still to play for.

I'll let you into an embarrassing secret here. As first man, with your race over after 18 seconds, you circle the top of the banking, enjoying a ringside view as the rest of the race unfolds. In Berlin, as I soft-pedalled around the top of the track, I did what I always did in that position: I did my bit to influence the outcome. When Craig went past me, with Jason tucked in behind, I puffed out my cheeks and blew as hard as I could; and when Jason passed me, alone now, on the final lap, I did it again. Conversely, as the two French riders approached me I turned around and blew *at* them, thus creating – ahem – a 'headwind'. OK, it's ridiculous, but if a butterfly flapping its wings can help create a tornado on the other side of the world, then my puffs might have ... OK, it is ridiculous.

But it wasn't superstitious. I don't have any superstitions, nor will I ever have, because I think it sets a dangerous precedent. If you 'need' your lucky socks, and something happens to your lucky socks, what then? It could play on your mind, so I prefer to rely on training instead of lucky socks and I take a dismissive approach to superstitions generally. As for the blowing, I suppose my justification would be that it couldn't do any harm.

Maybe I didn't blow quite hard enough, because Jason flashed across the line in 45.485 seconds – 0.637 seconds down on the French trio of Laurent Gané, Florian Rousseau and Arnaud Tournant. But wow! Our silver medals felt like golds. They were the only British medals at those championships, and were especially significant in light of the new lottery-funded era that was dawning for British cycling ... it also meant that we began Olympic year, 2000, feeling as though we were riding the crest of an almighty wave, with the unthinkable – an Olympic medal – coming very hazily into view on the shore.

I graduated that year, too, with a respectable 2:1. Finally my mum could breathe a little more easily, given that I now had something 'to fall back on' ... but her relief would have vanished had she seen the house in Rusholme that I moved into that same year, with Craig, three other male cyclists and one bathroom – a truly lethal cocktail. The only positive thing that could be said about that house was that it was quite near the velodrome. Also I could escape, for brief periods, to my girlfriend Claire's house. Claire was also a cyclist, from the Manchester area, who was more into mountain biking than track cycling, though we actually met at the Manchester Velodrome. To her I will always be grateful for providing sanctuary from my three housemates, their appalling habits and our house of horrors.

CHAPTER 8

'They'll Be Here in a Week to Ten Days'

'They'll be here in a week to ten days.' For Craig, Jason and me it was the most repeated statement of 2000, to the extent that it could be abbreviated – 'week/ten days' – and instantly understood, until it eventually became a euphemism for 'never'.

It was Olympic year, the Games in Sydney were fast approaching, and we still had no bikes. They would be arriving in 'a week to ten days', we were told in February. And then again in March, April, May ...

So much had changed and was changing in British cycling. For one thing, the national governing body, formerly the British Cycling Federation, was now a streamlined 'British Cycling', and Peter Keen, the new performance director, deserved huge credit for establishing a 'World Class Performance Programme' (WCPP) from scratch, putting a new structure in place with the assistance of the lottery and funding that was unprecedented in a sport like cycling in the UK. What's more, he had done it in a little over two years.

Peter had coached Chris Boardman to his pursuit gold medal at the 1992 Olympics, and he was and is an outstanding coach. From the outset, he had a very clear vision for the

WCPP: it would focus on track racing, which was obviously a very welcome development as far as I was concerned. And within the sphere of track racing, it would focus mainly on endurance events, in particular, the pursuit and team pursuit. From my perspective, this was less encouraging, but still, nobody could complain: the sport was moving forward, and we were all being pulled in its slipstream.

Leading the charge were the pursuiters. Huge efforts and resources, from coaching to equipment, were directed towards the track endurance programme in the first couple of years of lottery funding, leading up to the 2000 Olympics. We sprinters, meanwhile, were pretty much left to get on with it. We had a manager, Steve Paulding, but no sprint coach. We were still coaching ourselves, Craig, Jason and I taking turns to watch each other and offer feedback. It wasn't an ideal situation, and I felt the lack of a coach keenly (no pun intended). Now 24, I felt I was approaching the most important years of my cycling career. I was, by now, a fully-fledged specialist sprinter, and had been for several years; but I had still never had specialist sprint coaching. People like Ray Harris in the early 1990s and, later, Marshall Thomas, gave their absolute all to help me, but, though I have the utmost respect for them, they didn't have world-class sprinting expertise, either as riders or coaches.

I don't blame Peter Keen; in fact, I completely understand where he was coming from. There was a lot of pressure on him to provide a return on the lottery funding – one that would be measured purely and simply in medals won at world championships and, especially, at the Olympics. He obviously assumed that the team pursuit squad had a better chance of a medal, and the assumption was a perfectly reasonable one. In contrast, there was no reason for him to think that we sprinters had any chance at all. And, given that he had limited resources – albeit more than British

Cycling had had in the past – why would he channel them our way?

Peter was confident, having coached Boardman so successfully, that he could produce world and Olympic medal-winning individual and team pursuiters. These disciplines are, by their nature, relatively controllable, as they are about times rather than tactics. Plus, it was natural for him to want to focus on the area of the sport, and the riders, that he knew best, and in which Britain had something of a tradition. We sprinters were seen as a bit of a maverick bunch. We were considered, I found out later, 'difficult' and hard to manage. To Peter, it must have seemed a risk to invest significantly in an area of the sport in which Britain had enjoyed only isolated successes, roughly once a century, and that thanks to Reg Harris.

Did we feel neglected? Yes, of course. It was difficult to watch the endurance guys getting so much help and attention, while we struggled to get proper racing bikes. Not that it was attention that we craved. It was support that we needed – support to do the job to the best of our ability.

We felt a little like outsiders, and we had no one to fight our corner. We were, therefore, always arguing with the powers that be, fighting for a better deal, which, on top of the demands of training and racing, was a draining and stressful distraction. It all came to a head when we got to May and the first World Cup of the season in Moscow ... and we didn't have proper bikes to race on: we were still racing on very basic steel bikes. We had French-made carbon fibre Corimas on order. They had been on order for weeks but finally, after what seemed like an eternity, we were told they would arrive in 'a week to ten days'. Then, almost laughably, we were told: 'They're in the country.'

In the country? It was tantalizing. We could almost touch our new carbon bikes ... but when, exactly, would they be here, *with us*? 'A week to ten days'.

A clear-the-air meeting was arranged on the eve of the Moscow World Cup. At the meeting were Peter Keen, his number two Dave Brailsford, Jason, Craig MacLean, Craig Percival and me. As an exercise in clearing the air, however, this was about as effective as a scented candle on a typical morning in the bathroom of our house of horrors in Rusholme.

The atmosphere was confrontational from the start. Jason accused Peter of being 'up there in your ivory tower', which, not surprisingly, didn't go down too well. But it set the tone, and the meeting ended with us basically being told that we should be grateful for what we'd been given. It was pointed out to us that Yvonne McGregor, Britain's leading female pursuiter, made do with some old bike, while here we were demanding this and that ... but there was a crucial difference between Yvonne and us. At about 60 kilos, Yvonne was generating up to about 800 watts, while we 90kg sprinters were, briefly, kicking out a couple of thousand. We needed strong, carbon-framed bikes that could turn that power into forward motion; we weren't looking for all-singing, all-dancing machines, just bikes that were fit for purpose.

In my desperation for a proper sprinting bike I even phoned another British rider, Gary Edwards. I didn't really know Gary, but I did know he wouldn't be using his bike for a while: he was serving a doping suspension after testing positive prior to the Commonwealth Games in Kuala Lumpur. I hummed and hawed about phoning him, then thought: why not? I felt I had nothing to lose. But it was an awkward conversation.

'Hi Gary, it's Chris Hoy [who you barely know] here; I just wondered if I could borrow your bike for the World Cup in Moscow ...'

'... Er, well, I can't lend it, Chris, I'm sorry ... And, er, can I just ask – where did you get my number?'

He was friendly and apologetic, but he said he couldn't lend me his bike, worth a few thousand pounds, and, on reflection, it seems fair enough.

As for the Corimas, the problem stemmed partly from the fact that we were British: I'm pretty sure of that. The bikes were being supplied by the manufacturer on some kind of special deal arranged with the federation, but I can imagine that we were slipping down the pecking order every time a frame was ordered by a paying customer. From the French manufacturer's point of view, there was little in it for them – we were British, so it wasn't as if their bikes were going to be seen winning Olympic medals, was it? I'm pretty sure that's what they would have been thinking.

I started the year riding a carbon monocoque frame, which I'd bought with my own money in 1999, but in February, while I was at a training camp in Perth, the UCI outlawed all monocoque bikes. That left me in a real fix for Moscow, and in the end I rode the World Cup on a Hotta bike, which wasn't really a sprinting bike, but it was all I could get my hands on.

And guess what, we returned to Manchester to be told that the Corimas, though now allegedly 'in the country', would arrive in 'a week to ten days'. When they eventually did turn up you could have knocked us down with a feather. The important thing, however, was that this was before we left for the Olympics.

In the midst of all this there was a positive development, with the official appointment of a dedicated sprint coach. Martin 'Marv' Barras was someone we had got to know gradually over the last couple of seasons, and we'd been properly introduced at our winter training camp in Perth, a couple of months earlier. Marv was a French-Canadian who'd spent most of his coaching career in Australia – he was therefore a rare commodity: a top sprint coach who also spoke perfect

English, albeit with an amusing accent, not dissimilar to Kermit the Frog.

He seemed the ideal appointment, and I got on well with him immediately. Marv had great experience and he was a relentlessly upbeat, positive guy. I had the feeling, from our first meetings, that he believed in me, which is absolutely fundamental in any coach–athlete partnership. And when I started properly working with him, I knew for certain he believed in me when he told me he thought he could get my 200 metres time down to 10.5 seconds within a season. My reaction to that was: 'Are you mad?'

Upbeat and positive doesn't necessarily mean confident, though. My God, could Marv be nervous! In Moscow, the first time he worked with us, he was as jumpy as a kitten. On the morning of the team sprint, at breakfast, he wouldn't shut up – he just kept talking and talking. And talking. At one point he even said: 'Oh man, I'm so fucking nervous!'

This was a little bizarre, because by now, having developed as an almost autonomous unit, our group was quite experienced. It led to a curious role reversal, whereby we, the riders, found ourselves reassuring our coach. Marv was and is an emotional guy, and he was the 'newbie', so it was natural, to some degree. It also had something to do with the fact that he was super-excited. And he was even more hyper when we finished second in Moscow, again to the Poles, to make it a positive start to the season, even *without* new bikes.

My role that year was very simple: I had to improve my standing start. My Olympics – if I was selected – was going to be all about my ability to ride one lap very fast. Previously, I'd seen myself as an all-rounder, but the team sprint was far and away my best chance of ... a medal. At the time, I couldn't have said that out loud. Not for superstitious reasons – I don't believe in such nonsense, as I've said – but because I simply couldn't comprehend it. Winning an Olympic medal was the kind of thing that happened to other people, not me. Despite our silver medal at the world championships the previous year, the idea still seemed faintly ridiculous.

Marv began to supervise my training, which focused mainly on my standing start. I'd do sessions which, after my warm-up, would comprise 12 flat-out starts – each one perhaps amounting to an effort of between seven and 11 seconds. Then I'd warm down and go home to rest for the next session. It doesn't sound like much (the hard work totalling 132 seconds, maximum) but flat out really meant *flat out* – Graeme Obree-style flat out, leaving everything on the track, holding nothing back. I could be absolutely knackered after these sessions.

Initially, Marv didn't work quite as well with Jason and Craig as he did with me. Though we had been crying out for a coach, when we finally got one it was a bit strange, a culture shock, and it required a readjustment to the way we worked. While I was younger, and eager to learn, the more experienced and mature pair of Jason and Craig were more resistant to a 'newbie' infiltrating our little team, telling us what to do. And Marv did, initially, try to tell them what to do. Just about his first act was to produce a document detailing week-by-week training programmes, with everything stipulated, from the length of the session to the gear ratios we should use. For me, it was the best thing that could happen. For Jason and Craig, it was a bit difficult, because they had developed quite clear ideas – and enjoyed some success. Their reaction could be summed up as: 'Whoa! You can't walk in here and tell us what to do.'

It led to a bit of a stand-off between them and Marv, which left me in the middle. It wasn't as if this was an industrial dispute and I was breaking the picket line by working with him, and embracing his ideas. I explained to Jason and Craig, 'I'm going straight in here, and getting stuck into the training

he's suggesting ...' and they were great about it; they understood where I was coming from and supported me.

I loved having Marv around; I relished the feeling of
having someone to discuss my training with, to bounce ideas
off. With Marv, there was the bonus of him being someone
with knowledge and a real passion for working closely with
athletes. It was what I had been crying out for, and it felt as if
a door had opened. He helped demystify lots of aspects of
training for me, but, more than that, we at last had someone
on our side, fighting our battles. It wasn't easy for him – it
was still a struggle to get the sprinters treated as equals,
which is shown by the fact that there is a missing generation.
After Jason, Craig and me, no one else emerged until Ross
Edgar, several years later. But, overall, things were better, and
just in time.

It was a big year, 2000, but not just on the sporting front.
There was a serious family development, too – an addition to
the family. And it was a very unusual addition. I gained an
uncle.

CHAPTER 9

Uncle Mick

The appearance of my uncle Mick, at an early season training camp in Australia, wasn't a surprise. We had been in contact before I travelled Down Under, to arrange this first meeting.

I had been training in Perth, then travelled to Camden, near Sydney, where we stayed in a vets' college and tried out the new track – the track that would be used for the Olympics later in the year. I had finished training one day, and was back at the college, waiting for Mick at the main entrance, when I spotted him walking across the car park. As soon as I spotted this tall, imposing and fairly sturdy figure, I knew immediately that he was my mum's brother. We went out for dinner, Mick with his wife and two daughters, him speaking in his curious hybrid accent, a mixture of Scottish and Australian, and we got on like a house on fire. Afterwards, I phoned my mum and told her about him – because she hadn't yet met him, having only quite recently found out that he existed.

My mum, Carol, and dad, David, come from quite different backgrounds. Dad is Edinburgh born and bred – though the Hoy name probably originated in Norway, where it would have been Hoj – while Mum grew up in the west of Scotland, in Wishaw, on the outskirts of Glasgow. It's interesting, though perhaps inevitable, that both seem to have adopted traits that owe something to where they grew up: my dad is calm and quite reserved, the stereotype, almost, of the Edinburger. My mum, it is fair to say, is more typical west of Scotland: gregarious, outgoing, garrulous. There is a great Scots word, 'gallus', which encompasses all three of these traits. Mum will walk into a crowded room and not see strangers, only friends she hasn't met yet.

Mum was given up for adoption when she was ten days old. She knew from a young age that she was adopted – and she was lucky to be adopted by a loving family, the Reids. But she knew nothing about her real mother, not even her name, and it wasn't until she was working as a nurse in the 1960s that her curiosity took her to Register House in Glasgow, where she was able to check her birth certificate. (Apparently, at that time, Scotland and Poland were the only two countries where adopted children were actually allowed to see their birth certificates.)

When she checked hers, she discovered that her mother was called Catherine Gallagher; that her family had been Irish immigrants; that Catherine had worked as a cook, and that she had lived in the Gorbals. The Gorbals was a very poor part of Glasgow and, curiously enough, it has a cycling connection. Robert Millar, Britain's best ever Tour de France cyclist, was born just around the corner from where my natural grandmother lived. (I should give an honourable mention here to my British team-mate, Bradley Wiggins, who in 2009 equalled Millar's best overall placing of fourth.)

When my mum went to see her mum's old house, it was gone – like much of the Gorbals, it had been flattened. And that was it, really. It seemed that the demolished house represented a dead end; that the trail had gone cold. After that, Mum made a conscious decision to forget about it, suspecting

it would cause grief and upset for her adoptive mother –
whom she always regarded as her real mother – if she ever
did track down Catherine Gallagher.

My mum then met my dad, to whom she was introduced
by mutual friends. But when they began going out – 'court-
ing' I believe the expression was in those days – she still lived
in Glasgow, he in Edinburgh, and so it required quite an
effort to see each other. It is only about forty minutes by train
now, but in those days it must have been difficult, travelling
between the two cities by horse and cart.

Once my mum was married and had a family she kept any
thoughts of tracing her biological mother at the back of her
mind. But inevitably her curiosity would periodically return;
she would do some digging, and find out some new piece of
information. She managed to find out that Catherine Gallagher
also lived for a time in Arrochar, a small village near Loch
Lomond. But every time she found something out, she left it at
that – almost as if she couldn't quite bring herself to try and
make contact, or find out whether her mother was still alive.

Then, in the mid-1990s, Mum was attending to a patient at
the Edinburgh Royal Infirmary, and got chatting to him –
probably not an uncommon occurrence – and he told her
that he helped adopted people trace their biological families.
My mum told him about Catherine Gallagher, gave him her
contact details, and a few days later he phoned and
completely shocked her. 'You've got a brother, a sister and
your mother's alive,' he told her. Mum, who had been about
to go out to work, was absolutely stunned, and almost overwhelmed.

But it turned out to be a case of mistaken identity, as the
guy discovered when he phoned the wrong Catherine
Gallagher. I imagine she was even more shocked – not to
mention confused – to be told that she had a daughter she
knew nothing about.

Not surprisingly, that traumatic experience deterred Mum from continuing her search. A few years later, however, another patient of hers mentioned that he was going to Arrochar to stay with his wife's parents. Mum's ears pricked up. But she was cautious. 'It's a lovely part of the world,' she said to him, just making conversation. He said he was surprised she even knew Arrochar. So Mum mentioned that she was trying to trace someone who had lived there, whom she named as Catherine Gallagher but described only as a long-lost relative. 'My mother-in-law knows everyone,' said the patient. 'I'll ask if she knows.'

The patient phoned Mum later, telling her that the person Mum had mentioned (her mother) was dead. But then he told her that Catherine Gallagher's sister, Mary Mackenzie, still lived there – and he had her number. Mum phoned, though still she didn't say why she was interested in Catherine Gallagher. Mary, who referred to her late sister as 'Kitty', seemed friendly anyway, and invited her over. Mum said she'd think about it; then she asked whether Catherine had had any children. 'Yes,' said Mary. 'A son, Michael, who's in Australia.'

She didn't mention a daughter. But when Mum called back later, saying she would like to take her up on the offer of a visit, Mary said: 'I might know who you are – you're Kitty's daughter, aren't you?'

When she visited Mary she found out more about her mother, who died in the early 1990s, by which time she had been working in a pub in Oxford. Her son, Michael, who was four or five years older than Mum, hadn't been adopted; neither had he been brought up by Kitty. He was raised instead by Kitty's mother – my mother's biological grandmother, who had another five daughters and one son – in Arrochar.

She might not even have known that her daughter was pregnant with my mum. When Kitty left hospital, it seems that she gave my mum up for adoption as quickly as possible.

Michael, meanwhile, joined the merchant navy when he was 17 and trained to become a chef. His home base was in Scotland, with his aunt and uncle, where he later met his wife. He left the navy when his first daughter was born, and in 1972 he left the UK to live in Wollongong, near Sydney. By the time I met him – my mum and the rest of my family finally met him later in the year, when they came over for the Olympics – he had a wife, Sue, and two daughters, Val and Bev, and he was, in many ways, an archetypal Aussie male. He was big, six foot plus and well built. Yet there was a Scottish twang still present in his accent.

We became close, and he really did become part of the family, another uncle to join my dad's brother and sisters Joan, Derek and Rosie, and my mum's brother Jim. From that first meeting in 2000 I met Mick and his family whenever I was in Sydney for World Cup meetings, which was every year. He always took me out for dinner, and always insisted on paying. On one occasion I managed to sneak my credit card to a waiter when I went to the toilet, and Mick, when he realized what I'd done, was genuinely annoyed. He was a great guy, and we were all devastated when he was diagnosed, a few years later, with cancer.

His poor health meant he couldn't travel to Athens for the 2004 Olympic Games, as he and his family had planned to do. However, they did all make the trip down to Melbourne for the 2006 Commonwealth Games. I last met him during the Sydney World Cup, just before Christmas 2006. He died in March 2007.

CHAPTER 10

I Believe the British have Pastries for Breakfast

New bikes – check.
New coach – check.
Tip-top condition – … check, I think.

After an uncertain start to the year, the planets seemed to be gradually coming into alignment as the Sydney Olympics drew closer. To be selected was, of course, a huge deal – I'd dreamt of being an Olympian ever since I wrote, on a goal-sheet given to me by my old Dunedin Cycling Club coach, Ray Harris, that my long-term ambition was to go to the Olympics. In actual fact, I wrote: 'Become Olympic champion'. I was about 16 at the time. But now, eight years later, I wasn't really thinking about winning; it felt like a triumph to be going at all – and going with a chance of a medal.

After a reasonable but unspectacular World Cup campaign we travelled to Brisbane for a pre-Olympics training camp. Actually, it was a pre-pre-Olympics training camp, because it was followed by another one, in Melbourne. But it was in Brisbane that I began to *feel* like an Olympian. We travelled to a school that had been converted into a clothing ware-house, like a very exclusive branch of T.K. Maxx – one that

distributed only official Team GB Olympic kit: the branded
racing and training outfits, the T-shirts and bags, the track-
suits and leisure gear. Yes, I was a serious athlete; no, I definitely wasn't there for the T-shirt; but ... I'm not too
embarrassed to admit that I got a thrill. You tried to appear
unimpressed as you inspected the bounty in the company of
your peers, but I suspect that others, like me, were as excited
as seven-year-old kids on Christmas morning when they got
back to their rooms and rummaged through their new gear.
Just to be dressed in the official Olympic kit was incredible.
I immediately felt about three feet taller.

While in Brisbane we trained on an outdoor concrete
track, which had one very unusual drawback: killer magpies
– that is, magpies that were infamous for dive-bombing
cyclists. This was a serious problem, to the extent that a lot of
local cyclists had taken to drawing a pair of eyes on the back
of their helmets; apparently if the birds thought they were
being looked at, they didn't attack. They're unique to
Queensland, these magpies, and when we were there it was
the season for them to attack. We were therefore on our
guard. But fortunately we managed to avoid any serious incidents.

In fact, one concern as I arrived in Brisbane was that I was
a little bit lighter than I would normally be. I was aiming to
be 90 kilos, but I was about 86. It was nothing to worry
about, but I was quite young and inexperienced, and I was
entering a new, slightly scary environment. There were six
weeks to go until the Games began, and I knew that, in that
time, I could afford to eat a bit more than usual, and gradually build towards what I considered my ideal racing weight.
In this sense, I was in luck.

On my first morning in the small hotel in which we were
staying I went down to breakfast and was confronted with
the most incredible spread. I felt like Charlie entering Willy

Wonka's chocolate factory. My normal breakfast then, and now, is a large bowl of cereal, but at breakfast that morning there were some delicious-looking Danish pastries that really caught my eye, so I ate one. It tasted as good as it looked, so I had another. And then another. And another. And another. And another. This was the great thing about being 24-years-old and in heavy training: my metabolism would just speed up no matter what I fed it. When I'd finished with the pastries, I counted up how many I'd had and it came to fifteen. (The strapline to the advert I would later do for Kellogg's Bran Flakes – 'I believe the French have pastries for breakfast' – takes on an ironic quality. But these pastries *were* delicious.) Apart from the pastries for breakfast, the food was a highlight of the Brisbane camp, the chef having told us on the first day, 'Whatever you want to eat, we can get it.'

'What, anything?' we replied.

'Yes,' he said. 'Anything.'

For a few days, we requested staple dishes, all the usual pasta and rice combinations, and he always came up with the goods. It was impressive. So we decided to test him, and asked for haggis. Next day, we got delicious haggis.

Brisbane was great; it was still far enough out from the Games to be fairly relaxed. And we had a good environment, with a positive atmosphere. All was going well.

Did I say *positive* atmosphere? I'll blame a Freudian slip for that, because it was while we were in Brisbane that we received some shocking news. As well as Craig MacLean, Jason Queally and myself, there was a fourth rider in the sprint team – someone who'd emerged to replace those such as Craig Percival who had drifted in and out of the squad. Neil Campbell was there as a reserve for the team sprint, and, like Jason, to ride the kilometre time trial.

I didn't know Neil very well, though in Brisbane we shared a room. Even then he kept himself to himself, and while

Jason, Craig and I were close, and trained together most of the time, Neil was very much an individual and tended to do his own thing, almost, it seemed to me, for the sake of it. It was as though he wanted to cultivate an air of mystery. Not that it seemed to do him much good on the track, because he wasn't going particularly well.

Then, one morning in Brisbane, came the bombshell: Neil wouldn't be riding the Olympics. He was going home with suspected cancer. Urine tests, taken at the World Cup in Turin in July, and at the British championships two weeks later, had shown high levels of chorionic gonadotrophin, a hormone produced by some types of tumour that also stimulates testosterone production; this suggested he could be suffering from testicular cancer. Although we weren't close to Neil, it was shattering: he was a 26-year-old who had one minute been about to ride his first Olympics, and the next was sitting on a plane home for urgent medical tests. It must have felt as though his world had collapsed. I remember his mum phoning to speak to him – I answered and spoke to her briefly, long enough to realize how distressed she was. I then had a similarly upsetting phone conversation with my own mum about it.

It was only later – after the Olympics – that Craig, Jason and I discovered that Neil didn't have cancer at all. All his subsequent tests had come back clear – and, given that you don't suddenly recover from cancer, the explanation could only be that he'd taken a banned substance. That was what the British Cycling Federation decided, anyway. He was banned for a year and fined £1,600.

Unfortunately, people make an automatic association between drugs and cycling now, but it's funny – here I was at the Olympics and I was very naïve about that whole world. Some people may find this hard to believe, but I hadn't encountered drugs; I knew very little about them; I had never been offered them, and I wouldn't have a clue how to go about getting them. My experience with Neil was as close to 'home' as it got, though I did know – or know of – others who'd tested positive. One of them was Gary Edwards, the guy whose bike I'd asked to borrow earlier in the year. And, strangely enough, Gary and Neil were in the same team. There were other riders, from home and abroad, around whom there was some suspicion – but there were only rumours, nothing more. Anyway, Neil was going so badly that you'd never have thought he was taking drugs. I thought they were supposed to make you go fast ...

I say that flippantly, but this, I think, is where I've been very fortunate: I have never thought that they can make much of a difference. Not that drugs were something I ever considered, but I have never, at any stage in my career, felt that I would have to take them in order to go fast. In road racing – the pinnacle of which is the Tour de France – a drug culture has apparently developed that is so ingrained that some riders seem to feel it is impossible to succeed without doping; in track racing I know that is not the case. Perhaps things are changing. I mentioned, briefly, my British team-mate Bradley Wiggins's performance in the 2009 Tour de France, in which he placed fourth. I have known Bradley a long time; we have both been involved in the British team for more than a decade, and I would vouch for him. For me, at least, his emergence as a Tour contender gives me hope that clean riders can win the Tour.

Perception is so important; and so are role models. Whereas on the road a lot of the 'heroes' have allegedly been dirty, my 'role models' – from Graeme Obree to Jason Queally – were clean. I believed 100 per cent in my team-mates Craig and Jason – I could see every day what they were doing in training, and I knew what they both thought about drugs. It didn't occur to me that I would *have* to take drugs if I wanted to reach the top; that it might otherwise be impossible. I can see why, in road racing, and perhaps in other sports, young athletes might not have that same confidence. In this sense I count myself lucky.

From Brisbane we travelled to Melbourne for our final pre-Olympic training camp. The change of venue, in particular the change from a big outdoor track to a 250-metre indoor track, was intended to give us a big lift. On the faster track in Melbourne we would ... well, we would go faster. Wouldn't we?

That's what we thought. More than that, it was what we assumed; what we had bargained on. And so, when we got to Melbourne, and began doing times that weren't spectacular, the doubts started. Incredibly, we were going slower than we'd been going outdoors. There were three weeks to go to the Olympics. The idea was that, by now, we'd be feeling fresh, and starting to go really well. That was so far from being the case that the doubts quickly turned to full-blown panic, even if none of us would admit it.

Then the team pursuiters arrived, and that compounded our sense of panic. They were fresh. They looked to be going well. 'How's training going?' we would ask. 'Yeah,' they'd reply, exuding confidence. 'Good, thanks.'

Shit.

It was cold-ish in the velodrome, only about 14 degrees, which makes a big difference, but it didn't fully account for our sluggish times. We did a couple of dress rehearsals – again, these were calculated to put us 'in the zone', and to give us the extra 1 per cent to allow us to raise our game, and finally get the confidence we needed. In our full race kit, on our racing bikes, with our racing wheels, in our racing helmets – everything was as it would be in the velodrome in Sydney. And, for the opening lap, I recorded 18.3 seconds – slower than I'd been going virtually all year. Doubt had been replaced by panic, which was now being replaced by outright fear: what the hell was going on?

The art of peaking for a major championships is just that: an art. And as such it is mysterious, hard to pin down or explain rationally. It's something you only really try to do once a year, and you always do it a slightly different way, tweaking aspects of your training and recovery here and there. The theory is great: train hard, taper and peak. But it is so easy to get wrong – and, here in Australia, was the first time we had really done it properly, with Marv having worked it all out, and dictating things.

The problem is that if you start to doubt the process, and then begin to worry about it, you can be doomed. In Melbourne I wasn't doing much training (which is the whole point of tapering), and so I had a lot of time to think, and to wonder: have I got my preparation wrong? Even if I was watching a film, or reading a book, it was always there, in the back of my mind, stressing me out. Next morning I'd wake up, think about that day's training session, and feel apprehensive – which, of course, only compounds the problem. By now we were only training every two days, which gave us 48 hours between sessions to worry about how bad the last one had been, and to worry that the next one might be just as bad, or even worse.

There was no comfort in the fact that we were all going just as badly: Craig, Jason and me. In our team sprint dress rehearsal Craig did the second lap in 13.8 seconds – he was looking to do 13.1 at the Games. Jason did a flying kilometre in one minute, one second – normally he'd go five seconds faster.

Each of us was asking the same question: What the hell is going on? And Marv, our coach ... well, he virtually rode every pedal rev with us, and he's an emotional guy, so you can imagine how stressed he was getting. As for me, after feeling three feet taller wandering around the camp in

Brisbane in my British Olympic team gear, now I felt I'd lost that, and some more.

If you think this sounds a bit over the top – more like the confessions of a paranoid lunatic than an athlete – I'd have to agree, to some extent. But that's what the Olympics, in particular, does to you. I don't know if there's any comparison; an event that you've thought about, and dreamt about, for years; that you've made so many sacrifices for; that could potentially change your life. It's pretty intense and pressurized. I was going to compare it to exams, but, to be honest, I can't think of any exams that *feel* like the Olympics. You don't have the world watching you sit exams.

Craig, Jason and I talked about our bad form in Melbourne, but we couldn't offer each other much comfort. We weren't exactly experienced in competing at an Olympics. Had we been more experienced in trying to peak – really peak, rather than the mini-peaks you'd aim for in other competitions – we'd have recognized some of the patterns, as I do now. Now, I know that you can suffer huge dips in form just before big peaks, and so I'm more relaxed and laid back. Back in 2000, however, with the Olympics a couple of weeks away, it was horrendous.

And then, on the final training session in Melbourne, just before we left for Sydney, something changed. In my one-lap trial I did 18.1, which was not an earth-shattering time, in fact still a tenth of a second slower than I'd gone the previous year, but suddenly I was heading in the right direction again – I was in the ballpark. It was just enough to put my mind at rest, and as soon as my mind was at rest everything else started to click into place. We flew to Sydney, had a day's rest, and then an eight-day lead-in to the Games, and I was flying. So were Craig and Jason. Marv had got it spot on! (And in the future I wouldn't worry quite so much about apparently alarming dips in form in the build-up to a major event.)

In Sydney, we didn't stay in the athletes' village, but instead rented a big house. This was a decision made by Peter Keen, the idea being to preserve some semblance of normality. Given that it was our first Olympics, I think he was worried we'd be distracted by the village, and by the presence of so many other athletes, so we were put up in one house, with the endurance guys in another. The consolation for not staying in the athletes' village was that we'd be allowed to move in there later, after we'd competed, to enable us to enjoy the whole Olympic experience. Or so we were told originally, before travelling to Australia. In Brisbane it was changed: we'd have to return home, we were told, just two days after competing. We were gutted. No village; no closing ceremony.

It's true that the world championships were due to start three weeks after the Olympics, in Manchester, and that these were important – important for lottery funding, and, potentially, as an insurance policy should we fail to perform in Sydney. But I think there was more to it than that. To be honest, I think they were worried we'd go out and get hammered. We had a reputation for being wild, which – like our reputation for being 'difficult' – was completely unfounded, and I have no idea where it came from. There had been a couple of nights out in Melbourne in 1998 after a training camp, but nothing to earn us any real notoriety. In fact, it was the endurance riders rather than the sprinters that they should really have been worrying about. At the 1996 Olympics in Atlanta one rider, Matt Illingworth, went on a night out and didn't come back for three days – an incredible feat of endurance for one of the country's most talented endurance athletes.

Stuck in our house, we did feel we were missing out a bit. It was the perfect place to be before and during competition – it was just afterwards that we had itchy feet, and wanted to be in the village. And so we forced the issue. We spoke to the British Olympic Association (BOA), who told us that the British Cycling Federation couldn't deny us the right to attend the opening and closing ceremonies; it was up to them, the BOA. We never had any intention of going to the opening ceremony, which was two days before our competition started, but we'd been looking forward to going to the closing one, and finally letting off a bit of steam after living like monks for nine months.

We were told by the Federation that 24 hours was all we needed in the village. We fought that and eventually were granted a longer stay with our fellow athletes, but it came with an implicit threat: if you don't medal at either the world championships or the Olympics then your funding will be cut. I have no doubt at all that the Federation thought they were acting in our best interests, but the problem was that they didn't really know us back then; they didn't know how we operated. I think they thought we'd climb out of hotel windows for a night out, which could hardly have been further from the reality. We were disciplined, self-motivated – we didn't need the big stick.

There was still this conflict; this sense of 'them and us'. But not for long. Day one of the track cycling programme changed all that – forever.

Day one included the kilometre: Jason's event. Craig and I went to the Dunc Gray Velodrome in a state of excited anticipation. I was looking forward to seeing how Jason did, and sampling the Olympic atmosphere ahead of my own race, the team sprint, with Jason and Craig, the following day. But as I approached the velodrome I was struck by the silence.

As I entered the stadium I saw that the women's 500-metre time trial had started. And there was a big crowd; it's just that they weren't making any noise, until the French girl, Félicia Ballanger, got into the start gate, and then the chanting started – 'Aussie, Aussie, Aussie', followed, of course, by 'Oi, Oi, Oi' – to try and put her off (it didn't work: Ballanger won ahead of the Aussie, Aussie, Aussie, Michelle Ferris).

When the Aussies were in action, there was lots of noise – otherwise, it was very muted. On the one hand, it was a bit disappointing; on the other, part of me was relieved that I hadn't been overwhelmed by the atmosphere; that I didn't walk in and think, 'Oh my God, this is the Olympics!'

When it came to the men's kilo, the pre-race debate revolved around how much Arnaud Tournant, the French prodigy, would win it by. Tournant, though he was still only 21, was considered unbeatable. Jason had won a World Cup in Valencia, but a more accurate gauge of his form was in the previous year's world championships, where he was fifth. His relatively low seeding meant he was one of the first up. As he sat on the track, while our mechanic, Sandy Gilchrist, attached his bike to the start gate, Jason tugged at the zip on his predominantly blue GB skinsuit; he looked a little on edge, though I think it was nervous energy. He got up in a bit of a hurry, climbed on to the bike as the clock showed 30 seconds to go, and then he blasted out of that start gate, out of the saddle as he accelerated around the track. I could tell immediately that he was on a good ride – he didn't exactly keep a straight line, wobbling around the track a little, but that was a sign of the effort he was making, and the speed he was going. He was fast. Over half a second up at half-distance, but his time as he crossed the line was stunning: one minute, 1.609 seconds – a personal best by over a second and a half. That was incredible enough, but even more so were the initials that appeared by Jason's time on the scoreboard: 'OR'. Olympic record – he'd broken Florian Rousseau's Olympic record.

Wow. My heart was thumping against my ribcage. I was so pleased for Jason, but it's amazing how quickly doubts – or negative thoughts – start to flood into your brain. There were lots of riders still to go – all the big hitters. Maybe the track was just unbelievably fast – perhaps everyone would break their personal best by a second and a half and Jason would eventually finish where we expected him to finish. But Stefan Nimke, the German, and another fancied rider, went a second slower than Jason. Then it was Shane Kelly, the Australian. There was an almighty roar from the crowd and he seemed to respond to that: he was up on Jason at half-distance. My heart sank. But a lap later, at 750 metres, he had slipped marginally behind – and that was it for him. Jason was still leading with just one rider left: Tournant.

Tournant was stocky, punchy and unbelievably fast. There had been a very funny incident a couple of days earlier, when we had been sitting around in the centre of the track at the Dunc Gray Velodrome, waiting to start a training session. They were trying out the arena's PA system, playing music, which stopped briefly. Then it started again – this time it was the familiar funky intro to the theme from *Shaft* – and at *precisely* that moment Tournant's head appeared, bobbing up the steps almost in time to the funky chords, wearing his shades and looking like 'The Daddy'. It was as if the show could really begin now that Tournant was here. We fell about laughing. 'He's a porn star!' said Marv. And that's what he was like: he *was* The Daddy, the superstar – the theme from *Shaft* could have been his soundtrack.

Now, as Tournant began his ride, Jason was riding around the centre of the track on his road bike, watching all these other riders step up and fail to beat his time. By this time he was contemplating a silver medal, at worst, and I'm sure he was as shocked as I was, sitting in the stand. But I was about to be even more stunned, because Tournant, though he was up at half-distance, also did what Kelly did – he faded over the second half. Jason was still top of the leaderboard: he was Olympic champion. What's more, he had won by eight-tenths of a second from Nimke. Kelly was third; Tournant didn't even medal.

Before I knew what I was doing, I was running around the concourse, ignoring the golden rule – don't walk if you can help it, and never, *ever* run so close to a competition – as I tried to get to his family, who were at the other side of the stadium. All the time I was thinking: 'My God, we've got an Olympic champion in our team!' The bronze medal had been his dream.

I also thought about what this would mean for our prospects in the team sprint. It was kind of a form guide for the final lap, which was Jason's job. It gave us a lot of hope. But just so that we didn't destroy our hopes by knackering our legs sprinting after him, we stopped running, and went down to the track centre instead. We only saw him briefly, after the medal ceremony, when he had the gold medal round his neck, but he was warming down on his road bike, mindful of the fact that he – we – had another event the next day. It was weird: there were no real hugs or handshakes; we just grabbed him, patting him on the back, and only for a moment, because now he was being ushered away to a press conference. He looked as though he were in a dream – he appeared shellshocked. And so were we.

I didn't get the chance to congratulate him properly until the following day, because he stayed in a different apartment that night. After the medal ceremony and the press conferences he had to go for dope control, and by the time he'd finished with that it was late, and they didn't want to disturb us. Which is ironic, given that I couldn't sleep anyway. I was running Jason's race over in my mind, again and again, and thinking about what it must be like for him now, to be the Olympic champion. Even if he does nothing else in his life now, I thought, that wouldn't change: he would always be the Sydney Olympic champion.

Jason's gold medal-winning ride in Sydney was by far the most significant thing that had ever happened during my career. It opened my eyes to what might be possible; it brought new horizons into view; and it altered the course I would take in the years after Sydney.

But that night, lying sleepless in my bed in our house in Sydney, I wasn't thinking quite so lucidly, or looking so far into the future. After I had finally digested the fact that Jason had won, having pinched myself a few times to make sure I hadn't dreamt it, I focused on the following day, drawing huge confidence and belief from the fact that Craig and I would be going in to bat with the Olympic champion on our side. Now I felt about six feet taller.

CHAPTER 11

Sydney, Silver and Stig of the Dump

I woke up – I suppose I must have got to sleep in order to be able to wake up – on the morning of 17 September feeling as nervous as a kitten. I got out of bed as soon as I was awake because I couldn't lie in bed a second longer. Then I couldn't sit still. I wasn't dreading the day ahead: I felt so ready to go. I couldn't bear the idea that there were still hours to go, with nothing to do but wait. I wanted to ride now.

We had all started to go much better in Sydney. It was warmer, and there was a feeling that it was almost over; we were there. You realize that you've done the work, there's nothing else you can do, and this helped our confidence to grow. We went in optimistic – not confident, because we didn't know what the others would do. There were the Australians, the Greeks, the Germans, and of course the French, who had beaten us to the gold medal at the world championships the previous year.

Sitting around the house on the morning of the race, just waiting, was torture, but as soon as we got to the track I was fine. It was an environment I could control; I knew the routine from here: get ready, warm-up … the countdown to our team sprint qualifying ride started as soon as we arrived, with every minute accounted for. But I still hadn't really seen Jason. When I finally met him, sitting in the track centre, I said, 'It's Jason Queally, the Olympic champion.' Still there were no hugs, no manly embraces – just a handshake. He still seemed a little dazed, and in a state of shock (I didn't want to shock him even more by embracing him). But he seemed strangely relaxed, almost Zen-like. I wasn't sure if this was good or bad, but then I remembered: he's the Olympic champion. And he was in our team.

In qualifying, we were guaranteed a big reaction from the crowd – though it wasn't for us. We were paired with Australia, meaning that they started on the other side of the track from us. What mattered was our time, and that's what I was focused on. The worries and stresses of the training camp in Melbourne didn't figure at all. It had only been nine days ago that I had been thinking we had got our preparation hopelessly wrong, yet here I was, sprinting out of the start gate, with Craig tucking in behind me as man two, and Jason behind him as man three, all three of us nailing it, doing a close to perfect ride. My time for my opening lap was 17.921 seconds. I had hit my target for the year just when it mattered.

We weren't racing the Aussies, since this round was purely about qualification, but there were bragging rights at stake. It was bloody close: after my lap we were 0.073 seconds ahead; after lap two we were 0.095 seconds down (I obviously didn't blow hard enough that lap), which brought a huge roar from the crowd. Then it was Jason, Olympic champion, and he brought it back – we crossed the line 0.060 seconds before, on the other side of the track, the Australians stopped the clock. We had beaten them and qualified second. The arena was transformed, in that instant, from cacophony to eerie silence.

In the second round we were up against the seventh fastest team, the Czech Republic, and this was the crucial ride. We had to beat them; but we also had to do so in at least the second fastest time of all the four heats. If we could do that, then a medal would be ours, and it would be silver or gold. We would be in the final.

We were last to go, meaning that we knew what time we had to do to reach the final. And I would get to watch! As the first rider, who swung up and had the ringside seat after my opening lap, I would see the race unfold, keeping one eye on the scoreboard, so I'd know immediately whether we'd done it. We beat the Czech Republic by about a tenth of a second, but it was the time that mattered – and, glancing at the scoreboard, I saw it: we were second fastest. It would be us versus France in the final.

The French team was awesome: Arnaud Tournant, Florian Rousseau, Laurent Gané. Arguably three of the greatest sprint cyclists of all time, but that didn't mean we intended to lie down and hand them the gold medal. In our minds, we hadn't settled for silver – we intended to give them a good race. In reality, it was a one-sided final: we were almost half a second down, with 44.680 seconds to their 44.233. We were smoked. But any disappointment didn't last too long. We had lost to formidable opponents. And we had the pretty amazing consolation prize of Olympic silver medals.

On the podium, that began to sink in. And yet ... there was a part of me that was a little bit disappointed. A private ambition I'd had was to do the fastest first lap of the competition, and I hadn't quite managed that. I would describe my mood as happy, but not fully satisfied. It was a team achievement, and in my mind I knew that it was Craig and Jason who'd really brought home the bacon. It was they who had raised the bar; who'd made this Olympic medal a possibility. I knew that my performance was adequate, but that there was vast room for improvement.

Still, standing on an Olympic podium for the first time was an unforgettable experience. And we weren't the only ones to be moved by the occasion. Tournant broke down in tears on the podium. Having finished only fifth the previous evening, he now had his gold medal, but I think he was also thinking about what he'd missed out on: the double that everyone had expected him to collect, almost as a matter of course. I didn't know Tournant then. Though he was younger than me, he *seemed* older, simply because he had been a star for so long; I also found him a little bit cold and aloof back then. What I didn't yet know was that he was destined to become a great opponent, and also a great friend. Our rivalry would last the best part of the next decade, and yet it is strange to think that Sydney was, as far as the Olympics were concerned, as good as it got for him. Incredibly, that team sprint provided Arnaud's one and only Olympic gold medal. In 2000, on the eve of the Sydney Games, you'd have got very long odds on that possibility.

That silver medal hardly left my sight, or my clutches – other than at night, when I hung it on my bedpost – for the remainder of the Olympics, but my Games weren't over yet. Which came as a bit of a shock. I had come to ride the team sprint, but Craig said, afterwards, that he might not ride the keirin. He was riding the individual sprint as well, in which he got through to the last eight, and to do all three events would have been asking a lot. So the opportunity presented itself: did I want to ride the keirin?

And did I have a choice? Not really. If you're asked by your coaches to ride something at an Olympic Games, even if you have never ridden it before, and are totally unprepared for it, you ride it. I have to be honest, though: I was champing at the bit to get into the athletes' village, and to experience that side of the Olympics. Maybe I'm just not very good at waiting – OK, patience definitely isn't one of my virtues – but the three-day interlude between team sprint and keirin seemed like a very long three days, especially when all my preparations – physical and mental – had been geared towards the team sprint, and only the team sprint.

I had never ridden an international keirin before. I had ridden exhibition-style races in Trinidad and Barbados, as I mentioned earlier, but I had absolutely zero chance of doing anything in the Olympic keirin, which wasn't negative thinking on my part, just realism. It was the first time it had been in the Olympics, but it was a feature of the world championships, and there was an art to it – an art that I didn't have much chance of mastering in three days.

In the keirin, six sprinters line up, and then fall into line behind a pace-setting motorbike. The motorbike gradually increases its speed until, with two and a half laps remaining, it swings off the track, and that's when all hell breaks loose. And all hell really *does* break loose – or it did in those days. If you think back to what football was like before they outlawed the tackle from behind, or the two-footed challenge – well, in 2000 the keirin was a little like that. OK, so there weren't many two-footed challenges – but it was a case of just about anything goes in the mad scrap for the line, with shoulders, elbows and possibly even helmets all used to impede an opponent. They might as well have put me in a boxing match. These days, it's a bit cleaner.

I lined up for the first round in a heat that was stacked with some of the best keirin riders around, including the great Frenchman Florian Rousseau. Two went through, and in the mêlée I managed to cross the line fourth – remarkably, Rousseau was one of the two behind me. But this didn't mean it was all over, either for him or for me. There was a way back into the competition, through the 'repechage' heats – a kind of last chance saloon; in fact, Rousseau did get back in, and went on to win the gold medal.

I didn't. Not quite. But first, after my heat, I got a bit of an ear bashing from Marv for the way I'd ridden. 'What was that?' he asked. I had ridden a nothing race. I didn't make a single move: I didn't do anything at all. It was partly because I had no idea what to do, but in Marv's eyes my 'crime' was more serious than that: it had looked as though I wasn't trying and didn't really care.

'Do you not think you deserve to be up there?' Marv asked. 'Do you not think you're as good as these guys? You didn't even race that race.'

Then he started talking about the next race, the repechage: 'Look, I don't care what happens here. I want to see you *commit* and make something of the race. Shake it up a bit. Be aggressive. If you don't make it through, there's nothing lost. But I want to see you take the race on. I want to see you do *something*.'

His words had the desired effect: I lined up for the second keirin of my life, alongside my five opponents, listening out for the hum of the approaching motorbike, in a completely different frame of mind. I really wanted to do something in this race that would, at the very least, impress Marv.

The six riders rode around in a fairly orderly line, and I was about half-way down the string, in third place, when the motorcycle swung off, acting as the cue for the real action to start. But just as it swung off, I heard a Japanese rider, sitting in front of me, shout something; something that seemed to be directed at the rider in front of him, a Polish rider.

Right, I thought, there's something going on here, these two have some kind of arrangement. And that was it: I didn't waste any more time thinking, I nailed it, passing the Japanese and cutting back down the banking to squeeze him out, and slot in behind the Polish rider. This is brilliant, I thought, I've got the perfect lead-out here ... the Pole was going flat out, there were two laps to go ... I couldn't believe my luck.

I sat there, biding my time, and with half a lap to go I started to come off the back wheel of the Polish rider. What now? Sprint for the line, but I hadn't been in this position before, and I didn't really know how to judge it. There's a reason why, in cycling, you ride close behind the rider in front of you, and remain glued to his back wheel as long as possible. At the kind of speed we were now travelling – probably close to 40mph – the wind resistance is considerable (try sticking your hand out the window of a car at 40mph), and that hit me full in the face as I left the shelter of the Pole's back wheel. And now that I was on the front I found that my legs didn't have that extra bit of acceleration that I needed; I began tying up within sight of the line, and Ainars Kiksis, of Latvia, came over the top of me to cross the line first.

But I was second. Yes! I was through to the next round. I couldn't believe it.

And I was right not to believe it: because it wasn't true. After a few seconds I realized I'd been disqualified – apparently for impeding the Japanese rider when I dropped down in front of him with two laps to go. I hadn't: it was an extremely dubious call. But, to be honest, I wasn't that bothered. I was just pleased to have animated the race, and Marv was happy that I'd shown a bit of fight.

Now my Games really were over – the racing, anyway. It was time, finally, to let my hair down and experience the athletes' village.

Now, too, I could properly reflect on my silver medal. Every time in sport that you do a significant thing for the first time it's the same feeling. My first Scottish title gave me that feeling; my first British title – when I won my first national champion's jersey in the 1995 team sprint and hung it up in my room, rubbing my eyes in disbelief every time I saw it – gave me that feeling too; and my first time riding for Scotland and for Great Britain also gave me it: the feeling that I had climbed up another rung of the ladder, or gained another foothold on the climb to the summit.

I didn't have any idea where that summit was – or how far the ladder reached into the sky – but it didn't matter, it was all about moving up. It wasn't elation I felt; and I certainly didn't think, 'I've made it.' It was more a feeling of intense satisfaction, if that makes sense. As long as I was moving up, progressing, I could justify this extended 'year out' – this journey – I had embarked on a few years earlier. On some level, it was a validation of what I was doing, I suppose. And what made it extra satisfying was that my family were there in Sydney to witness it – Mum, Dad, my sister Carrie and her boyfriend Garry, and my auntie Joan and uncle John. Oh, and my uncle Mick and his family. Mum and he had finally met, and they got on as if they'd known each other all their lives.

When Craig, Jason and I moved into the Olympic village, we were in high spirits, as were most of the British team. Not everyone, though. We moved into a block within the village that we shared with some of the swimming team management, who weren't quite so buoyant, because the swimmers hadn't enjoyed a successful Games. When we arrived, screaming 'Waaaaaahaaaaayyyyyyyy!' – or words to that effect – we were promptly told to calm down. Oh, and turn our music down while we were at it.

There can be a perception, from the outside, that the British team – or any other national Olympic team, for that matter – is a happy ship, full of positive, optimistic athletes, in the best condition of their lives, all 'up for it'. That, of course, would be a hopelessly naïve view. It is a group of people like any other: it contains the usual wide range of people and personalities, with all the issues and tensions you'd expect.

This time, on the whole, Team GB was a pretty happy ship, apart from the swimmers. There has traditionally been a closeness between the cyclists and the swimmers, with each team paying particular attention to what the other does. There are things we have in common in terms of dedication and volume of training. We tend to get on well – sometimes very well, as in the case of Hugh Porter and Anita Lonsbrough, who married after meeting at the 1964 Olympics, and, more recently, Rob Hayles and Vicki Horner, another Olympic swimmer.

Overall, the Sydney Games was the start of things getting better, in terms of the atmosphere and sense of cohesiveness within Team GB. It was certainly an improvement on Atlanta 1996, when GB returned with one gold medal. It was the calamity of those 1996 Games that prompted the drastic review, and eventual overhaul, of sport in the UK; it also led to the introduction of lottery funding, and to greater professionalism in the governing bodies.

In Sydney, Team GB finished tenth in the medals table, with 11 golds, 10 silvers and 7 bronzes. It was a more than decent return on the first two or three years of lottery funding, which was just as well. Had we managed the almost impossible and performed worse than in Atlanta, then I can imagine there would have been a lot of questions asked about why all this lottery money was being squandered on our hopeless sportspeople.

Not that I was too concerned with the bigger picture at that point: I'd just had the best week of my life. And now, with the competition over, I could enjoy myself. It wasn't difficult. It felt like Hogmanay every night for a week, with Sydney Harbour the place where everyone gathered and partied like it was, well, like it was the Olympics. Prior to the Games I hadn't had a drop of alcohol in six months, and it wasn't that long ago that I'd been a student, which is what I felt like again; albeit one with a silver medal in my pocket. Because, yes, the silver medal didn't remain on my bedpost when I was out. For – ahem – security, we kept them on our person, tying them to our belts and hanging them in our pockets, like a set of keys. You also had your accreditation on, so people would come and talk to you, ask what your sport was, and how you'd done ... if they then asked to see your medal, well, you would have to reluctantly dig it out of your pocket.

OK, there was serious kudos in having an Olympic silver medal, and I may have flaunted it a little. But there was an incredible atmosphere in Sydney; an atmosphere of sheer excitement, and that – never mind the famous cold Australian beer – was intoxicating. People were so friendly, and just so proud to have the Games, that it made for an incredible feel-good vibe. Then there was the power of the Olympic medal, which was extraordinary. When I did, reluctantly and discreetly, produce it from my pocket, to let people see, you could sense their wonder: they were just amazed to touch and hold it. It helped that the Sydney medals, of the three Games I have now been to, were the most impressive of the lot: big, heavy, clunky things.

Then there was the closing ceremony. Or, as Craig and I will always remember it, the Night That Jason Lost His Dignity.

Let me explain. We, in common with everyone else, thought it would be a good idea to add a drop of alcohol to the drinks we would be carrying around the stadium with us. Strictly speaking, of course, this wasn't permitted, so it required some forward planning. Simple: Craig, Jason and I visited an off-licence close to the village, and bought a half-bottle of vodka. Not that we wanted to get roaring drunk, just pleasantly tipsy. The idea was that we'd decant the vodka into our plastic sports bottles, all set for the closing ceremony later in the evening. It needed to be decanted because, as well as the alcohol ban at the opening and closing ceremonies, the village itself was designated 'dry', mainly to encourage the athletes to leave the village and go into Sydney itself to meet and mingle with the other party-goers.

Up we walked to the off-licence, bought the half-bottle of vodka, and then Craig and I decanted ours into our Lucozade bottles. 'Aw, no,' said Jason. 'I threw mine out.'

Our Olympic champion had absent-mindedly tossed his bottle into the bin on the way into the shop, which meant he had no receptacle for the vodka. So what did he do? Buy another bottle of Lucozade, then empty it? No, not Jason. While Craig and I looked on in horror, he began rummaging in the bin, trying to find his old bottle. Before long he's virtually got his head in the bin, rooting around for this bloody plastic bottle, while a small crowd starts to gather, no doubt wondering why this guy in a GB tracksuit is behaving like Stig of the Dump. Eventually he emerges, holding his bottle, a daft smile on his face as he gives it a wee polish and then proceeds to fill it with the vodka and Red Bull concoction. You could see people thinking, 'Isn't that the guy who won a gold medal …?'

Our good mood that week owed to our silver medal, but also to the bond that we had as a team. Craig, Jason and I had all been on an identical journey, with all the same sacrifices and the same highs and lows. They were the only ones who knew exactly what I'd been through, and vice versa. When it came to letting off steam together, that added considerably to the sense of relief, elation … and all the many other emotions we were feeling in Sydney.

Coming home to Scotland, I was struck again by the power of an Olympic medal. A lot of my friends knew I cycled, that I was serious about it and that I had been doing reasonably well, but it shocked some of them that I was suddenly an Olympic silver medallist. Other races, even the world championships, meant absolutely nothing to them, but they all understood the Olympics. Their reaction tended to be: 'Wow – hang on, let me get this straight ... you won an Olympic medal?'

Although we were still buzzing from the Olympics, it was straight back to work at the world championships in Manchester. It was difficult and yet also very easy to race there, if that makes any kind of sense. It felt odd to be racing again so soon, but we had our Olympic silver medals, our 'insurance policy', which meant that our year would be judged a success, no matter what. And we backed it up in Manchester with another team sprint silver, our second in successive world championships after Berlin the previous year. Once again we lost out to the formidable French, with Spain third. Jason slipped back a little in the kilometre, winning bronze behind Tournant and Sören Lausberg of Germany. Did it really matter, though? Stig of the Dump – as we were now calling him – had the big one.

Still the memories of the Olympics were hard to shake off as the year drew to a close. I suppose the experience was life-changing, in the sense that other people's perception of you, as an athlete, altered. It is hard to define exactly how, but I was now a member of one of the most exclusive 'clubs' in sport: the Olympic medallists' club.

It was also life-changing, in a less obvious way, in that it fired my enthusiasm even more. I was already committed and ambitious, but now I didn't just *want* to win an Olympic gold medal, I felt I *had* to. I had an Olympic silver medal but that, I felt, couldn't be the pinnacle, or the end of the journey. So I suppose you could say – though I didn't really think this at the time – that anything less than a gold medal at the next Games would be considered a failure. The question was, how? Did I want to continue in my highly specialized role as the lead-out man in the team sprint, and hope that Craig,

Jason and I could overhaul the French? Or was it time to try something different?

In the meantime, I did something that provided external proof of my pride in my status as an Olympian. I 'branded' myself with a tattoo of the five Olympic rings. This actually dated back to a discussion I'd had with school friends when I was about 14, on the subject of tattoos. At the time I wasn't that keen; I worried about regretting it when I was in my seventies. The only thing I'd get, I said, was the Olympic rings, if I ever went to the Olympics. I was pretty sure I wouldn't live to regret that.

And so, back in Manchester, I paid a visit to a local tattoo parlour – 'tattoo artist to the stars', as it said outside the shop. The stars from *Coronation Street* were among his clients, apparently. Olympians, however, were not. That much was obvious as I explained that I wanted the Olympic rings etched on my shoulder.

'The what?' responded the tattoo artist.

'The Olympic rings,' I said.

'What do they look like, then?'

Fighting heroically to hide my amazement, I persisted. 'They're the five rings that symbolize the Olympic Games.'

'I'm not really into sport,' he said.

Fortunately I had a picture, with the colours clear, and the exact overlap, and so he went to work – and made a right pig's ear of it. The rings were wonky, one of them looking square rather than circular, and I got a lot of stick when people saw them. Finally, in 2003, I got them touched up in a tattoo parlour in Perth. You can still see the imperfections if you look very closely; my Olympic rings perhaps aren't as impressive as Craig's on his ankle, but you can still tell what they are. They shouldn't cause me too much embarrassment in my seventies.

CHAPTER 12

Primero?

I knocked on the door, and a voice shouted: 'Come in!'

It was Martin 'Marv' Barras's office. I had come to chat to him about my plans for the following year. Or not so much chat, as tell him where, after thinking about little else since the Sydney Olympics, I believed my future lay. And it wasn't as the lead-out man in the team sprint. After two years specializing in this role, I felt it was time for a change.

'Hi, Marv,' I said. 'I just wanted to speak to you about next year.'

'Let me guess,' he smiled. 'You want to go for the keirin, don't you?'

'No, no,' I said. 'I want to go for the kilo.'

'What?'

Marv seemed surprised, yet to me it was the obvious path to take, as there seemed to be a question mark over the future of the team sprint team. Jason had taken his foot off the pedal – to capitalize on his Olympic gold medal he was pursuing as many commercial opportunities as he could, which took him away from traditional, mainstream racing: he was going for land speed records, and other promotional activities. Craig, meanwhile, was thinking of specializing in the sprint and keirin. Despite my introduction to the keirin at the Olympics, I didn't feel that it was the best event for me. I wanted something less chaotic, more controllable; something where, if you put the work in, you got the result you deserved. I had been fascinated by the kilo ever since I'd watched it at an East of Scotland championships at Meadowbank when I was about 16; when, one by one, these riders stepped up on this cold, blustery night, went hell for leather until the lactic acid started to burn, the tank emptied and they all 'died' – in cycling parlance – on the final lap, crossing the line in a wheezing, panting mess. For some reason that appealed to me.

The last time I'd ridden a kilo was in 1998 at the Commonwealth Games in Kuala Lumpur, when I hadn't trained properly for it. Now I was 24, about to turn 25, which felt – ridiculous though it might seem now – to be quite old to be taking up a new discipline, with a view to specializing in it. It felt as if I were taking a step back in order, I hoped, to take two forward.

Marv wasn't disappointed to hear my plans. Far from it. As my experience of watching it at Meadowbank all those years ago demonstrated, it's a tough event – a 'hard bastard' event – and Marv relished the challenge of turning me into a kilo rider. He saw it as a project, and one he couldn't wait to get his teeth into. Not that he said any of this initially.

'Interesting. Let me have a think about it,' he said. He was going to keep me stewing for a bit.

There was a changed atmosphere within the British cycling team in 2001. There's no doubt that our Olympic gold and silver medals raised the status of us sprinters, particularly since the endurance riders didn't do quite as well as us in Sydney, though they still won two bronzes, through Yvonne McGregor in the women's pursuit, and the men's team pursuit squad. Four medals was a very decent haul for

Britain's cycling team – the best ever in an Olympic Games – but Jason's gold and our silver stood out and increased our bargaining power. There would be no more waiting an interminable 'week to ten days' for new bikes. We had leverage now, and could ask for more support and services. And not only ask, but get!

But the dynamic also changed within our sprinters' group. Jason wasn't around so much; Neil Campbell was banned; and Craig and I were following different programmes. In terms of the team sprint, it meant that the order of our trio would change. As a kilo rider, I could move to man three; Craig, with his sprint training, could become a very fast man one; and Jason, when he came back to the track from all his extracurricular projects, could slot in at short notice to be man two.

Once Marv gave me the green light to re-style myself as a kilo rider I had a great winter, really relishing the new challenge. The 2001 season began well, and the first World Cup of the year, in Cali, Colombia, gave me a memorable debut as a kilo rider. I was on Jason's old bike, which he was a little annoyed about. It was the one he'd won the Olympic gold medal on; he thought it should have been in a museum or otherwise preserved for posterity. I completely agree now, though at the time my attitude was probably less sentimental and more pragmatic. It was fast – Jason had proved that – and so I was only too happy to use it.

My best kilo time, prior to Cali, was one minute, five seconds. Given that Jason had won in Sydney with a time four seconds quicker than that, it wasn't a PB that would give the likes of Arnaud Tournant any sleepless nights. Yet in Colombia, even if I didn't have much of a reputation in my own right, I did detect a different reception. Just as the Olympic medals had lifted our status within the British team, so, on the World Cup circuit, we seemed more visible, less the second-class citizens of previous years. Everyone was a bit friendlier, a bit more chatty – perhaps because it wasn't embarrassing to be seen talking to us any more.

One of the Spanish coaches, who was always one of the friendlier people on the circuit anyway, came and chatted to me. 'What are you riding?' he asked. 'The team sprint and kilo,' I said. 'The kilo?' he said, laughing. He knew me as man one in the team sprint, and couldn't imagine why, or how, I'd suddenly step up from doing 18-second efforts to one minute plus. It would be a little like Usain Bolt switching to the 400 metres – not impossible, but slightly strange.

'I'll be watching you,' smiled the Spaniard, tapping his nose.

As it was, he missed the kilo – he wasn't at the track when it was held. But when I met him in the hotel later, he asked me how I'd done. 'I won!' I said.

'Primero?' he replied.

'Si! Si!' I said. He looked shocked.

He wasn't the only one. I was, too. It was a fast track, at altitude, but my time of 1.02.499 blew me away. It would have been good enough for a bronze medal at the Olympics – though that is a tenuous claim, given the different track and conditions – and it was much quicker than I thought I was capable of. I was one of the early starters, and once I'd set down that time there was only one rider, the Frenchman Hervé Thuet, who was likely to threaten it. Poor Hervé was known as the 'eternal fourth' – a jokey reference to another great French cyclist, the 'eternal second' Raymond Poulidor – because he always seemed to finish fourth in the world championships. On this occasion he flew around the track, stopping the clock on 1.02.501: two thousandths of a second slower than my time. I felt as if I'd won the world or Olympic title, rather than 'just' a World Cup. Standing on the podium – the first time I had done so on my own, rather than with team-mates – gave me that feeling again, of being at the start of a journey, not knowing where it would end.

When I say I was surprised by my time, and by the result, I really was. Though I'd been training for it all winter, I went into that kilo genuinely not knowing what time I'd do, partly because you don't ride the full distance in training. With Marv, I'd broken it down, focusing on the start, then on the stamina needed to sustain the effort – but I hadn't actually ridden a full kilo against the clock. A minute might not sound much, but it is horrific. The tank gets emptied all right, but it's not in the final few metres: typically, the oxygen runs out at around 40 seconds, leaving another 20 or so of sheer agony. At least doing it in one minute, two seconds meant three seconds less suffering.

From Colombia I went to the more familiar Meadowbank Velodrome for the City of Edinburgh Grand Prix, an event at which my mum and dad have taken on important roles. For years Mum ran the canteen, just as she used to do at BMX races. And Dad was and still is the announcer, providing the commentary from the track centre, like Scottish cycling's answer to John Motson. Actually, with his calm way of speaking he's more like Peter Alliss, the golf commentator.

In Edinburgh there was no kilo, so I rode the keirin and tried an unusual tactic, but one suited to a kilo rider: I went hard from the front. I just put my foot down and nobody could come past me. I don't know what my dad, in his commentary gantry, said about that, and I'm sure I would have been embarrassed by it, but I was pleased. I was feeling really strong; in fact I'd probably never felt stronger. Everything was going so well. And then, with one slip, my whole season went pear-shaped.

I was at my girlfriend Claire's parents' house when I had a freakish accident. Reaching for a glass from the cupboard, I dropped it, and in order to prevent it smashing on the floor I tried to cushion its fall with my foot. Bad move. It severed a tendon, which meant that my foot – in fact, the lower part of my leg – was in plaster for a month. I went to the world championships in Antwerp soon after, but the month off meant that I had lost all the form I had, and only managed eighth in the kilo. In the team sprint Jason, Craig and I scraped a bronze.

There was some tension in the team; we weren't the tight unit we had been. Jason was struggling with the post-Olympic feeling, which is something I would come to identify with, and there was a more general feeling that we were doing our own things now, following our individual routes. This created a bit of antagonism, especially between Jason and Craig, who, as I have said, are similar characters. Cross them once and it's difficult to build up trust again. I don't know what the reasons were for the tension, but I knew how stubborn both could be, and that it would be difficult to revert back to the great friends we'd all been.

Some of the tension was due to the sudden departure of Marv, on the eve of the championships. His wife had been keen to move back to her native Australia, and Marv intended to go at the end of the season, but when the bosses at British Cycling heard that he would probably be working with the Australian team the following season, they told him to clear his desk. It was pretty unceremonious, and unnecessary, the team felt. And I also felt that we were back to square one: going to Antwerp without our coach. Bad things come in threes – the foot injury, the departure of Marv ... maybe eighth in the kilo was the third one.

Meanwhile I had been a little worried that Jason might feel some resentment towards me, since I was now doing 'his' event. How wrong I was. There wasn't an ounce of that from him; he was unbelievably supportive and helpful, sharing tips and advice, especially after Marv went. Jason could see that I was feeling a bit lost, and he said, 'If you want some advice planning your training, I'd be happy to help.' How jammy: I had the Olympic champion as my mentor! It's an incredible testament to the guy: he could have kept all that knowledge and experience to himself, having learnt the hard way, but he was genuinely keen to help me. I'll always be indebted to him for that.

Over the winter of 2001/02 I followed Jason's training programme. 2002 was another important year, with the 'home' Commonwealth Games in Manchester a huge target. But following Jason's programme initially made me very nervous. You remember what I said about Jason's propensity for rest? When we sat down together and began writing a training programme, I was struck by one thought: there's so little in there. Next, a question: where's the training? Then came a conflicting thought: but this guy's Olympic champion. He should know what he's talking about.

Still, I was a bit unsure. Jason sought to reassure me, telling me that the rest is important because the training – what little there is – is so hard. 'When I train, I train 100 per cent,' he said. There were echoes of Graeme Obree, but perhaps I still hadn't fully absorbed the lesson. 'There's a difference between thinking you're giving 100 per cent and actually getting 100 per cent out,' said Jason. 'If you're fatigued you can't get 100 per cent out.'

Typically, the training would be two or three days on, two days off. And those two days off would involve – as Jason would say – high-quality rest. The idea was to be almost competition fresh for training, to get the maximum benefit from it. I began following it, and went out to Perth, by now the regular winter training retreat, with our new sprint coach, Iain Dyer. After a while I realized that I wasn't going that well; Jason's programme wasn't really working for me. It needed tweaking, taking into account my strengths as an athlete, relative to Jason's. I was younger than him, and my recovery had always been good, so I thought I could add more volume. I was used to doing a lot more training, and missed the stimulus of that; of feeling knackered in the evenings. Shane Sutton has claimed that I can't relax at night unless I know that I've really pushed myself during the day, and I think there's something in that.

So I changed the programme – it was a work in progress over that winter – and gradually found a way of working that was based on Jason's ideas, but which was tailored for me. It makes sense, because no two athletes are the same. And it seemed to work, with a victory in the Sydney World Cup in a personal best of 1.02.4, with Ben Kersten over a second back in second place. That would have got me silver at the Olympics – and it was a more relevant comparison than my time in Cali, since it was in the same Dunc Gray Velodrome.

Jason was also back that season, and really gunning for the Commonwealth Games. They were a big target for him, and he was flying. He didn't ride the Sydney World Cup, but in training he was always a bit ahead of me, always the hare for me to chase. We travelled to Cottbus in Germany for a pre-Games training camp, when suddenly I leapt ahead of him. But Jason wasn't himself; he was going through a very tough time, having recently suffered two bereavements in his close family. It was painful to see this guy, clearly not himself and struggling badly, when less than two years ago he had been on top of the world at the Olympics.

As our build-up for Manchester reached its final phase, we travelled from Cottbus to Frankfurt Oder, to stay in a sports school. We were left with Bill Huck, a former world sprint champion from Germany, to overlook our stay and assist us with the training sessions. Bill is a lovely guy, with a very laid-back nature, and I keep in touch with him to this day;

but no matter how good a guy he is, he wasn't able to make our time in Frankfurt Oder a happy one.

Unfortunately, unlike the environment in Cottbus, it was awful. The school was like an army barracks. No, actually, it was like a prison. The beds were fold-down seats: wooden boards with skinny bits of foam for a mattress. The sleeping bags we were issued with were stained; it was disgusting. And the canteen-style food was similarly disgusting. We looked at each other and asked: why? It was old-school training, from the days when people thought there was a correlation between suffering off the track and suffering on it. Which, frankly, is nonsense. The whole point of a training camp is to be in a *better* environment; an environment conducive to turning up at a major competition in the best possible health and shape. It's not that we expected (or ever experienced) five-star accommodation, but we preferred not to fend off cockroaches at night, or run the risk of catching a skin disease from the bedding.

If there was one silver lining it was that I was doing a video diary for the BBC. This at least provided an outlet for my frustrations and helped to dispel any notion my friends and family might have had that what I did was glamorous.

After two nights in this hellhole – which made my old house in Manchester seem like the Ritz – we staged a mutiny. The whole sprint squad, about eight of us, had a meeting, and there was just one item on the agenda: why the hell are we here? Why couldn't we move into the athletes' village in Manchester? Yes, there would be distractions there, but it would be better than this ...

When we communicated our issues with the training venue to the management they responded pretty quickly in arranging for us to return to Manchester. But while the others went to their homes, I couldn't. I had nowhere to live at that time, having moved out of the house of horrors in Rusholme, into my girlfriend Claire's. Now she was moving, and was in between houses, so instead I went straight into the village, which had just opened and was still virtually empty. I ended up being there for 10 days before I raced, which is a long time, but my performances were great in training and I could feel my nervous, excited anticipation building with every day. It was a bit like the morning of the team sprint in Sydney: by the day of the event, I could hardly contain myself. I was hugely excited, but also aware that even an excellent performance might still mean finishing in fourth place, and out of the medals.

For Jason to even make the start, after what he'd been through in the build-up, was amazing. I take my hat off to him. As well as him, there was Jamie Staff, who was new to the GB sprint squad, having switched to the track from a successful BMX career in America. Jamie was – and is – a phenomenal athlete: he is sheer power. There was also Ben Kersten, the Australian. Including me, that made four favourites; and, of course, only three medals.

On the night, I travelled to the Manchester Velodrome, such a familiar place as my daily training venue, but transformed for the Games, and really buzzing with the atmosphere of a major event. There was a Scottish 'pen' in the track centre – at a track meeting all the teams have fenced-off 'pens,' which are pretty much identical to sheep pens, in the middle of the track – but I also became aware of the support we had in the stands. My mum and dad were there, and lots of others too. I don't know whether the Scottish flag sticks out because of its colours, but I saw so many blue and white Saltires that they seemed to outnumber the red and white cross of St George. There was this feeling of huge expectation – tinged with desperation, since the Scotland team was yet to win a medal at those Games.

Jamie was the first of the favourites to go up. He did a mid 1.02, and I thought: That's quick, but I can beat that.

Then Ben Kersten went up and did a long 1.02. And I thought: I know I can beat that. I wasn't thinking I could win it; I was thinking of a medal, so I'd have something to show for it.

I was second last to go. I nailed it out of the gate; I came out of the blocks like a banshee. I'd done a 17.9-second opening lap in the team sprint at the Sydney Olympics – and then swung up, my job done – but here, on the first of my four laps, and on a bigger gear, I did 18.0. I was flying. And I knew it. But I had started obscenely fast; I could still 'die' in the second half. I was up after a lap, still up after two ... and that's when the pain started. My legs and lungs felt as though they'd been flooded with poisonous acid: they were screaming. I didn't think any of my senses would still function, but as I crossed the line I heard this almighty roar. I steadied myself, tried to get some oxygen in, and then looked up at the scoreboard: 1.01.

1.01. The only people who'd ever done a 1.01 at sea level were Jason, Arnaud Tournant and Sören Lausberg. It was an elite club, and I was elated to join it – that was my first reaction. My second was: I've got a silver medal at worst.

I was so pleased that I did about five celebratory laps, punching the air, acknowledging the support, while Jason waited to go.

Even though it was a fast time, I couldn't imagine Jason falling short. I fully expected him to beat me. After my five laps I came to a halt, with the adrenaline starting to go, and my legs turning to jelly. I was in a bad way, and collapsed, realizing how much the ride had taken out of me. By now I was in the track centre, with the cameras on me, watching Jason's ride. People said later that it must have been horrendous, but it wasn't. I'd done my job – I was delighted with my ride. To me it was almost irrelevant what Jason did.

Jason went through the first lap in 18.6 seconds – 0.6 seconds down. 'He's got a serious amount of work to do here,' said Chris Boardman in the commentary box. He pulled back a couple of tenths over the next lap; then another couple in the third lap. He was catching me; it looked as if he was going to steamroller the last lap and just pip me on the line, but then he started tying up. The clock stopped at 1.01.9. I was staring at the clock, but couldn't do the mental calculation (so much for my year of maths at university), and so I looked instead for the little symbol beside the time: either '–' or '+'. Minus meant he was quicker; plus meant he was slower.

And there it was, Jason's time: 1.01.9 (+0.2)

I'd won my first individual title. And the first to congratulate me was Jason. He came and gave me a big hug, then said some really nice things in his media interviews. He said he was delighted for me, and I knew he really was, even though he was obviously disappointed for himself. It was a lesson in how to be gracious in defeat – and I hope it's something I've also managed to emulate, because I really do believe that the real measure of someone is how they react to defeats and setbacks. Success tells you little about yourself – it's easy to be modest and gracious after winning.

What followed was the proudest moment of my career to date. Hearing 'Flower of Scotland' at the start of rugby internationals had always been rousing. Now here was I, on the top step of the podium, flanked by Jason and Jamie, and they weren't playing 'Flower of Scotland', but 'Scotland the Brave'! With the Saltires in the crowd, so many of my family among them, and friends watching at home, it was a moving moment, which explains the tears.

After adding to my medal collection with a bronze in the team sprint – with Craig, Ross Edgar and Marco Librizzi (who rode the qualifying round, Ross coming in for the final) – I travelled back to Cottbus for another training camp, this one leading up to the world championships in Copenhagen. I had an amazing feeling at that training camp, as though I were flying; everything was easy, effortless. I would push myself really hard in training but it all seemed to flow easily. As Shane said at the time, I was riding on morale. I was on a high from winning the Commonwealth Games, and I didn't seem to be able to come down from it. I was on the crest of a wave, sitting right in the sweet spot, and my only fear was that the bubble would burst – that the wave would crash to the shore before Copenhagen.

It didn't. I carried that form to Denmark, not just thinking but *knowing* I had a really good chance of a medal, and confident that my form was not only as good as it had been in Manchester – it was better. Even Tournant, who can't have had a clue what the Commonwealth Games was, seemed to have heard about the time I'd done. I could tell in his attitude towards me; something had very subtly changed.

When I stepped up for my ride, eighth from the end – on account of my lowly seeding from my eighth place at the previous year's world championships – I had that same feeling. I was still floating, though I went fractionally slower than in Manchester, mainly because it was colder. Still, my 1.01.893 put me top of the leaderboard, and prompted an 'Ooooooooohhhhhhhh' from the crowd. I sat and watched, and with three to go, when Poland's Grzegorz Krejner failed to beat my time, I looked at Iain Dyer, smiled and gave him a high five. I knew I had a bronze medal at least. Next it was the previous year's silver medallist, Germany's Sören Lausberg. He also fell short, meaning that only one man was standing between me and my first world title – Arnaud Tournant.

When I first met Tournant he seemed the epitome of Gallic insouciance. He was cool and aloof to the point of seeming cold and arrogant. He had been an amazing talent, just 19 when he burst onto the scene, and now, in Copenhagen, he was going for his fifth consecutive world kilo title. That was what made his defeat in Sydney, when he only finished fifth behind Jason, so astonishing. Arguably his most impressive ride came at high altitude, in Bolivia the previous year, when he set a new world record for the kilo – a remarkable 58.875 seconds: the only ever sub-60-second kilo. In every race he had been unbeatable; he was used to winning, it came easily to him.

In Copenhagen I watched him race, in a scenario similar to Manchester, with a TV crew focused on me. When he crossed the line and, once again, I spotted that '+' symbol, I was caught by those cameras mouthing something I shouldn't have – but I couldn't help it. I had just won; I was world champion. It was only a few seconds later that I noticed the number after the plus sign: 0.001. I had beaten him by the smallest margin possible: a thousandth of a second.

Tournant was distraught. He slumped to the ground, surrounded by his support crew, and that was the last I saw of him until the next day, when we had the medal ceremony. But even overnight he hadn't got used to the idea that he had lost; he was still sulking. Incredibly, he never won another world kilo title after that. But he told me, much later, that he had realized that he learnt more from his defeats than his victories. He became more humble, more human – and he appreciated his victories more, rather than taking them for granted. As I said earlier, I really do believe you learn more from failure than from success.

It wasn't until after the kilo medal ceremony that Arnaud finally acknowledged me. As we warmed up for the team sprint – which Craig, Jamie and I also won, finally beating the French to complete a memorable double – he rode up behind me, and patted me gently on the back. I turned to see the trace of a smile. We would go on, over the following years, to become good friends, but it really started there, in Copenhagen. The pat on the back signalled that he had come to terms with his defeat, and that he respected my victory. Coming from Arnaud, who really wasn't used to losing, it was a nice gesture, and it meant a lot to me.

CHAPTER 13

The Chimp is in Its Cage

All this stuff about learning more from defeats than victories ... and how failures are, in the long term, better than successes, for keeping your feet on the ground, and making you appreciate your successes more ...

In sport, this is received wisdom – it is drummed into us all the time. But if anyone had tried to tell me that in Stuttgart, on the evening of 30 July 2003, I would have struggled to accept it, because it is the kind of knowledge that comes with perspective, that you can only appreciate looking back through a long lens. At the time, you just have to put on a brave face, to be a gracious loser, even while inside you are hurting, and asking yourself lots of questions.

In Stuttgart, scene of that year's world championships, I was confronted with a brilliant opportunity to practise being a gracious loser, because that evening I was given a brutal reminder that sport can be fickle indeed. One minute I am on top of the world, looking forward to consolidating my status, defending my world title, and then entering Olympic year as a strong contender for a gold medal. The next, I'm failing to medal.

Even worse was to come a few weeks later: a bronze medal. Not in the world championships, but in the national championships in Manchester. In a matter of weeks I went from being best in the world to third in the country; from being an Olympic gold medal contender to nothing more than a contender for a place in the British team for Athens in 2004. In the autumn of 2003 I faced the sobering, dispiriting prospect of not even going to the Olympics. At that time one question kept recurring: will I look back and realize that 2002 was as good as it got?

In the build-up to the world championships there were echoes of the lead-in to the Sydney Olympics. The 2003 season started well, and I won the World Cup in Cape Town quite easily, but then my form dipped. One bad session you can deal with; but when it's followed by a second bad session, a third, a fourth ... then you start getting nervous before training sessions, worrying that there's something wrong, and putting pressure on yourself to turn it around. That nervousness turns into anxiety, which only compounds the problem. You try harder, trying to force it, but in the process your technique becomes ragged. As with anything, trying too hard can be counter-productive. It's the very definition of a vicious circle.

Looking back on that year now, through the long lens, I can see where I went wrong. I would deal with a slump like that very differently now. But at the time my attitude was: if I'm not going well, then I should train harder. Instead of resting, I thought I should put in more effort; that I should just try harder. I can say without hesitation or reservation that a big turning point for me – and the reason for later improvements – was that I learnt that less can be more. I have come to appreciate that you don't have to flog yourself half to death every day. (Not *every* day.)

The real difficulty in 2003 had more to do with my psychological state than my physical condition. Up to then I'd been on a steadily rising curve of improvement, which is like winning: it's easy to deal with. I hadn't yet peaked; I hadn't even plateaued. I had just kept getting better. The challenge for any athlete always comes when you stop improving – and in 2003 I seemed to stop improving.

There was also the pressure of being world champion, especially in the weeks and days building up to Stuttgart. I'd never dealt with that burden before, of being the favourite. I also began having continual muscle spasms in my legs and gluteus maximus (basically, my buttocks), which would sometimes last for hours on end. I'd be lying in bed, and as soon as I felt the first twitch, I knew I was in for an uncomfortable night, kept awake by this constant repetitive twitching. And it would continue – like a minor case of cramp – until the muscle became so fatigued that it just ran out of steam ... by which time I'd feel as if I'd been punched in the leg. With various physiotherapists and doctors, over several months, we looked into all possible causes, from hydration to electrolyte balance to biomechanical problems, but in the end it seemed to be down to too much training and not enough recovery time, meaning that the muscles were in a constant state of tension.

I'd wake up having had little sleep, with what felt like a dead leg, and then try to train. There was another thing, too, which I now appreciate was a source of stress, and probably contributed to my dip in form. I broke up with my first serious girlfriend, Claire, which, like any relationship break-up, was painful and difficult.

It certainly contributed to a less than smooth build-up to Stuttgart, where, as world champion, I was last man to go. It was hot in the arena, about 33 degrees. And the track was fast. I didn't feel great, but, as in Sydney, I'd had what I thought was a last-minute reprieve. Training had suddenly started to go a bit better; and as a consequence, I felt more relaxed. I had also made a decision, the week before the race, that I would put a bigger gear on my bike: 99 inches rather than 98. That meant it would take me marginally longer to get up to speed, but I felt that I could wind it up more, and finish a lot faster.

On the night, Stefan Nimke, the German rider, was up quite early and did a 1.01.2 – half a second quicker than I'd ever gone. When I saw his time I reacted irrationally. That is, I thought: I'm going to have to hit this really hard, get up to speed early and hang on. In other words, I made a last-minute change to my game plan, based on what someone else had done, which is a classic mistake (identical to the one committed, at the Sydney Olympics, by none other than Arnaud Tournant, who also panicked and reacted by changing his gearing when he saw Jason's time). It meant that I went out far too quickly in the first half of the race, and as a result tied up badly and slowed dramatically at the end.

Ironically, due to the fast conditions, I did end up doing a personal best – 1.01.7 – and as I crossed the line there was a huge roar. I thought it was because I'd won. Brilliant! After all the problems I'd had in the build-up, I felt that I'd got away with it. But before I began my celebrations I realized the truth: the cheer was because I had lost, and Nimke, the local rider, had won. In fact my personal best was only good enough for fourth.

To say I was devastated would be an understatement. I was really shattered, and I felt my confidence evaporate. Next morning we had the team sprint, but after a fitful night's sleep I was woken at 6 a.m. by the anti-doping testers. The International Cycling Union (UCI) testers come at random early in the morning to collect blood samples, and this morning they decided it was our turn. Though I fully support drug tests, and am in favour of as many as possible, I found the timing of this one frustrating. They test certain teams, and not others, very early in the morning during competition, when you need all the rest you can get – it can put those teams who get woken up earlier than usual at a slight disadvantage, which doesn't seem fair. Still, it's all done for the right reasons.

We qualified quickest, slipping back to third fastest team in the second round, and so only making the bronze medal ride-off. I was in the team for the first ride, dropped for the second, and brought back for the medal ride, when we managed to get bronze. But it wasn't much to do with me – I wasn't going well. Craig was the strong man that year.

He underlined that at the national championships in Manchester three weeks later. I was then feeling down after the world championships, and in need of a break to recharge my batteries. I didn't want to ride in Manchester, but I was told I had to. It was to be stage one of the Olympic trials, and because I hadn't medalled in Stuttgart, I was starting from scratch. In fact, I had only missed a medal by a few hundredths of a second, but it meant I didn't have the priority on World Cup places the following season. There were four World Cups, and four kilo riders – Craig MacLean, Jason Queally, Jamie Staff and me. We would get one each, but we all wanted the same one: Manchester. Had I medalled in Stuttgart, I'd have got first choice. As it was, that would go to the winner of the national championship.

Prior to the championships I tried to force myself to train but, to be honest, it was a struggle just to get out of bed for training. I had no motivation at all; I just wanted the season to be over, to go back to the drawing board and formulate a plan for 2004 that would return me – I hoped – to where I'd been in 2002. As last man, I watched Craig step up at those national championships and do a 1.01.5 – a national record. He was flying, and Jason wasn't too far behind him. I was half a second down, which was only good enough for third, and another hammer blow to my confidence. I remember sitting in the velodrome's reception area after that ride, thinking that my future as a kilo rider looked bleak. At that point I didn't see how I could make the Olympics – not as a kilo rider, anyway. My best bet, I thought, looked like being the team sprint.

With hindsight, if Stuttgart hadn't happened – if I hadn't bombed so abysmally there – it's possible I might not have gone on to win the gold medal in Athens. Had I successfully defended my world title, I wouldn't have changed a thing in my training programme. I'd have carried on doing the same, with the likely result that I'd have had my Stuttgart experience in Athens.

As it was, I went back to basics, and reassessed everything.

Someone I have only mentioned in passing so far, but who was becoming increasingly important, is Shane Sutton. Despite my *annus mirabilis* in 2002, morale in the sprinters' camp was poor after the abrupt departure of Martin Barras. At the time there was no one with the big personality, or influence, to take our group by the scruff of the neck and really go out to bat for us, and get the support we needed. In the wiry, fidgety bundle of energy that is Shane, who gradually got involved towards the end of 2002, we found someone who wasn't just willing to go out to bat for us – he would to go to war for us.

Shane was known as a tough Aussie road rider in the UK, having been one of the top professionals on the British circuit in the eighties and early nineties. He then became Welsh national coach before joining the British set-up. When he was assigned to manage the sprinters it raised a few eyebrows. Shane is ... how can I put it? Well, my first impression was that he was a complete nutter. I think most people think that when they meet him.

My initial introduction to him had been a couple of years earlier, en route to a World Cup meeting in Sydney. We were in Singapore airport, travelling along the moving walkway, heading towards the gate – our flight was due to board in about half an hour. Shane glided past us on the other walkway, heading in the opposite direction. I think he was going for a fag. He's often rushing somewhere for a fag. 'Flight's delayed, mate,' he said as he passed. 'Three hours.'

'Oh God,' I said. 'OK.' I was with Alwyn McMath and Andy Slater, and we stepped off the walkway, turned around and headed for the shops. It was in one of the shops that we heard the announcement: 'Final call for passengers Hoy, McMath and Slater ... please proceed immediately to the gate ...'

After a Usain Bolt-style sprint – of the kind that really isn't recommended for cyclists, who aren't accustomed to using their legs for running – I boarded the plane, and there was Shane, laughing. I thought: I'd better watch this guy. But what I also learnt, pretty quickly, was that he puts in as much, if not more, than most of the riders. He's the most hands-on coach you could imagine, as well as being the biggest wind-up merchant.

For such a big personality he had a low-key introduction to our group. Shane appeared at the training camp in Cottbus, which fell between the Commonwealth Games and the world championships in Copenhagen, and his enthusiasm was infectious. He didn't know all the nuances of sprinting, but he picked it up quickly. His main role in any case was as a motivator, and as the person who would bind us together and lift us when we were down. Beyond the technicalities of sprinting – and that, really, was the domain of Iain Dyer, our other new coach – he could see from your body language how you were feeling. He is the ultimate 'people person'; he's in your face, intense and scarily perceptive. Shane can tell, from how you are riding, whether there's something up – it could be a cycling problem, or a personal issue. He knows. And he'll ask you about it.

'C'mon mate, what the fuck's up with you?' is a typical Shane question. 'You got a face on you as long as the back straight.' When someone challenges you like that it isn't really an option to bluff it. (Only on one occasion have I managed to pull the wool over Shane's eyes, when Ross Edgar and I sneaked out for a night on the tiles in Perth, during an off-season training camp. The rest of the team had flown back the day before, but for Ross and me it was our penultimate night there, we had trained hard for two months solid and fancied letting our hair down, but didn't think Shane would approve. So we sneaked out; and sneaked back again several hours later, without Shane suspecting a thing. We were both feeling a little rough the next day, but hiding it well, when Shane said: 'Well lads, you've worked hard – you've earned the right to a night out. Go out and have a few drinks.' 'Ach, you're all right, Shane, we'll take it easy,' I said, earning even more brownie points, when the reality was that I was feeling far too delicate to contemplate it.)

Other things you should know about Shane. He has incredible enthusiasm – he is always up for it. His willpower is astonishing. And he's a stubborn bastard. At some point he has clashed with everyone, and he and I have had some huge arguments. He is of the Brian Clough school of management, in the sense that, if you don't agree with him, he will behave as Clough did when players disagreed with him. On those occasions, as Clough once said: 'We talk about it for 20 minutes and then decide I was right.'

With Shane, you could talk for 20 minutes ... 30 minutes ... an hour. But if you – sorry, if I – attempted to reason with him, or looked like beating him with a solid, logical, rational argument, his typical response would be: 'Ah, here we go, it's the captain of the school debating team ...'

Still, for all our fall-outs, I confess to being a fully paid-up member of the Shane Sutton fan club. He is a force of nature, a bundle of contradictions – not least the fact that he is such an archetypal Aussie, who says he has 'green and gold runnin' through me veins', but gives his all to the British cause – and he can be frustrating at times, but Shane is a brilliant guy to have on your side. He sees his job as being there to make life easier for us, doing little jobs, checking we're OK. He treats us like children sometimes, but you feel that he is there for you all the time.

Shane has claimed that, following my disappointment in Stuttgart, 'I had Chris sitting on me bed in tears.' Which isn't strictly true (that's another thing: he does tend to exaggerate), but it is fair to say that he was a huge support, and really came into his own as we went into the winter, as I wrestled with how best to put my 2003 season behind me and prepare for the biggest year of my career.

Shane wasn't the only one I turned to. In fact, this was a deliberate strategy. Feeling that it was a time to take stock, and in some respects start again, I wanted to leave absolutely no stone unturned. I decided to speak to people I'd not previously thought of consulting – simply because I didn't imagine they'd have anything to offer me – and to pick their brains and see if there was something, anything, that I could apply to my preparation. For example, I went to see Chris Boardman, who'd been involved with the British team as a consultant for a couple of years, but who I hadn't had many dealings with. Chris fell squarely into the category of people I've just described. I assumed that, because he had been an endurance rider, who spent much of his career road racing, his knowledge and experiences wouldn't have much relevance for me as a sprinter. This was wrong, but it wasn't an arrogant assumption, more a pragmatic one – it simply isn't possible to pick everyone's brains. But it would be good if you could, because everyone potentially has something to offer. My meeting – and subsequent chats – with Chris were fruitful if only for one nugget of advice.

Chris talked me through the methodical way in which he and Peter Keen planned his training, spending hours writing and honing his plan for the year ahead until he was 100 per cent happy with it. 'It's like a recipe for the perfect cake,' Chris said. 'You have to believe that if you follow the guidelines you will get the result you're looking for. It should give you confidence, and allow you to see the bigger picture; if you have one bad session there's no need for it to affect you too much – you can always relate it to the big picture, and see how insignificant it is in a year-long plan.'

The gist of Chris's advice was this: 'The piece of paper with your final training programme has to excite you.' Which might sound a little geeky, but I could identify with it; it is the scientist in me, I suppose, who enjoys the process of working out a puzzle – and showing your workings, like the inside of a machine. Here it was a case of working back from my ultimate goal, filling in all the blanks, and creating a document that stands almost as a blueprint for ... an Olympic gold medal in the kilometre time trial in Athens. When I came to write my plan for Athens I wasn't happy with it, so I scrapped it. I went through about four drafts until I could hold the piece of paper in front of me and say, with confidence, 'This is it.' You can't be 90 per cent happy with it, because you have to commit 100 per cent to it. If you don't believe in it, it won't work.

Next, I went to see another individual connected to the British team, but not yet fully involved. One of the problems I had, as a direct result of what happened in Stuttgart and then a few weeks later in Manchester, was a complete loss of confidence in myself. There's this myth that top athletes are very confident people, full of self-belief all the time. But it is a myth because, put simply, there is so much uncertainty about sport that you cannot be 100 per cent confident all the time. One of the things that you do as an athlete is to constantly ask questions: it is a healthy curiosity and a constant quest for answers that provides a lot of the drive. But the problem is that when things aren't going so well, and the answers don't appear to be forthcoming, you can feel a bit lost – and become a little bit introspective.

To help me understand all this I decided to go and speak to someone who might be able to help: a psychiatrist. Steve Peters had started working with British Cycling on a part-time basis, and I'd heard great things about his work with some other members of the team. It was Jason who said I should see him. 'He's a top bloke,' he said, and that convinced me to ignore any fears I had and drive to visit him at the Sheffield hospital where he was based. And I suppose there were fears, if only because it seemed a bit of a drastic step.

The idea of seeing a psychiatrist was, I admit, one that I initially struggled to get my head around. And as I drove to Sheffield it began to seem like a ridiculous idea. I didn't need to see a psychiatrist: I knew that I didn't have any real mental health issues. So what was I doing?

My apprehension only increased as I walked into the hospital, and was directed to the psychiatric ward. The psychiatric ward! What the hell was I doing here? I consider myself to be open-minded when it comes to something like this; if someone told me they were seeing a psychiatrist I wouldn't bat an eyelid. But when it's you, it's different; it's as if the stigma that you don't believe is there in the first place suddenly becomes very real.

I was shown into Steve's office and sat opposite this slightly built, grey-haired man in his early fifties. He said, 'What's up?'

'I'm not really very happy at the moment,' I said, feeling fairly self-conscious. 'I've not had a good season. I don't know why, but things are going pretty badly across the board. I want to turn it around; I want to feel happier about life in general, and perform better on the bike, and I think the two go hand in hand.'

Then I relaxed; he was very easy to talk to. It wasn't a case of lying on a sofa talking about your childhood. I wasn't there for psychiatric help. In fact, I don't really know what I expected, but I do know that his approach surprised me. It was just like having a very relaxed – albeit very frank and personal – chat with someone. What made Steve a good listener was his manner, but he was also someone who clearly understood sport. He appeared to know why I was doing what I was doing, and why it was important to me. He seemed to know where I was coming from.

Clearly he was also very good at sussing someone out very quickly; at getting a feel for the type of person you are, and how you tick. After he had listened for a while, not really saying much, he offered some practical suggestions. The biggest thing was not to worry about things that are outside your control. There were no lightbulb moments; in fact, I spent most of the time waiting for the 'session' to start. And then I realized that it had. We talked about everything. I mentioned the muscle spasms interrupting my sleep. He asked me about Stuttgart, and I talked him through it.

He said, 'Why didn't you say to yourself, before your ride, that the reason your rivals are going so fast is the quick track and conditions?' Then he explained the difference between emotional reactions and logical reactions. And I began to understand the distinction; I was able to recognize that my decision to change my strategy before my ride was an emotional one, a reaction to what I'd just seen. Whereas the decision I'd taken earlier in the week, to ride it in a different way, had been based on logic. In the heat of battle, he said, it is very easy – natural, even – to be 'hijacked' by your emotions. The trick was to override them with logic, and he said he could help me do that.

I came away from the psychiatric ward of the hospital in Sheffield, and my first meeting with Dr Steve Peters, feeling upbeat. I even felt positive about the year I'd just had; he'd helped to give me a new perspective on it. It wasn't the end of the world, as he said; potentially it was just a blip, one I could easily recover from. I drove home in a much better frame of mind.

That was the only time I met Steve at the hospital. As time went on he was to be found at the Manchester Velodrome with increasing frequency. He was approachable, and lots of cyclists – and other athletes – began to see him on quite a regular basis. Though I saw him around all the time, and he chaired some meetings involving the coaches and riders, I only went to speak to him again a couple of times in 2004. I didn't feel that I needed to see him on a more regular basis, as long as I was implementing the points he raised.

But we did have one important chat before the Athens Olympics, one that I think helped set me up mentally for the Games. I'd had a great winter, and then gone to the world championships in Melbourne and won by four-tenths of a second from Arnaud Tournant. I was ecstatic. In my mind I'd spent a lot of the winter focusing on the team sprint, thinking that would be my best chance of another Olympic medal. But in Melbourne, on an average track, I recorded a personal best for the kilo. There were eight weeks to go to Athens. I was the best in the world. And I thought I had more scope to improve.

What's more, as world champion I gained Team GB an extra place in the kilo. There had been four of us going for one place; now there were two places. Craig got the other one, though he was enduring a difficult year, blighted by illness. Which just goes to show how cruel sport can be: in 2003 Craig was arguably the best in the world at one point; a few months later, when it really mattered, he found himself in a frantic race against time to be fit and healthy for the Olympics.

At our pre-Olympics training camp in Newport, Steve Peters and I sat down for a chat. 'OK,' he said, 'so talk me through what's going to happen on the night.'

'Well, I'm last off …' This is an honour that falls to the reigning world champion.

'So what's going to happen,' said Steve, 'if, like in Stuttgart, someone posts an amazing time?'

'I'll be fine. I won't think about it.'

'So if someone does a world record you're not going to think about it? How can you not think about it? If I tell you not to think of a pink elephant, what's the first thing that pops into your head?'

'A pink elephant.'

'Exactly. You can't say: "I'm not going to think about something." What you can say is: "I'm going to think about something else." In that way, you override emotional thoughts with logical ones.'

Later on – around the time of the Beijing Olympics – Steve became quite famous for his 'chimp'. If you do a Google search on Steve, you'll find that 'Steve Peters chimp' is about third in the list of most popular searches in connection with him. What he was trying to do here, in his pink elephants chat, was to provoke my chimp – the chimp being the emotional part of the brain.

It's a metaphor, and an effective one. When you're going mad, and reacting emotionally, you can imagine this chimp having escaped from its cage, going ballistic. Everyone has a chimp – in other words, everyone has that emotional part of their brain. What Steve does is to help you try to keep emotional responses in check during competition; to defeat that chimp – to keep it locked in its cage – with logic.

Now, I consider myself a reasonably balanced person. Most of the time I am fairly rational and logical. My chimp comes out of its cage sometimes, but no more than with anyone else. However, I certainly do become aware of it in the high-pressure environment of a major competition, and that's when it can hijack your rational thinking, which can then affect performance.

Other people, including a lot of athletes, are more emotional more of the time. Someone like Victoria Pendleton, for example. Vicky would be the first to admit she is a highly emotional person. It is what makes her who she is – she is open; she wears her heart on her sleeve. But this was also her biggest problem in major competitions, when the pressure increases, and she could easily be hijacked by her emotions. It is no coincidence that since she began working with Steve Peters she has dominated women's sprinting. She is still the same emotional person; she hasn't become cold and clinical. But what Steve has taught her and the other riders he's worked with is to cage the chimp when it matters – which might only be for a few minutes in a year. That way, in the case of Vicky, she can be as mental as she likes the rest of the time. (I'm joking, Vicky.)

That year, leading up to Athens, everything seemed to be falling into place. Apart from having rediscovered my form I had a good support team around me. There was Shane for 24-hour, in-your-face support – for keeping motivation high and morale good; Iain Dyer to act as a sounding board and to discuss the technical details of training; Dave Clark, from the Scottish Institute of Sport, and formerly with the Springboks and Welsh rugby teams, who had been helping me with my strength and conditioning training; and Steve

Peters, who provided, for want of a better expression, mental coaching.

At the top of the organization, Peter Keen was still in overall charge, but Dave Brailsford, his deputy, was preparing to take over, and he was an increasingly important figure in 2004. Dave is a hugely impressive guy, not least because his skills have improved a lot over the years he's been involved – and he first became involved with the World Class Performance Plan very near the beginning, back in 1999. He would be the first to admit that in the early days he seemed unable to delegate; he wanted to be in control, and involved in everything. These days, Dave's managerial skills are the envy of other teams and organizations around the world. I think Steve has helped him, too, as he has helped so many people, coaches and athletes, in the team. Steve's is the voice of reason (or logic) within the organization, and he works as much with the coaches as with the riders, if not more. More often than not, he's like a buffer between the two camps, but his real skill, perhaps, is that you speak to him and then feel that he's fighting your corner, even though he's on no one's side. In fact he's on everyone's side, fighting everyone's corner.

I detected another subtle change in myself in Olympic year, which may or may not have had something to do with what Steve told me. According to my training plan, I had particular objectives for particular training camps or sessions; and I stuck to them, always keeping the bigger picture in mind, rather than focusing too much on an individual session, or measuring myself against Jason's or Craig's performances. That used to be a bad habit of mine. At the end of training I'd check my times, but I'd also look in the book at Jason's and Craig's times. And these, I realized, were important to me, despite the fact that Jason and Craig might have been in a different phase of training, and have had different objectives.

It was one of the most fundamental pieces of advice Steve gave me: don't worry about things you can't control. I couldn't control what Craig or Jason, or anyone else, was doing. So I stopped sneaking a look at their times. Logic was winning the day. The chimp was in its cage.

CHAPTER 14

Some of My Bark
is Missing

In September 2008, not long after I'd returned from the Beijing Olympics, I was sitting in a café in Edinburgh when a middle-aged woman hesitantly approached. 'Excuse me,' she said. 'It's Chris Hoy, isn't it?'

'Yes,' I replied. This type of encounter was happening quite a lot in September 2008, which didn't make it any less bizarre.

'Well done!' she said. 'Was Beijing your first Olympics?'

That was happening quite a lot, too. Athens – never mind Sydney – seemed not really to register, at least not with the general public. It certainly registered with me.

The last few weeks before the 2004 Olympics, and what I thought was the biggest opportunity of my life, were inauspicious, thanks to two incidents. A few weeks before leaving for Athens I was cycling through Manchester, on a deserted road, with no vehicles around, when I approached a junction with traffic lights. Actually there was one vehicle: a police van. It was facing me, on the opposite side of the road, waiting to turn right, across my path.

I carried on – the lights were green and I had right of way. But as I drew almost level with the junction the van began to turn. I thought he was coming half-way, but no: he kept coming. I had a nano-second to wonder if perhaps he hadn't seen me; but I was in my red, white and blue Great Britain kit – I could hardly have been more visible. When he was within five feet of me he seemed suddenly to realize what was about to happen, and slammed on the brakes, just as I slammed on my brakes too ... we collided in slow motion and I fell.

It could have been a lot, lot worse; he had slowed to walking speed by the time we hit each other, and so I was really just nudged off my bike. In the van, which had been idling – it wasn't as though it was on its way to an emergency – there were three policemen. The driver quickly jumped out, and I think he was apologizing, but I couldn't stop myself: I went ballistic and, in a state of shock and anger, turned the Manchester air blue as I yelled at him. His response was to laugh. I don't know if he thought that would defuse the situation. It didn't. It only increased my rage. 'What's so funny?' I screamed.

'I'm not laughing at you,' he said. 'I've just come from an RTA [road traffic accident] and then I almost cause one ...'

Hilarious, eh?

Then another police car appeared, and from it another policeman got out. He said he'd seen everything. He did help defuse things, and I carried on to the velodrome, but I was shaken. I felt that my whole life had been building towards the Olympics, I'd put so much into it, and someone's carelessness could have cost me the chance of going. But more than that, this guy was in a big steel box – effectively a lethal weapon as far as cyclists are concerned. It wasn't my first near-miss, it wouldn't be my last, but it did remind me how fragile you are, and how careful you have to be, when you're on the road on a bike.

The second incident was more serious. I was in Athens by now, ensconced in the athletes' village. The Games were six days away – the thing to do now was to wrap yourself in cotton wool, to try and make sure nothing happened at the last minute to derail you.

How ironic. The village was big: there was a road around it, which, on a bike, took about 10 minutes. A handy distance for a short recovery ride – you could do a few laps in the relative safety of the village. Again, how ironic.

I had just finished my last turbo session, which in itself was significant. It was a particularly nasty session: seven alternations of 20 seconds 'on,' 20 seconds 'off.' That means absolutely 100 per cent flat-out effort for 20 seconds, with just 20 seconds to recover before the next one. It was the best session I'd ever done for this particular drill; I put myself in the dark place to get that performance out, and it was incredibly painful – I curled up like a foetus after it, trying hard not to be physically sick. Had my mum seen me she would definitely have said: 'That can't be good for you.' And she might have had a point …

Anyway, the session was completed; the box was ticked; the work was all done. Cotton wool time. But first, a gentle warm-down in the village. I set off for a half-hour spin and to get some fresh air. As I approached a roundabout, at about 20mph, I noticed a bus approaching the next junction. I knew, by now, two things about the roads in Greece: that vehicles don't really give way at roundabouts, preferring to just keep going; and that the bus drivers are the worst offenders.

By now I was on the roundabout, watching the bus approach the junction, and thinking: he doesn't look like he's going to stop; and if he doesn't, it looks like he could hit me. Two options: slam on my brakes, or go faster and try and beat it. I accelerated, taking the roundabout at speed, leaning more into the corner than I would have otherwise. As I rounded the apex of the bend I realized something else: that the scorching heat was melting the tarmac. It was turning into goo, and as I leant into the corner, my front wheel lost its grip.

Down I went, straight on to my left side. Fortunately the bus was able to stop before it went over the top of me – unwittingly, I had discovered what it took to make a Greek bus stop: not a road junction, but a stricken cyclist.

There were a lot of people around, and ordinarily my reaction would be: oh no, how embarrassing. But on this occasion the stakes were a bit higher, and my first thoughts were: wrist, collarbone, hip, knee: is everything OK? I was stinging and sore from the open wounds on my left side – my shin, back and arm taking the brunt – but my bones and joints all seemed intact. Phew.

I picked myself up, remounted my bike, and headed straight for the British team's medical centre to get cleaned up. Usually shock kicks in within a few minutes of a crash, but here my thoughts remained lucid. The overriding one was: that could have been it. Four years of ups and downs, all over in the second it took for my front wheel to lose traction. And I knew that I was in the shape of my life.

As per normal after a crash, I had an uncomfortable couple of nights, with the large wounds refusing initially to scab and weeping quite a lot. I couldn't sleep on my left side. But as I went to bed the first night my main concern was less about that than about how I would feel in the morning: that was the big test.

It could have been worse. But my scars were pretty impressive. The one on my shin was obvious when I was wearing my cycling shorts, but Shane told me I should keep hidden the fact that some of my 'bark' was missing, as his brother, Gary, put it on the TV commentary. Although the crash became known about, I downplayed it. My mum and dad helped with that, my dad laughing it off when some journalists asked about it, saying it was a sign of good luck.

*   *   *

On the night the missing bark proved not to be a factor at all. I had got away with it. I still felt I was in the form of my life, and, keeping Steve Peters's advice in my head, I was pretty sure I was in the right frame of mind, too. As world champion and last man off I would be confronted with the same scenario as in Stuttgart: I was going into the competition with the pressure of being the favourite, and I would have to watch the others do their rides before I stepped up. But the key thing to remember was this: my training had gone almost perfectly. I was in the shape of my life. The others didn't matter. Well, they *mattered*. But nothing I could do could influence their performance – so why even waste time thinking about what they might or might not do? At the risk of sounding selfish, it was all about me. I had to focus entirely on myself.

It wasn't easy. First the Australian, Shane Kelly, broke the Olympic record with 1 minute, 1.224 seconds. Phew, fast. I clocked his time, felt my stomach lurch, and then remembered Steve's lessons. Or, rather, I focused back on myself; and I reminded myself that it was very warm, and therefore very fast, in the Athens arena. By now I was on my road bike, slowly circling the warm-up area in the middle of the track. Next up was Stefan Nimke – the 2003 world champion. 1 min, 1.186 seconds. Another Olympic record: incredibly fast. But I dealt with this better than I had dealt with Kelly's time: I was expecting it now. The emotional response would have been to panic. The logical one was to remind myself, again, that conditions were very fast; and not only that, but this was the Olympics: everyone was in the shape of their lives. Including me.

Theo Bos, the Dutchman, was next, but he messed up his start and fell short of Nimke's time. At this point, with just one rider – Arnaud Tournant – between me and my ride, it was time for me to stop what I was doing. I got off the bike, handed it to Iain Dyer, then sat down on the hot seat while Gavin Thomas, our physio, gave me chalk to rub into my hands, to grip the handlebars better. I've said it before, but it's the only description: it feels like the gallows. The clock is ticking, there's no escape now; it's just this awful countdown to this one moment that you've thought about more than any other moment for the last four years. And the strange, paradoxical thing about the kilo, because you only have one shot, and because of the sheer pain involved, is that in these final moments you don't want to be there. You'd rather be anywhere else. People don't believe me when I say that, but it's true: those final moments are absolutely terrifying, and you wonder why on earth you've put yourself in this position. I doubt that even Steve Peters could talk me out of having such thoughts – but, equally, I am sure that everyone else thinks exactly the same way: it's part of the process of preparing to produce the ride of your life. So it's natural. Logical, even.

Shane then took over, standing at the side of the track with my bike while I remained in the chair, visualizing each part of the race. Now was not the time for conversation, even from motormouth Shane. Half an hour earlier he had said, 'Just go out and express yourself', but now he, and Gavin, kept quiet and were deadly serious. They were maybe concerned about the two Olympic records the arena had just witnessed. Make that three, because, as I was sitting in the chair, the goalposts were moved again. There was another huge roar: Tournant stopped the clock at 1.00.896 seconds. The first ever sub-61-second kilo at sea level: an Olympic and sea level world record.

What happened next could have thrown me. At one time it would have. I heard a shout – there was a lot of noise, but I distinctly heard 'Chris!' and recognized the voice: it was Jason's. He was in the crowd, about 10 rows back, but was beckoning me towards the start gate, having noticed that the clock – which is supposed to start its 50-second countdown at the moment when you sit on your bike – had already started. An official had made a mistake. But Steve Peters must have done a very good job because even now, in the heat of the moment, I found that I was able to rationalize it: I knew I could go through the routine of walking – awkwardly, like a penguin, in my cleated cycling shoes – up the gentle slope of the track, then mount my bike, which had been fixed to the start gate by Shane, in less than the allotted 50 seconds.

So I didn't panic. I didn't rush. This was my moment, and I wanted everything to go exactly as I'd rehearsed it, on the track and in my head. The missing bark from my left shin was a livid red, but the crash was ancient history. I adjusted my helmet, and as the clock ticked down to 10, I gripped the handlebars, stood up on the pedals ... five ... four ... three ... two ... one – and blasted out of the start gate. I wasn't aware of my time but I was aware of my speed, and I knew, from the second I left that start gate, that I was on a good ride. I was totally focused on what I was doing, but I could hear a roar once every lap: whenever the time flashed on the scoreboard. I could tell I was up. Though I was oblivious, of course, to the size of the gap. After one 250-metre lap I was inside 18 seconds – the only rider to break that barrier, 0.07 seconds up on Tournant – and I just kept going, piling it on. The gap over Tournant opened to 0.141 seconds after two laps, half-distance, then closed to just 0.07 seconds with one lap to go. This is when it counts. I don't know if Graeme Obree's advice, issued seven years earlier in our shared hotel room in Perth, had lodged itself in my brain, but I followed it to the letter: just when I think I am digging as deep as I possibly can, I dig a little deeper. And then I dig a little deeper still. It's in the last lap and a half that it really starts to hurt, when the lactic acid starts to really scorch your legs, and the lack of oxygen sears your lungs. On the final lap I was in more pain than I had ever known, and I have never found hurting myself so easy. I cross the line and the clock stops at 1 minute, 0.711 seconds. It's an Olympic record. I am the Olympic champion. By 0.185 seconds.

I ride round in a daze. I pass three red-T-shirted GB coaches in the track centre – Shane Sutton, Iain Dyer and Dave Brailsford – and they look as if they're on pogo sticks, jumping up and down, throwing their arms around each other. In the stands my dad, large man that he is, is also visible, throwing his arms out, and I see my mum, sister Carrie, her partner Garry and another eight family and friends there with them, flying the Union Jack and home-made 'Real McHoy' flag. I take my helmet off but I'm still in a daze. Shane hands me a Union Jack as I pass him and I begin to celebrate, but I can't believe it, can't take it in.

What to do now? My mental preparation for the kilo hadn't included this bit. I really didn't know what to do. I had been so focused on the ride itself, on getting everything out, that my head was as empty as my body as I rode around the track, my head slumped between my shoulders, before finally I began to celebrate.

As I think about it now I realize how an athlete's career can be defined by one performance, from Jonny Wilkinson with his drop goal in the 2003 Rugby World Cup Final, to Lewis Hamilton passing Timo Glock on the final bend of the final Grand Prix of the 2008 season, and how fickle sport is. So much can go wrong, both in the build-up and at the time, when the pressure is at its most intense. I had never known anything like the pressure I experienced in Athens, but somehow I managed to ride what I consider now to be an almost perfect race: and I did it when it most mattered. When that sunk in, my emotions finally caught up. I stopped shaking my head in disbelief and let myself go. To finally register that I was Olympic champion was … well, I don't know if I did register it for a long time: it was unbelievable.

As events transpired, it was probably my only chance ever to win the Olympic kilometre title. And, if anything, my kilo in Athens seems even more significant – and gives me more satisfaction – now than it did at the time.

Part of the reason for that is that the kilo was so closely followed by disappointment, when we failed to medal in the following day's team sprint. A combination of things conspired against us; but also there was the fact that Craig, who finished seventh in the kilo, wasn't himself. Throughout the year Craig had been fighting a losing battle in trying to regain his 2003 form for Athens, and he was far from his best in qualifying. Jason came in to replace him in the second round, against Germany, and we went very fast, partly because Jason, ironically, was in the form of his life, doing his fastest ever last lap. But the Germans, as a trio, went even faster, breaking the world record (we recorded the second fastest ever time) and dumping us from the competition without a medal. For Jason, Jamie, Craig and me it was a bitter disappointment, though not one – from my point of view – that detracted too much from the kilo, or the fact that I would be an Olympic gold medallist for all time.

One of the things Steve Peters stresses, which fortunately comes quite naturally to me, is to focus on processes rather than outcomes. It would be an unnecessary and unhelpful distraction to think about how life might or might not change when you are Olympic champion, when you should be focused only on doing the work that could ensure that you have a chance of becoming Olympic champion. As I say, this comes naturally to me: I enjoy training; I enjoy the process of working towards a goal. I suppose you could say I like the idea of being on a journey, without necessarily thinking about the destination.

But it meant that I had been so focused on the journey to the Olympics that I hadn't given a second's thought to life after Athens. In fact, as my dazed reaction to winning demonstrated, I hadn't even considered what I would do as I crossed the line at the end of my race.

It is quite common, I think, for people who achieve their dreams to struggle a little afterwards. I've heard some Olympic champions say that they had difficulty coming to terms with the fact that an Olympic gold medal *didn't* change their life. A bit like lottery players who dream of winning millions, I think some imagine that a gold medal will solve all their problems – and make them happy – in a single stroke.

That wasn't a problem for me, because it never occurred to me that being Olympic champion would fundamentally change my life. Yet it did for a while change my attitude to my sport – or rather, to my event – and not in a very positive way. The difficulty I encountered after Athens was that no kilo was ever going to measure up. There was never going to be the same drama, the same excitement, the same pressure. Other races seemed like an anti-climax. Even when I only finished third in the 2005 world championships in Los Angeles, behind Theo Bos and Jason Queally, I was disappointed, but not distraught. Which was a sign, I think, that it didn't mean that much to me – after Athens, it couldn't. I wanted to win, and I certainly didn't enjoy losing, but the real desire had gone.

The thing is that training for the kilo is bloody hard. You have to put yourself through the wringer in every session. And you have to be in the right frame of mind to do that.

But I imagined and hoped that this was a temporary lapse, and that the desire would return in time for the Beijing Olympics. I certainly wasn't prepared for the phone call I received as I sat having lunch in a Manchester restaurant in June 2005.

It was Shane. 'G'day mate.' The usual greeting. 'You sitting down, mate?' Again, a typical Shane question, just before a wind-up. 'The kilo's gone,' he continued. 'UCI have dumped it from the Olympics.'

Not for a second did I think he was serious. I knew that the UCI, cycling's governing body, had decided to drop two events from the Olympics to allow them to add BMX to the programme. But I also knew Shane. I assumed this was just another of his wind-ups. Still, I phoned him back after lunch. 'You are joking, aren't you?'

'Nah,' he said.

He then convinced me that he *was* serious – that the UCI had dropped the kilo and women's 500m time trial. It seemed preposterous. Perhaps it's not for me to say, but the kilo in Athens must have been one of the most exciting and dramatic events on the track cycling programme. What's more, it was an event that the wider public – not just the cycling audience – understood.

Later that day I spoke to Jason about it. He was as gutted as I was. Like me, he'd assumed that it would be a case of last event in, first event out. In which case the keirin would have gone – it had only been added in 2000 – or perhaps the madison (a bunch endurance event for two-man teams). But there was also a strong case for the road time trial – introduced in 1996 – as a contender for the chop. This isn't the greatest spectator event, and it had been discredited in 2004 when the winner, Tyler Hamilton, subsequently tested positive for blood doping.

It seemed so unjust, and that the UCI had done the sport a big disservice. Personally, it felt like a kick in the teeth. It also created a big dilemma for me in terms of what I did now. Did I keep going with the kilo, to try to add to my two world titles? There was also the Commonwealth Games in Melbourne in nine months, where I would defend the title I'd won in Manchester, and which, as my first major individual title, meant so much to me. But it was out of the Olympics, meaning that the biggest target that it's possible to aim at had been removed. And the difficulty, as I've described, is that you can't do the kilo half-heartedly. Given the punishment you put your body through in every training session, you have to be 100 per cent committed to it. When Jason dipped in and out – after his gold medal at the Sydney Olympics in 2000 – his performances suffered. It was only when he dedicated himself to it that he was able to pull it out of the bag. It is an event of no compromise.

My initial reaction was, 'What's the bloody point?' It was the off-season, so I was just returning to training, and thinking about the season ahead, and what my targets should be, and it threw me. As far as the Olympics were concerned, I thought that I would simply have to put all my eggs in the team sprint basket. The idea of altering direction and trying the other Olympic sprint events, the keirin and individual sprint, seemed ridiculous. The guys at the top in these disciplines had been doing them for 10 years; they were highly technical and tactical.

But surely – people will counter – riding your bike over a short distance is not that complicated. If you have the speed, can you not adapt to the different sprint disciplines? To a certain extent, yes. But it was the kilo that had appealed to me most, and which I put five years of my life into, in that period hardly riding a single sprint or keirin. In my two events – the kilo and team sprint – there were no tactics. In the other two, you would often see them won by someone who wasn't the fastest, but the most tactically astute. That's what makes them exciting: they're unpredictable, there's more chance of an upset. But this is precisely why the kilo appealed to me: it was a test of pure physical effort. It levelled the field. There was no hiding place: you got the result you pretty much deserved.

I would liken the sprint and keirin to a foreign language or a musical instrument. You were at a serious disadvantage if you hadn't started learning at quite a young age. As a relatively old dog – 29 – it was asking a lot for me to learn some new tricks.

Yet, by a strange coincidence, I was, at the time of the kilo announcement, preparing to head to Japan for a six-week period riding the Japanese Keirin Association circuit. It wasn't because I wanted to brush up on my keirin skills, it was because this was something most sprinters did at some point in their careers; in fact, it is near the top of the 'to-do' list, along with racing in the West Indies, which, as I have described, is one I ticked off fairly early in my career. Like Barbados and Trinidad, Japan would prove to be a fascinating cultural experience, though very different – in many ways the polar opposite.

And, OK, it was also pretty lucrative – not as lucrative for the overseas riders as for the Japanese riders, some of whom were millionaires (the amount bet on the Japanese keirin circuit every year is around $7.5 billion), but it was possible to go out there for a six- or eight-week period and come home with a bit of money in your pocket.

It started with an induction at the Keirin School, where, for three weeks, we were cooped up in a college-style campus in the mountains and subject to a daily ritual of classroom lessons about how to ride keirins – with written and mechanical tests at the end. And then, following my successful 'graduation' from keirin school, there were the races themselves, which bore little relation to UCI-approved international keirins. For one thing, in Japan the pacer is not mounted on a motorbike, but on a normal bike. For another, the races are held on large, concrete tracks, rather than tight little wooden velodromes. Also, you have to declare your tactics in advance: there is no room for spontaneity. It's because in Japan the keirins aren't about sport, they're about betting. This is where Japan was so different to the West Indies, where the fans were so exuberant, and created an amazing atmosphere. In Japan, the spectators weren't fans, they were punters; the vast majority knew little, and cared even less, about cycling as a sport.

It wouldn't be accurate, though, to say that there was no atmosphere inside these vast – albeit virtually deserted – velodromes, of which there are around fifty throughout Japan (more than in any other country). Even if the venue was almost empty, it didn't mean no one was watching – they were watching in betting shops instead. The punters in the arena, meanwhile, were passionate, and they weren't afraid to shout abuse at you if you lost – and if they had money riding on you. Typically, they didn't know much English, but they knew one or two important words when it came to dishing out abuse. 'Hoy you ****!' And if I won, then I'd hear a gleeful 'Hoy!' For much of the time we felt less like cyclists and more like horses or greyhounds – it was abundantly clear that we were not athletes, in the punters' eyes, but potential cash cows.

You hear a lot of rumours about how much you can earn on the Japanese keirin circuit. The first thing to say is that Japan is the *only* place a sprinter can go to make any money at all. The second is that it is less than has been reported, or rumoured. You could go there for eight weeks and possibly make £30,000, but only if you won every race. In recent years, too, the money has been falling. There are more cultural than financial reasons to go these days.

Each meeting lasted three days, from Friday to Sunday, following which your bike would be taken away from you, and transported to the next venue. It could be anywhere. I remember one week racing in Aomori, at the north end of the island, where there was snow by the track, and the next week travelling to the south end, where it was 32 degrees. That, to me, summed up Japan: it is such a contradictory place, a mix of ancient and modern, with the people so polite and deferential, and trying desperately not to offend you, yet also able to scream abuse at you at the end of a keirin race! I remember, before I went, watching the Bill Murray film *Lost in Translation*, and thinking it was OK, albeit that nothing much happened. But I watched it again when I returned from Japan and thought it was the funniest – and most spot-on – film I'd ever seen. As in the film, I had the bizarre experience of someone talking at me, 1,000 words a minute, for about five minutes, at the end of which the translator would say: 'He says, "Good luck and try your best!"' I would look puzzled, and say: 'Is that really what he said?' 'Yes,' the translator would smile.

From a racing point of view, my time in Japan was reasonably successful, with four wins from 15 races, but it was marred by what was, at the time, my worst ever crash. It didn't even happen in a proper race; it was in a training race. We were coming around the corner three abreast, with me on the outside, when the rider at the front 'threw a hook', meaning that he veered quite suddenly and drastically from his line. It happened so quickly that the guy next to him had no chance to react: he was taken out and, like a falling domino, he took the next one out: me.

I hit the deck very hard. And it was, as I've said, a concrete track, with this horrible non-slip surface, of the type you get at road junctions in the UK, as though it had been covered in paint with grit in it. You hit this stuff and don't slide: it just rips your skin off. I landed on my left hip, and was only saved from a really serious injury by my protective clothing. That's the other thing about the keirin races in Japan: they insist that you wear a lot of padding and open-faced motorcycle helmets. On this occasion, it was just as well.

After the way my event had been unceremoniously dumped from the Olympics, my big crash in Japan seemed an appropriate way to end the season. I returned home to Britain to lick my wounds and think about the next stage in my career – there were some big decisions to be made. Should I continue with the kilometre, even though it wouldn't feature in the Beijing Olympics? The team sprint would be an even bigger priority for Beijing – I knew that already. The question was, did I have time, less than three years out from the next Olympics, to learn some new tricks, and become a competitive sprinter or keirin rider?

CHAPTER 15

'Would You Like Me to Lap Dance for You?'

This seems like a good time to take a step back from the chronological order of events to look at something that affects every elite athlete: drugs and drugs testing.

As I write, this topic is hotter than the tarmac on an Athens roundabout. But as an athlete I have experienced the evolution of the anti-doping system from all but non-existent to omnipresent; from being a subject that was discussed in whispers, to one that can sometimes seem to dominate much of the discussion around top-level sport.

I began competing in the days when heads were buried deep in the sand, and I have witnessed unbelievable changes as the full extent of the problem has been first acknowledged and then, finally, tackled with some seriousness. Much of the credit for that belongs to the World Anti-Doping Agency, set up to tackle the scourge of doping in all sports in the aftermath of the 'Festina Affair' at the 1998 Tour de France – when the world's number one professional road cycling team was discovered to be running a systematic doping programme.

Since then, the landscape has changed beyond recognition. As athletes, the price we've had to pay for many decades of ignorance, or neglect, has perhaps been the loss of the presumption of innocence. That precious principle has been eroded and replaced, in a lot of people's minds, by scepticism and cynicism – which is painful for me to write, but unfortunately true.

The cost to us athletes, as a consequence of that erosion, has been high. It entails increased, round-the-clock testing and putting up with the 'Whereabouts' system, whereby you have to state where you'll be for an hour every day of the year, three months in advance. Whereabouts is often perceived as a hassle and inconvenience, but what a lot of athletes seem to overlook is the fact that it's there to protect us, and to level the playing field. It has become an important responsibility of being an athlete, and the administration of it – the constant updating of your schedule, which you can do online – has to be as important to you as any aspect of your training.

I'm an ambassador of UK Sport's '100% ME' anti-doping initiative and I support Whereabouts unequivocally. I believe it is imperative, given the extent of the drugs problem in all sports, and I hope it survives the legal challenges to it, which are, at the time of writing, being made in Belgium and Spain, among other places. The credibility of sport now depends upon having a credible dope-testing system, so the stakes are high.

The irony is that, while scepticism might be at an all-time high, sport has perhaps never been cleaner. If half the stories I've heard about earlier eras, including the era when I started competing, are true, then drugs were rampant in sport for decades. Maybe I'm being naïve, but I don't believe they are now. I don't for one second think they've disappeared, but I *can't* believe that they're as prevalent as they were – not with the testing that's now in place, and with an athlete's reputation, career and livelihood at stake.

Whereabouts has the potential to be the weapon that finally defeats the cheats. It leaves them nowhere to hide, in or out of competition. Athletes gossip, and in the past I heard stories of athletes, including very high-profile ones in sports other than cycling, disappearing to far-flung places; they had their own coaches, organized their own trips and would go missing for weeks on end, during which there was no way of contacting them. Now, no matter where they disappear to, they have to tell the anti-doping authorities.

One high-profile athlete was rumoured to have a bum bag with him at all times, stuffed with $10,000 in cash, so that at any time he could up and leave. The cash was to ensure he didn't have to use a credit card, which would have enabled his pursuers to trace him.

As a sportsman you would hear these stories – some no more than urban myths, I'm sure – and it would irritate you. If these guys were cheating, then what chance did you have to beat them? For me, though, the Sydney Olympics were hugely significant in dispelling a lot of myths, urban or otherwise. Even if drugs were prevalent, they weren't the be-all and end-all – if they were, Jason wouldn't have won. Simple as that. It is one reason why it annoys me so much when you hear the old 'they're all at it' arguments; or so-called experts proclaiming that it's impossible to become an Olympic champion without drugs. It's funny how many of these experts are either people who weren't quite good enough to make it, or who resorted to drugs themselves.

Since Whereabouts has become such a fundamental part of being an athlete, I think I should explain how it works. And how strange it can be, at times, to have strangers turn up at your house to watch you go to the toilet.

As I have said, you have to be available for an hour a day. As my own whereabouts I always nominate my home address, and a time as early in the morning as possible – typically between 7 and 8 a.m. If for some reason you're not there, it counts as a missed test and a 'strike' against your name. Three strikes and you're out. It was this rule that the 400-metre runner Christine Ohuruogu fell foul of, by missing three tests. She was hit by a suspension which technically, under British Olympic Association rules, meant she would miss not only the Beijing Games but all future Olympics as well. She appealed, had her lifetime Olympic ban overturned, and went on to win a gold medal in Beijing – but her case highlighted the risks and dangers of not being organized and keeping on top of the Whereabouts system. The next athlete who misses three tests might not be treated so sympathetically.

Whereabouts means, of course, that if you make spontaneous changes of plan – perhaps staying at a friend's house, or at your girlfriend's (on the sofa, obviously) – then you have to update your information, which you can do online, by phone or even text.

The testers' visits are not confined to the Whereabouts system. They also make random checks, and naturally they don't come at predictable times. For example, at the 2008 world championships, which were in Manchester, I was tested three times over the weekend. Then, on the Monday morning, I woke up to find the testers at my door again. I suppose the idea is to make sure you never assume that, just because you've been tested recently, you're going to be left alone for a while.

For all that I am an enthusiastic supporter of the Whereabouts programme, I must admit that I still find it a bit odd having strangers coming into my house to watch me pee. I accept it, but it's something you never really get used to. If it was feasible to arrange for the testing to be done at a training venue, I'd do it, but that would be fraught with risk, because my routine changes so regularly, and I just can't take the chance of not being where I'm supposed to be.

There's one problem, of course, with them coming first thing: if I'm not still in bed, then I'll just have got up. And what's the first thing most of us do when we get out of bed? That's right: go for a pee. Invariably, then, the cistern will have just started refilling when there's a knock on the door. Aw nooooo! Then it's a case of sitting down with the tester in the living-room – once you've been notified of a test, you have to stay within sight of the tester – watching breakfast TV, drinking endless cups of coffee or tea, waiting for my bladder to refill. Which can take considerably longer than the cistern.

In fact, in extreme cases of dehydration it can take hours rather than minutes. One of my worst experiences wasn't a home visit, but a post-race dope control on a hot summer's day in Hanover in 2000. I had just finished competing and was very dehydrated, but in the waiting room for dope control they provide you with drinks to help the process – in this case, beer. Since I was building up to the Olympics I hadn't had an alcoholic drink in a long, long time ... so I opened a can of the supplied beer with some trepidation. I took a glug. Whoof! As the smell hit my nostrils, and the liquid flooded my dehydrated body, I felt instantly giddy. It went straight to my head.

Other riders were there, tucking into the beer, and the atmosphere was becoming quite convivial – in contrast to the more sombre, impatient mood that you usually find in these places. Until someone noticed that it was non-alcoholic beer. That had the effect of simultaneously sobering us up and making us feel a bit stupid. It was strange – it must have been the association of the smell and taste, almost like a case of psychosomatic drunkenness.

Back to the home visit, though. How do you pass the time with a stranger who's waiting to collect your pee? It's quite strange. Some testers are very pleasant, very down to earth, and easy to pass the time with. Others ... are a little different. Naturally, we athletes discuss the testers among ourselves – we get to know them, and their quirks and foibles, just as they get to know us. It's an odd relationship we have.

For strange drugs-testing procedures, however, nothing really matches the experiences I had in Australia prior to the 2006 Commonwealth Games in Melbourne. We had a pre-Games training camp in our usual place, Perth, where we received a visit from the Australian anti-doping agency.

In Australia I've detected a subtle difference in the attitude of some of the testers and the relationship between them and the athletes. Whereas in Britain I feel that we're on the same side as the testers, working towards the same goal, Down Under there's more of a 'them and us' atmosphere, and the testers can sometimes appear a bit more heavy-handed.

Anyway, they came to test us in Perth in 2006, and the testing procedure was odd. It's standard practice to take your top off – so they can see you're not storing bulbs of clean urine in your armpits and transporting it in tubes wrapped around your body (don't laugh: apparently it has been done) – and also to drop your trousers and pants. You are, therefore, essentially naked.

So far, so normal. But at the track in Perth the tester then asked me to do a full 360-degree pirouette, presumably to check that I didn't have any paraphernalia containing clean urine strapped to my back, the backs of my thighs ... I didn't really question it, I just did it, albeit feeling very self-conscious, and just a little bit like Steve Coogan's character Alan Partridge, when he does his excruciating pole dance for a BBC executive, and asks: 'Would you like me to lap dance for you?'

The full 360 was unusual, but I thought it must be stand-ard practice in Australia and I didn't think too much of it until I arrived in Melbourne, and received another visit from the drugs testers. I went through the ritual of undressing and, when I'd dropped my pants, asked the tester: 'Do you want me to do a full 360?'

I might as well have gone the full Partridge and asked him: 'Would you like me to lap dance for you?' He looked at me as if I'd asked whether it would also be OK to take a crap on the floor. 'Er, no,' he said.

'Oh,' I said. 'It's just that the last time, the guy asked me to do a 360 ...'

I don't know which of us was more embarrassed, but he looked at me again and eventually said: 'Well, er, that's not normal.'

Something else that's impossible to ignore is suspicion. It goes hand in hand with success, unfortunately, and it's going to take a while to turn that perception around. You'd have to be incredibly naïve not to be aware of it. And I understand people's scepticism, I really do, but there's one assumption in particular that I do also find annoying, which is the 'he's got massive legs, so he must be on drugs' argument.

When people meet me in the flesh a common reaction is: 'Oh, you're a lot smaller than I thought you were.' On one level I could find that quite disappointing, but on another it comes as a bit of a relief. The sub-text is: so you're not the muscle-bound freak that I thought you were.

Television has a lot to answer for; that and the Lycra. Craig MacLean, in particular, can look like a bodybuilder – his physique looks very impressive on TV (not that I'd ever tell him that to his face). But in 'real life,' and in casual clothes, both he and I look pretty normal. If you look after yourself, and eat a good diet, which Craig was meticulous about, you become very lean. And it's really about how lean you are rather than the size of your muscles. The leanness enhances muscle definition, but it doesn't come overnight. It takes years of dedication and work.

But I am aware – and I was certainly made aware after the Beijing Olympics – of this perception that I am some kind of weird cross between the Incredible Hulk and Mr Universe on a bike. One newspaper ran a feature asking where I bought my jeans. My girlfriend, Sarra, was quoted as saying that my thighs are thicker than her waist. But she is very slim! OK, so I'm not going to carry off the Russell Brand skinny jeans look, but it's really not that difficult to find trousers that fit. Compared with some sportsmen I am positively lightweight. I took part in an exhibition race at the Manchester Velodrome with the English rugby legend (and now coach), Martin Johnson. As I rode behind him, he resembled Gulliver and I looked like one of the Lilliputians.

Suspicion – based on gold medals or body shape, or a combination of both – can be frustrating, but it doesn't cause me to lose any sleep. I honestly believe that the truth comes out in the end; that all the samples that have been taken and stored will come back to haunt anyone who has cheated. In Beijing, for example, all the blood and urine taken was tested at the time, while the B-samples were frozen, to be kept for up to eight years, so that they can be examined against new tests. Personally, I am convinced that most – if not all – cheats are found out eventually.

CHAPTER 16

Taking On the Tour de France

Going back to 2006, I had that big decision to make: where should I focus my efforts in the future? And there was an even more immediate dilemma: when should I call it a day with the kilometre?

It was with huge reluctance that I contemplated turning my back on the kilo, because it had always fascinated me. Apart from my post-Athens blip, when I struggled a little with motivation, it continued to do so. Had it not been dropped from the Olympics then I have no doubt that I'd have continued to find it an interesting challenge up to the London Games in 2012. There are ways of staying mentally fresh, and Shane Sutton is particularly good at helping you look outside the box, and coming up with innovative ways of approaching it.

But the most important thing is to have a stimulating goal. For an event that's in the Olympics, there isn't a problem. For one that isn't, there is. So if I wanted to continue doing the kilo for a little while longer – and I did – I had to find a new challenge. The 2006 Commonwealth Games in Melbourne was one target, and was coming up shortly, but it wasn't enough in itself. I needed something else. And it was my dad who suggested it. Why not go for Arnaud Tournant's world record of 58.875 seconds? There was only one place to do it – the same place where Arnaud set his mark in 2001: the rarely used track in the velodrome at La Paz, Bolivia, where the thin air at high altitude made conditions ideal for record attempts. The plan was to go for it in 2007, then officially retire from the kilo and turn my attention to the Olympic disciplines, with the team sprint my priority, and the individual sprint and keirin offering possible back-up. It seemed like a good plan to me. Dad, who was in his element managing a project like this, and attacked it with the same gusto as he did his *Grand Designs*-esque project with the family house, got to work sorting out the logistics to make it happen.

Unfortunately, Melbourne provided a big setback. After losing my world title in 2005 I was determined to re-establish myself in 2006 as the best kilo rider in the world. Not that the winter of 2005/06 had seen me as down as I'd been in 2003, after losing my kilo title in Stuttgart. By now, I found I could deal with setbacks a little better, and rationalize them. After all, I wasn't the only Olympic champion who struggled to perform at the same level the following season; in fact, at the world championships in Los Angeles none of the Athens gold medallists managed to add world titles in the discipline in which they won their Olympic titles.

I finished only third in the kilo at the Commonwealth Games, behind Ben Kersten and a rejuvenated Jason Queally, and I was well beaten. Ben did a 1.01.8; Jason was only three-hundredths of a second behind him; and I was a little behind the other two with a 1.02.071. It was a crushing blow: I'd lost my Commonwealth title, the first major individual title of my career, which had meant so much to me when I won it in Manchester in 2002. But I also really felt that I'd let down the Scotland team, because there had been such massive expectations of me, and also of Craig, who finished in the worst possible position: fourth. At least I had a bit of metal to show for my effort.

I remember returning to the athletes' village that night and feeling dreadful. We'd left, earlier in the day, in a very buoyant mood; and we could feel the optimism from the rest of the team. It was as if they were depending on us to get the team off to a flying start. When we got back, it seemed as if no one knew what to say to us, or could look us in the eye. I got the impression that people didn't know whether to say 'well done' for my bronze medal, or to offer their commiserations for my failure to win gold. I suppose this was another sign of how far the sport had progressed in Scotland – and indeed in the whole of Britain – in the eight years since the Kuala Lumpur Games of 1998, when any medal was deemed a success. Then I'd have been the talk of the team with my bronze.

Fortunately, we managed to bounce back a couple of days later, when Craig and I joined Ross Edgar in the team sprint, and we reached the final: a showdown with the Auld Enemy, England. This created an interesting scenario, since we were all team-mates – and very good friends – most of the time, the Commonwealth Games being the only time that Jason, Jamie Staff and Matt Crampton raced in different colours from us. Then there was the coaching staff – Shane Sutton, Iain Dyer, Steve Peters, Dave Brailsford … they were all there in Melbourne, but where would their loyalties lie? Shane must have felt the most conflicted, with these Games being in his native Australia, while he was on the payroll of the British set-up. As if that wasn't enough to leave his head spinning, he had previously been Welsh national coach. Ever the professional, Shane resolved the dilemma in the team sprint final by wearing a Scotland T-shirt and an England T-shirt – one on top of the other.

Anyway, to our final: against England. There was a lot of satisfaction in the fact that it was us against England, with the

Australians not making the final, and having to be content with bronze. It showed the strength in depth of the British squad, and augured well for the world championships and Olympics. We got off to a great start, Craig storming out of the gate as man one, Ross taking over, and me finishing it off on the final lap, stopping the clock on 44.282 seconds, 27 thousandths of a second before the English.

It was nice to claim gold, though by now the Scotland team wasn't quite so dependent on us, with the swimmers collecting a sackful of medals in the pool, and helping to propel Scotland to its best ever performance at a Commonwealth Games, and a final position of sixth in the medals table, with 11 golds. Doing well in your own event is your number one goal at any major games, obviously, but I discovered in Melbourne – and would have it confirmed in Beijing two years later – how wonderful it is to be part of a successful team, when good morale spreads throughout the squad, among athletes and coaches alike, and infects you like a virus – but one that you want to catch. What a contrast it was to Kuala Lumpur. Here in Melbourne, others perceived us differently; they respected us, and we wore our Scotland kit with even more pride than usual.

Looking back now, I think my problem in Melbourne was that I was a little behind in my training. Prior to the Games, we'd had a training camp in Perth, where there was some tension between Shane and me over this. The problem lay, I think, in me trying to cram too much into that Perth training camp; it meant I arrived in Melbourne tired.

Shane and I had a bit of a falling out, and didn't speak for a couple of days, though we eventually shook hands. He apologized for what was basically a misunderstanding (he had enraged me by calling into question my commitment to training). I apologized, too. But then he hit me with: 'What *really* pissed me off was what you said at the Tassie Carnivals ...'

He was referring to an incident after a race in Tasmania ... the year before! He'd got us up at 5 a.m. to go to the airport, but when we got there, we were early. At the time, I remarked: 'Oh god, we could have had an extra hour in bed ...'

It had been an observation rather than a dig at Shane, but it had obviously touched a raw nerve – and remained touching that nerve for more than a year! I couldn't believe it, but I learnt a lesson: when Shane does something for you (such as getting you to the airport on time), you let him know you appreciate it. That's all he wants. If he thinks you're acting even remotely like a spoilt brat – and I suppose I was, a little bit, in Tasmania – then it'll really irritate him. And it'll come out. Even a year later.

Shane likes to say that I hadn't 'done the yards' prior to Melbourne, which certainly wasn't the plan – I intended to arrive at the Commonwealth Games at close to my best form, and maintain it for the world championships in Bordeaux a few weeks later. As it turned out, I continued improving after Melbourne, and really did arrive in the French city in the best condition I'd been in since Athens. It was an opportunity for revenge, and I took it, winning my third world kilo title, and beating Kersten, my Melbourne nemesis, in the process, with a young Frenchman, François Pervis, third. In the team sprint there was a predictable result: we were second, again to the French, with Jamie Staff and Jason Queally joining me in the team to claim silver.

Another significant thing happened in Bordeaux, though – the significance of which wouldn't be properly appreciated for a couple of years. Shane approached a recently retired sprinter, Jan van Eijden, who was at the championships commentating for Eurosport. Jan was someone we knew well, not least because he had been, by general agreement, the most tactically astute rider of the last decade. He won the world sprint title in Manchester in 2000, but here he was in the commentary gantry. Shane, a great lateral thinker, had an inspired idea: why not bring him on board to sharpen up the British sprinters' tactics? After all, bizarre as it may seem, this was what we still lacked; indeed, we had never had someone dedicated to helping us with the tactical side of the sport.

We were often the fastest on paper, but when it came to beating people in man-to-man situations, we invariably fell short, although, somewhat ironically, Bordeaux saw the best performance by a British sprinter in about 40 years. Craig reached the sprint final, where he was beaten by the apparently invincible Dutchman, Theo Bos, who also won the keirin by an embarrassing margin. But one swallow does not make a summer, and Shane knew that if any of us were going to challenge for sprint medals in the Beijing Olympics then we needed a sharper tactical edge.

I knew first-hand how good a tactician Jan was. He knocked me out, by two races to one, in the Manchester World Cup in 2004. I was faster than him in qualifying, but he stalled; he used tactics to kill my speed; he controlled the race. It was as though he could get under your feet, pinning you against the barriers, generally making himself an obstacle – a pain in the neck, in other words. In football, the equivalent would be the defender whose job it is to stop the striker getting a shot on goal. Jan could do this better than anyone.

Another appointment to the sprint group post-Bordeaux was a real coup. Again it was Shane – he does have his uses – who was instrumental in persuading Scott Gardner, an Australian sports scientist who worked with the dominant Aussie sprinters at the Athens Olympics, to jump ship. Going into the final two years before Beijing, we now had a very strong team of coaches, who complemented each other perfectly: among them the almost Spock-like Iain Dyer, very logical and calm, and a great guy to have in the track centre.

Iain will come over and tell you what to do and when: 'OK,' he'll say, 'we'll get you on the rollers at this time ... I want you doing a little "rev out" here ...' He'll know exactly when you're going to be called up; he'll have your bike weighed (as it has to be, prior to each race, to make sure it's not under the regulation weight); he'll know all the tiny but important details, such as where the toilets are, and how long it takes to get there: 'The toilets are a two-and-a-half-minute walk,' Iain will announce. Believe me, knowing these details, or, rather, knowing that you have someone on your team who knows all these details, is invaluable; it reduces stress considerably.

Iain was a revelation. Though he had been a lifelong cyclist, in all disciplines, from BMXing to road, mountain bike and track, he had been involved in just about every sport, from working as a gym instructor in Reading and then Wrexham, where he did strength and conditioning coaching with young tennis players attached to the LTA training centre, to fitness training with Shrewsbury Town Football Club, as well as writing modules and lecturing on sports science. In summer 2000, he ran a coaching education course at British Cycling, and it was around the same time that the talent team programme was set up. When a regional coach post became available, Iain went for it, and he was appointed to look after the North West of England. After only four months he was encouraged to apply for the national sprint coach job, which had been vacant since Martin Barras's departure. His first day in the job saw him travel to Perth with Jason Queally and me for a training camp, and I think it's fair to say that he then embarked on a pretty steep learning curve.

Before he was appointed to that job, I actually remember Iain sitting in the stands during training sessions, and popping into the gym, watching us do our weights. I didn't know who he was, but he became a familiar presence. When he was appointed sprint coach, he was really dropped in the deep

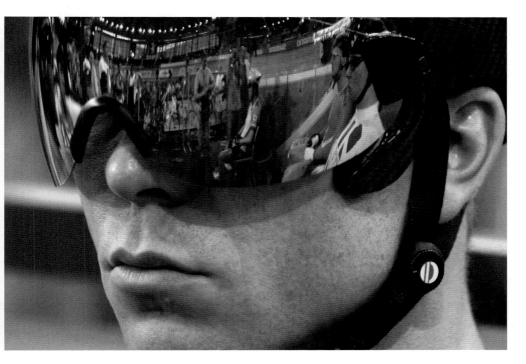

Photographers love the mirrored visor. It's the Palma world championships in 2007, and I'm running through the race in my mind.

En route to another world championship silver behind the French in the team sprint, Palma 2007. Craig MacLean is leading, Ross Edgar following, with me in third.

The Andes form a dramatic backdrop to my successful attempt at the 500 metres world record in La Paz, Bolivia.

The other pictures show me training for the Bolivia adventure (top), the aftermath of one of my gruelling turbo sessions (middle) and recovering from my unsuccessful attempt at Arnaud Tournant's world kilo record (bottom).

Above: Narrowly winning the keirin final in Beijing, 2008, for my second gold of the Games. No need for the photo finish on this occasion. Ross Edgar is second.

Right: Jason Kenny (left) and me sparring in the sprint final: neither wants to be at the front.

Below: Photo finish required here: beating Theo Bos at the Manchester world championships, 2008. It's the moment Theo lost his crown; I've never been so happy to win a quarter-final.

Above: Fortunately my dad has a big chest to absorb those tears, as my mum, girlfriend Sarra and sister Carrie look on.

Left: More man hugging and more tears in Beijing, this time with my coaches Jan van Eijden (left) and Iain Dyer (right).

Below: The Edinburgh bus parade, with rower Kath Grainger alongside me. An amazing day and probably the highlight of the post-Beijing celebrations.

The Save Meadowbank Stadium banners were out in force for the Edinburgh bus parade – and I was only too happy to be associated with the campaign.

Pumped up after delivering the match ball to the Murrayfield pitch prior to the Scotland–All Blacks rugby international, with some diminutive All Blacks looking on.

Meeting Lewis Hamilton at the Race of Champions, before our intended head-to-head had to be cancelled because the conditions were too dangerous for cycling.

A special day for the Hoy family at Buckingham Palace: me with my knighthood and Mum with her MBE for services to nursing. 'You got yours for actually doing something useful, didn't you?' as the BBC reporter said to my mum.

Left: BBC Sports Personality of the Year: the famous trophy is bashed up a bit, and the base is faded, but it's got character.

Below: Another bus parade, in London this time, and yet another incredible post-Beijing celebration.

Left: Her Royal Highness looks on as I chat to the Queen. With my good friend Rebecca Adlington and other Beijing gold medallists, Paul Goodison, Tim Brabants and Peter Reed (right to left).

Above: I wasn't superimposed: I did actually pose for this pre-Beijing. And yes, it was very windy and difficult to balance.

Right: Sarra and me on the carpet at the National Film Awards in London.

Below: Back to earth with a bump following my 40mph crash in the keirin final at the Copenhagen World Cup in 2009, in my first major race since the Beijing Olympics.

end, but he learnt very quickly. He developed some impressive ideas, showing particular interest in strength and conditioning, but over the years he has added great technical
knowledge, and now I'd say he is the world's foremost expert
on the technical aspects of sprint training. Iain's also great on
tactics, and he scores highly in his understanding of the theor-
etical underpinnings of performance. But perhaps his greatest
asset is that he doesn't think he knows it all. Sometimes you
get coaches who've had some success, and then think they
have the formula to repeat it. Iain is always tweaking, always
looking for new ways to work. He actually left the team after
Athens, and went to work in a friend's business for a few
months, but he was lured back. We were all delighted, none
more so than a young sprinter with whom Iain had been
working particularly closely: a teenager by the name of Jason
Kenny.

Then, of course, there's Shane: always bouncing off the
walls, able to gee you up, and analyse your races and opponents; Jan, who understands tactics like no one else; and
Scott, in the background, working out 'the numbers', meaning data on times, power output and so on. He'll come up to
you and say: 'Good numbers, mate. It's in there.' Scott was
the one who'd give you the information, the hard evidence –
the numbers that you couldn't argue with. He was set to
become a very important member of the team, who would
look after me, and the other sprinters, in 2007 – and help me
to master, belatedly, the black art of individual sprinting.

But the 2006 season wasn't quite over. Not yet. First, in July,
I had the Tour de France.

If I had a pound for every time someone has asked me why
I don't ride the Tour de France, or whether I might, then I'd
be a very rich – but still very irritated – man. It is usually a

joke. But sometimes there'll be a follow-up: 'No, but really ... why not?'

For the same reason that Usain Bolt doesn't run the London Marathon.

'Yes,' they say, 'but Mark Cavendish is supposedly a sprinter ... and he rides the Tour de France.'

'Cav' is an endurance athlete with a good sprint. I am an out-and-out sprinter. Hope that's clear!

Anyway, in July 2006 I did ride stage of the Tour de France. L'Etape du Tour – which means 'stage of the Tour' – is a mass participation event that sees 8,500 riders tackle one stage of the race, usually a few days before the *peloton* rides it; and the organizers usually select one of the hardest ones. They certainly did this time: 191 kilometres in the Alps, including the climbs of the Col d'Izoard, the Col du Lautaret and, the *pièce de résistance*, Alpe d'Huez.

As far as British Cycling was concerned, L'Etape challenge, as we'll call it, began as a bit of fun and a means of getting fit and losing weight for the support staff, management and sponsors, with Dave Brailsford, Shane Sutton and head coach Simon Jones all signed up. It was as if Gillian McKeith had come in and set them this target; it was that serious, and for a time it seemed more important to some than the Olympics. People were getting new bikes; they were having 'fruit days'; no question, it was, for all those involved, A Big Thing.

Then someone pulled out and Jason Queally said he'd fancy it, despite the fact that no other riders from the British team had signed up, only staff. You could see people thinking: Jason Queally?! A sprinter? Which made me think: I quite fancy it, too. So, in April, a few weeks after the Bordeaux world championships, Jason and I decided to go for it, mainly because it was in the off-season, so wouldn't impinge on our proper training.

What was I thinking, agreeing to ride close to 120 miles in the mountains? I'll be honest and tell you exactly what I was thinking: that, in a *peloton* of 8,500 people, there would be lots of bodies to shelter behind. I thought: I've been to Majorca; I've ridden over some big mountains there. Plus, I'm a veteran of the Junior Tour of Ireland. It can't be *that* hard.

Can it?

Later, I looked at the stage profile. The three peaks resembled shark's teeth: albeit shark's teeth that, in the case of the Izoard, climbed to more than 2,300 metres. And, in the case of Alpe d'Huez, we would finish up one of the Tour's most famous climbs, its 21 hairpin bends winding like a staircase to the ski station at the summit.

It is with a wry smile that I recall Shane's advice at the time. 'There's only one big hill really, mate,' he said. 'The Izoard. Get over that and you'll be fine. Alpe d'Huez isn't that hard.'

Having committed to doing it, I decided to do it for charity, raising money for Children with Leukaemia. But I couldn't train for it; not really. If I did too many long road rides I would compromise my sprint training; so the longest ride I did was about three hours on the flat roads of Cheshire, a bit more than 70 miles. And that was it: I travelled to France in a state of some apprehension.

On the morning of the race – sorry, the ride – we rose at the ungodly hour of 5 a.m. L'Etape would begin early anyway, but it was also important to eat – a lot – three hours before the start, to allow the food time to digest and to avoid being bloated when we set off. You didn't want to be lining up with any excess weight, especially with the prospect of no toilet stops. There was an atmosphere of nervous tension at breakfast. Everyone felt it, from Jason and me to guys in their late fifties, with their smart new bikes. None of us really knew what to expect. All we could reasonably assume was that we were in for a very tough day – potentially our toughest on a bike.

We rode to Gap for the start, along with thousands and thousands of other cyclists. It was an incredible blur of colour and glistening chrome, and it was mayhem. Like the start of the London Marathon, but with bikes to add to the chaos. And the obligatory portaloos, of course. In front of each was a lengthy queue of people, but as I got close to the head of the line, there was an almighty clatter, a door had been kicked open from the inside and one male cyclist found himself on full display in a compromising position. That's the problem with cleated cycling shoes – they slip. I would guess that he had been trying to hover above the toilet seat when his shoe slid across the floor and into the door, forcing it open. Cue an outbreak of nervous laughter.

It was hot, 35 degrees, and, as we took to the start, I decided to ride in my rainbow jersey of world champion. A foolish and slightly naïve move on my part.

The plan was to 'float' for the first hour: to ride in the middle of the group, being sucked along, hardly pressing the pedals. Shane agreed this would be our strategy as a group: 'We're gonna ride steady, mate.'

Then the flag dropped, and the GB contingent went off like a bunch of lunatics. We overtook about 1,000 people in the first hour. My intention had always been to stick with the British guys, because I didn't fancy being out there, potentially for six or seven hours, on my own, with no one to chat to. But as we bowled along at 45kph (28mph), I began to wonder.

When we hit the Izoard, many of those we'd overtaken began to come past us. We rode more sensibly up here – not entirely through choice. It was a brutal climb, more than 20 miles long, and taking almost two hours to complete. The worst thing you can do on a climb like this is allow your ego to kick in; you have to ignore the pace being set by other riders and stick doggedly to a pace you're comfortable with. If you 'blow up' – or hit the wall – on a climb like this, there's no hiding place; you can't freewheel. When it was finally over we stopped at the summit to regroup, waiting for about half an hour for Jason, who was really taking his time.

But Shane was, in fact, right: the Izoard was the hardest climb. Between the Lautaret and Alpe d'Huez I pressed on a bit; by now I was enjoying the sense of adventure, and the camaraderie – as well as Dave, Shane, Simon, Jason and me, there were sponsors and other people associated with the British team. It was a good group. And by the Alpe, when our group shattered into individual pieces, I began to be swept along by the atmosphere. There were huge crowds, camped out on the side of the mountain for days, maybe up to a week, awaiting the arrival of Le Tour. It felt like a sporting venue rather than a road; it was like an amphitheatre, and the atmosphere was truly amazing. You are in a place rich in cycling history, with every one of those 21 hairpin bends named after a previous winner at the Alpe; it is a magical place.

'Courage, Courage!' shouted the spectators in French as I toiled up the mountain. There's an important distinction here: for the riders of the Tour they shout 'Allez!'; for the riders of L'Etape it's 'Courage!' But that wasn't the only thing they shouted at me. 'Tom Boonen! Tom Boonen!' was another popular cry, particularly from the Belgian fans on the mountain. Boonen was the world road champion that year, and so would also have been wearing the rainbow world champion's jersey. I think it was the 138th scream of 'Boonen! Boonen!' that started me doubting the wisdom of wearing the same jersey. I didn't kid myself that they were mistaking me for Boonen (in any case, he was riding the Tour). Basically, they thought I was a groupie.

It wasn't that Alpe d'Huez was particularly steep. It was the fact that it came at the end, after more than six hours in the saddle, in suffocating heat. Looking at my handlebar-mounted computer, I saw, at one point, that my speed had dropped to 8.5kph (just over 5mph). I could almost walk quicker. A little later, I saw a sign that said there were 4 kilometres to go and I thought, Great – I'm almost there: that's only 16 laps of the track.

Then I thought, hang on: 4km at 8.5kph … that's nearly half an hour. Oh, shit.

Near the summit I struggled past Alun Owen, a Welshman who'd been a very good road rider a few years earlier. 'Bloody 'ell!' he said, 'Passed by a sprinter.' Clearly he had plenty left in the tank – the fact that he could talk was evidence enough. But to prove it he caught me again, and rode ahead, stopping to take pictures. I, meanwhile, wore a mask of pain. It required all my concentration to keep pressing the pedals, keep them going round – just. I hope Alun didn't think I was being rude; I just could not talk.

When, finally, I reached the finish, plonked right on top of the mountain, I rolled to a shaded spot, virtually fell off my bike, and then lay down, content to stay there for a long, long time. My body had never ached – all over – the way it did now. I had never suffered for that length of time before. My back hurt; my neck hurt; but most of all, my legs hurt: they were screaming. There was no relief, not even lying in the shade, finally separated from my bike.

I was used to dealing with extreme pain for a matter of seconds, not this low level of pain for hours. On this subject, in fact, there is an interesting passage in Mark Cavendish's autobiography, *Boy Racer*, which distinguishes between the different kinds of pain endured by a track sprinter and a road rider. Cavendish writes: 'There's a difference between hurting yourself and suffering. A track sprinter like Chris Hoy can hurt himself more than any road rider, but he doesn't suffer; for about one minute – the maximum duration of his full-on effort in a keirin or team sprint or an individual sprint – Chris can go 110 per cent into his reserves, but ask him to go at 80 per cent for ten minutes and he can't do it.'

I hurt; he suffers. That's spot on, Cav – I think he's nailed a fundamental distinction between sprinters and endurance athletes in this passage. I should add that I'm a big fan of Cav's, and watched him win four stages in the 2008 Tour de France, then topping that with an unbelievable six in 2009, with huge admiration. He also mentions in his book a little adventure we undertook together in LA in 2005, when, during the world championships, we went in search of Krispy Kreme doughnuts ... and eventually found some, after a bit of a trek through some quite dodgy-looking areas. As I watched him stuff his face with doughnuts I wouldn't neces-sarily have predicted that he'd go on to have the spectacular success he's had. But most of us involved with the British team knew Cav was special – and so he has proved.

Funnily enough, I recently found myself seriously thinking about riding L'Etape du Tour again. I can only put that down to the memory of the pain having faded a little. But recalling it in order to write this chapter, it suddenly seems very vivid again. It's a possibility. That's all I'm prepared to say at this point.

CHAPTER 17

The Final Kilo ...?

My legs had just about recovered from L'Etape du Tour when the track season got under way again. The 2006/07 season was set to be an interesting and important one, featuring my final bow as a kilo rider and my first as an all-round sprinter – though, if I'm honest, it was still the kilo, rather than sprint or keirin, that was uppermost in my mind. I was still far from convinced that, at the almost pensionable age of 30, I could pick up the skills to be competitive in these two events.

Still, the plan was to start riding some of the sprint and keirin competitions at the World Cups, but to make the kilo my main target at the world championships in Palma. From there I would go on to Bolivia, to tackle Arnaud Tournant's ultimate world record. My dad was still working on organizing track hire, flights, accommodation, the transportation of the start gate and timing equipment, as well as the travel arrangements for officials, and sponsorship, etc. It was proving an awful lot more complicated than we could ever have imagined.

As well as wanting more strings to my bow, my attempt to improve as a keirin and sprint rider could only improve my chances of helping GB to a gold medal in the team sprint at the Beijing Olympics. We thought that the keirin, especially, would sharpen me up, giving me more 'top end' speed. The next Games were now on the horizon; it's amazing how quickly the Olympic cycle passes, with only about six months of respite before the next ones start to loom in the distance. Once you're into year three, they seem very close indeed – and Beijing was coming into sharp focus.

And there was yet another reason for wanting to improve as a keirin and sprint rider: it could give me the edge if selection for the Games came down to a battle with, say, Jason Queally. Since his crash in Edinburgh, way back in 1995, Jason had stuck to his pledge never to ride a bunch race. As a result, he wouldn't ride the sprint or keirin – the former is hardly a bunch race, but you are racing against someone else, and crashes are not uncommon. So, for me, these could be my insurance policy. If Jason and I were considered equal in the team sprint, I might get the nod on the basis that I could ride other events. It sounds a little bit ruthless, given my friendship with Jason, and his generosity when I switched to 'his' event, the kilo, after Sydney; but I couldn't afford to be sentimental. I wanted to go to the Olympics as much as he did.

I began working in training with Jan van Eijden on the two new events, incorporating little things. One thing I did in my usual warm-down, at the end of each track session, was to ride looking backwards, rather than forwards. The reason for this is that, in the sprint, when you have your opponent behind you, you have to watch them – while riding in a straight line, obviously. There's quite a knack to this, but my warm-downs gave me the perfect opportunity to practise for around 20 minutes or so; riding for the entire period with my head tilted back. I even managed to avoid crashing, or cricking my neck.

With the keirin, it was more a case of thinking about it tactically. In this race, you spend most of it riding behind a motorbike, which swings off with two and a half laps remaining. The point of the motorbike is to set quite a fast pace; you are not allowed to overtake it, but, once it's away, there are no rules: it's a straight race to the line among the six riders.

Although I'd spent the previous summer in Japan, the races there do not really resemble international keirins: the pacer is on a bike rather than on a motorbike; the field is bigger; and the tactics are decided in advance.

One of my first international keirins was at the Perth Grand Prix in November 2006. I began with the intention of getting the place directly behind the motorbike, and then taking it on from the front – steadily increasing the pace in the last 500 metres and hoping that no one could overtake me. It was a tactic that would play to my strengths as a kilo rider, with the bonus that it could allow me to avoid the mêlée and inherent danger of battling for space on the track with the five other riders.

But someone had other ideas, and wasn't so keen on me slotting in behind the motorbike. It was Shane Perkins, a member of the Australian team. Back then, you were allowed to battle a bit more; contact was permitted, and the odd shoulder barge was OK. Now, like the tackle from behind in football, or the two-footed challenge, it has been outlawed. But on the Perth track Perkins kept battering into me in the early stages of the keirin, trying to dislodge me from my place as first man behind the bike. It was as puzzling as it was annoying. What was he expecting me to do? To back off and let him in?

Eventually, I turned to him and said: 'What the hell are you doing?!' Just to cement the idea – the fallacy – that I knew what I was doing, I then added: 'If you sit on my wheel you'll be guaranteed second!'

God knows where that came from, but, amazingly, it worked – he did exactly as I instructed! He dropped back, settled in behind me, and, when the motorbike swung off, I put my foot down. I really poured it on, and I won the race. As I was riding round after crossing the line, Perkins came up behind me, patted me on the back, and said: 'Thanks, mate, that was brilliant. You were like a motorbike.'

Two months later, in January 2007, I rode the keirin at the World Cup meeting in Los Angeles. In the first heat, I adopted the same tactic: from the front, foot down. And I won. Bloody hell, I thought, this is going well; maybe I'm on to something ...

It put me in the semi-final, where I was joined by my team-mate, Ross Edgar. That gave us an opportunity to put a little plan into action. I took the spot behind the motorbike, Ross slotted in behind me, and then let me open a wee gap as the bike swung off. I won that, too, with Ross second, so we were both in the final. And, guess what? I opted for the same tactic: from the front. But this time I almost messed it up. Two Aussies attacked in formation, and we had to counter, eventually going over the top of them. It meant making a huge effort, and I only just held on – but I did hold on. I had won the LA World Cup. It was a revelation.

But Jan, Iain and Shane were concerned. They recognized that my tactics were a bit one-dimensional. They weren't 'tactics' so much as 'tactic', because I only had one, and if for some reason I didn't find myself at the front, I could be in trouble. 'Once the big boys suss you out,' they said, 'you'll be screwed.' They were right: the idea that I could continue winning using this one, very straightforward tactic went against the logic of bike racing.

Why did it go against the logic of bike racing? Because there is such an advantage – in terms of shelter from the wind – in sitting behind someone; so for me to win from the front meant spending longer in the wind, while my rivals sat in my slipstream. Theoretically, all someone had to do to beat me was to sit behind me, conserving energy, before coming round me.

Then again, my kilo background gave me one advantage: I was used to riding fast on my own, and sustaining the effort for a relatively long period, while most other sprinters were perhaps more adept at brief bursts of speed.

The real test, though, as Jan, Iain and Shane noted, would come when I met the top riders. They meant one in particular – Theo Bos. At the time Bos was the sprint and keirin world champion, and he was considered untouchable. But that season he was being quite elusive, picking and choosing which races he rode, and I didn't meet him in competition in any of the World Cups. At the Manchester round, just a few weeks before the world championships in Palma, I was drawn against him in the sprint, but he'd crashed in an earlier round, and withdrew with an injured wrist. Then he pulled out of the invitational Japanese keirin, too.

The final of the Japanese keirin – a standard keirin, with motorbike, but held to promote the Japanese Keirin Association – came at the end of a busy weekend. I was exhausted starting the keirin, but there was a lot at stake: ten thousand pounds, to be precise. It isn't often track cyclists race for such a big prize, and there was big cash for the podium places, too. I used the same tactic, going from the front, and winning, while Ross Edgar did what he does so well: ducking and diving, and emerging from all the flying bodies to claim second. So we both went home considerably richer, and very happy with our weekend's work.

The fact that Ross and I were combining so well – purely as a result of us having complementary skills, with him able to accelerate sharply, and sprint through gaps, and me relying on horsepower – meant that some people assumed we were working as a team. Theo Bos was among those who seemed to think that my victories were coming as a result of Ross's help. I remember him being quoted in the press saying that I was only winning because of Ross – that it was a team effort, and we were clearly riding together. It wasn't, and we weren't; but, while we weren't riding as a team, we wouldn't ride against the other either.

Going into Palma at the end of March, we had some good news on the planned world record attempt. My dad had managed to get everything in place. The key had been the BBC coming on board, agreeing to travel out to a pre-attempt training camp in Florida, then on to La Paz in Bolivia, to make a documentary for BBC Scotland. The people involved, Jill Douglas as presenter, John Graham as producer, had become great supporters of track cycling, broadcasting the world championships each year since 2003. It was great to have them on board for what would prove an incredible adventure – and one I was really excited about.

But first came Palma de Mallorca and the world championships. On the first night we had a predictable result in the team sprint: second. Behind the French, naturally. The timetable meant that on day two I would attempt my first ever keirin at a world championships, while day three would witness my last ever kilo. This was already prompting some gentle mockery from those such as Craig MacLean – a silver medallist with Ross Edgar and me in the team sprint – who accused me of having more retirement events than Frank Sinatra. And, actually, I regret being quite so definitive about it – saying that Bordeaux, Palma and Bolivia would be my 'final' kilos – because, who knows? As I write, in the middle of 2009, I wouldn't rule out returning to the event at some point in the future ... but more on that later.

In the meantime, it's probably best to adopt the description I recently saw applied to Joe Calzaghe, the boxer. Apparently Joe is 'currently retired'. I like that, and it's probably a useful description for boxers, who tend to make more returns than Lazarus.

So, day two in Palma, and the keirin. I was nervous, knowing that this was the real test, when the French and Theo Bos would be out to knock me off the perch I'd built for myself with my wins in LA and Manchester. I didn't know what to expect, which is pretty much to be expected with the keirin. I thought of Jamie Staff, who went to the Athens Olympics as world champion, and with high hopes of at least a medal. He chopped someone in a repechage round, not dangerously, but enough to earn a disqualification, with no right of appeal, no chance of coming back in, nothing. To me, watching at the time, it seemed very unjust, but it summed up the shortcomings of putting all your eggs in the basket marked 'keirin'. I liked being master of my own destiny, and wasn't so keen on the unpredictability of the keirin.

In Palma, I reached the semi-final to set up, at long last, a showdown with Bos, who really had lived up to his nickname, 'The Boss', in this event. I remember watching him in the previous year's keirin final in Bordeaux, where he won by an embarrassing margin – about the length of the finishing straight. He rode across the line with his arms up, his tongue out – he looked completely unbeatable. That final can be seen on YouTube, and the commentator says it all: 'It looks like Theo just has to decide when to drop the hammer to make the others look like also-rans.' The commentator observes that Bos has ridden 'a contemptuous last lap'. But I also noted that the margin of his victory was exaggerated by the Spanish rider, José Antonio Escuredo, who was renowned for stalling and blocking. In Bordeaux, Escuredo had been doing his usual tricks when Bos jumped clear – he therefore opened a big gap very easily, and then managed to hold it. I knew that the gap between him and the others wasn't as significant as it looked in that final – but it certainly added to Bos's aura of invincibility.

In Palma, I wasn't sure that Bos was the same force that he had been in Bordeaux. Certainly his confidence didn't seem what it had been 12 months earlier, and in that semi-final I was hardly aware of him. I adopted my tried and now tested tactic, going from the front while all hell broke loose behind me. While I won, Mark French, the Australian rider, tangled with Kévin Sireau of France on the final lap. French took Sireau up the track, a horrendous move, and Bos, who'd been fifth, sneaked through on the inside. French was disqualified, but there was no compensation for Sireau – he was out, too. So Theo was through to the final largely through luck.

As I say, he didn't seem to have the same aura about him, and before the final – which Ross also qualified for, having managed an incredible burst of speed, taking him from last to first in the other semi-final – Bos did a curious thing. He came up to me as we were warming up, just minutes before we were due to be called up to the track, and said: 'My odds have just got worse.'

In Japan, all the pre-race conversations were about your odds. I said, 'Why's that?'

'Because Escuredo's not in the final.'

He was acknowledging that the Spaniard's stalling tactics had helped him win the previous year. But my thought was: how weird. Even if he was joking, it was strange to show any negativity. Then he said something even more strange.

'Are you going "senko" today?'

Again, this was a reference to Japanese keirin racing – Bos and I had been there at the same time two years earlier. 'Senko' was the tactic that saw the rider go from the front – it was *my* tactic. But why would he ask me? This was the world championships, not Japan. More to the point, why would I tell him?

'What do you reckon?' I said.

'OK, OK,' he said, nodding.

As morale boosts go, this was up there with anything Shane Sutton – morale-booster-in-chief – could offer. What it told me was that Theo was basing his race around me; which in turn meant he was worried about me. As far as I was concerned it betrayed not so much a chink in his armour as a gaping hole. I felt my confidence grow.

In the race itself, Bos's behaviour was fascinating, and it confirms to me that, for him, it was all about me. He was reigning world champion. Yet he appeared to have no confidence in his own ability. At the start, he lined up behind me, obviously wanting to slot in behind me, hoping he could come round me in the finale. We rode the opening laps in that order, me behind the bike, Ross behind me, Theo behind him, but when the bike swung off, it was Perkins who tried to take the initiative, moving up the outside in a bid to come over the top. I was aware of him coming, and accelerated, just enough to stop him passing me; it left him nowhere to go, and he slipped back.

Then Mickaël Bourgain, who'd been sitting at the back, realized he was in a dangerous position, and put in a big surge. His acceleration propelled him right over the top, and, coming into the home straight, with two laps to go, he came past me and took the lead. The key thing, though, was that he'd put in a three-quarter-lap effort just to get there; he'd used up a lot of gas, in other words, and, once he hit the front, he didn't have much left. Sitting behind him, I could see that he was ragged rather than smooth, and I thought I'd leave him there: he could provide me with a good lead-out.

Still Bos was behind me, waiting. I looked back, and I could see Ross there, too. With 200 metres to go I made my move, attacking Bourgain. It meant going wide, but whoever was behind me would have to go wider still. I was flying now, and there was a rider coming back at me – Theo. I pressed harder and harder and just held him off, with Ross nipping through to take third.

The picture on the podium tells the story: Theo looks crest-fallen, miserable. But his theory that he'd been beaten by team tactics – by Ross and me ganging up on him – was discredited, not only by the way this final had gone, but also because he had a team-mate there too in Teun Mulder.

For me, it was a revelation. This was an Olympic event. I was world champion. Now for the first time it dawned on me that, despite the kilometre going, I could still go to Beijing with hopes of a medal in an individual event. At the age of 31 once again I had that feeling of excitement and anticipation of what might lie ahead – a feeling I hadn't had since the 2002 Commonwealth Games, after winning the kilo.

Next day, I won my fourth world kilo title, equalling the record held jointly by Arnaud Tournant and Lothar Thoms of Germany. It was one of the most satisfying kilos of my career – and one of the best. I won by almost a second from François Pervis, who had almost beaten me at the Manchester World Cup just a few weeks earlier, and did the second best time of my career, scraping inside the 61-second mark by a thousandth of a second. Only in Athens – in faster conditions – had I ever gone faster.

Bolivia, here we come.

The original plan was for Shane to come with us, but the budget was tight, so only one person could go, and it was Scott Gardner: a case of science coming before morale. Not that Scott wouldn't also be good for confidence – and in fact he was someone I was now working more closely with, since I liked his scientific approach, and his focus on 'the numbers'. Always the numbers.

Keeping going after the world championships wasn't difficult. Even though most of my team-mates were enjoying
some time off, I didn't have a problem, because the goal I'd
set myself – to claim the world record – was one that really
fired my enthusiasm. I was looking to leave the kilo on a
high. You couldn't get more of a high, both figuratively and
literally, than setting a new world record at an altitude of
3,408 metres. La Paz is the highest city in the world; its velodrome, not surprisingly, is the highest cycling track in the
world.

Back in Edinburgh, my dad acted as project manager, but
he depended greatly on some local people in La Paz, not least
Ruben Martinez, president of the Federación Boliviana de
Ciclismo. A sprightly 73-year-old – at least, I think that was
his age: he was cagey about it – Ruben reacted to Dad's
request for assistance with such enthusiasm that you'd have
thought my world record attempt was the biggest thing to
happen at the Alto Irpavi Velodrome in years.

Which – without, I hope, appearing immodest – it was. In
fact, it was the biggest thing to happen there since 2001,
when Arnaud Tournant appeared with two team-mates to
have a crack at various world records – the kilo, the 500
metres and the 200 metres. In offering his full support Ruben
didn't just talk the talk, he walked the walk. Literally. He
walked around the 333m concrete track with his video
camera, pointing out all the little cracks and holes – and some
bigger ones – and then posted the recording online for me to
analyse. Such assistance was invaluable. I could also appreciate that the track hadn't been used much in recent years, and
that it would be quite different to riding on the smooth
boards of modern velodromes.

When I arrived in La Paz, around 20 hours later than
intended, I headed straight for the track, and was pleasantly
surprised to see the improvements that had been made in the

weeks since Ruben's video. My mum and dad, who'd been there for almost a week by the time I got there, told me that the work had continued until the last minute, with teams of locals mowing the grass and cleaning up the inside of the clubhouse, and painting and repairing the exterior and the track itself. It was incredibly humbling, as was the reception at the airport, which featured, as well as a beaming Ruben, local photographers and a TV crew.

My delayed arrival was a hassle I could have done without. Everything had been going like clockwork – the training camp in Florida suggested that I was maintaining my form from Palma – until the flight from Miami to La Paz. The plan had been to arrive as late as possible, to minimize the risk of altitude sickness, which starts to significantly affect physical performance within 48 to 72 hours. But as we cruised at 40,000 feet the pilot came on the PA and gave us the kind of message that you really don't want at 40,000 feet: the plane's hydraulics had failed; he didn't want to land at the high altitude of La Paz, and so we would be diverting to a place called Santa Cruz instead. Inevitably, what seemed at first to be just a minor glitch turned into a bit of a major ordeal; we sat around in Santa Cruz airport for a long time, waiting for our connection to La Paz, only to eventually learn that it would be going from a different airport. That meant boarding a rickety old bus, having loaded it with my bikes and other baggage, then travelling across the hot city. Having been oblivious to the existence of the Bolivian city of Santa Cruz only a few hours earlier, I now learnt that it had two airports.

Finally, though, in the late afternoon of Friday 11 May 2007, we arrived in La Paz. As a precaution against altitude sickness I immediately hooked up to an oxygen canister – we had a doctor with us, Kenneth Baillie, an expert on the effects of altitude, who was advising me – and I would remain sucking on oxygen for almost the duration of my stay in La

Paz, removing the tube only for my world record attempt. Or attempts.

As I said, my first port of call was the track. The journey there was stunning – with La Paz itself nestling in what looked like an enormous crater – but nothing could have prepared me for the sight of the velodrome, which met us, incongruously, at the end of a dusty track. Surrounded by the towering Andes, it was, without question, the most spectacular place in which I had ever competed, particularly so on this evening, as the sun dropped down behind the mountains. I got out of the people carrier Dad had rented, and entered the building, through the clubhouse, with its toilet and little canteen (to illustrate how basic it was, there was no running water), and past a display of cycling memorabilia, before emerging on the track itself. Then I repeated Ruben's walk, taking it slowly, studying the lower part of the track, where I would ride for my kilo attempt. I was pleasantly surprised: clearly a hell of a lot of work had been done to improve the surface; I began to feel confident that I could go fast. Then came more solid confirmation: we unpacked my bike, which had travelled with me from Florida, and assembled it. And, in the warm evening, with the light fading by the minute, I began to ride. It felt fantastic: there was barely a breath of wind, the sun was poking through the jagged peaks of the Andes, and, with the oxygen tube removed from my mouth, I didn't even register that I was at altitude, where the air apparently contained a third less oxygen than at sea level. To be riding here, against this stunning backdrop, was exhilarating.

Perhaps I should have just gone for the record there and then. The next morning conditions were far less favourable: the cloud cover was low, and it was chilly, with the odd spot of rain. As a crowd began to gather, we faced an agonizing dilemma. Should we postpone it, and wait until tomorrow, when the forecast was better? Then again, as we were told, the forecast was notoriously unreliable up here in the mountains. There was no guarantee it would be better; it could be worse.

The biggest problem was the temperature. Scott, the numbers man, had done the sums, and he reckoned one degree was worth a tenth of a second: a significant margin. At 8 a.m it was 12 degrees in the track centre. Scott reckoned it needed to be a minimum of 16. By quarter to nine, it had risen to close to 14, which was encouraging; less so was the wind, which also seemed to be rising. So it was a question, now, of balancing out the warmer air with the stronger breeze, and deciding when would be the optimum time to go for the record. Scott reckoned it was now – and I felt ready, too. I'd done my warm-up, I was just sitting on my bike on the rollers, turning my legs, waiting. I removed the almost omnipresent oxygen tube, and headed for the start line.

Then I went through my usual routine: I sat on the track, arms hooked around my knees, focusing on the ride, while my bike was fixed into the start gate. (This had been one of the many logistical challenges faced, but ably handled, by my dad: we had to supply a start gate, and ship it from Manchester.)

I would be lying, though, if I said that the routine felt completely normal. I couldn't quite achieve the same intensity of focused concentration as I managed in Athens, for example. It was because I did feel some anxiety, based on my uncertainty about what effect the altitude could have. That wasn't an irrational emotional worry, the kind that Steve Peters would disapprove of; it was a perfectly logical one. All I knew was that I was about to enter unknown territory. I had been given chapter and verse by the doctor, Kenneth, about the dangers of competing in such oxygen-deprived air – the air that was the whole point of coming here, since it is literally 'thinner' than sea-level air, and offers less resistance.

But the lack of oxygen was a serious issue for an athlete, of course. I knew that, at best, it could be very painful; and that, at worst … well, it could be that I came round in the local hospital. But that was the point: I didn't know. And – as you might have guessed by now – I like to be in control; I hate uncertainty.

I also knew that worrying about the possible effects *was* pointless. So I tried to banish those thoughts, and I think I did a pretty good job, but I'm sure they still had an effect – however minuscule – on my ride. I started fast, and was a second up on Arnaud after one lap, almost holding it on the second, but the third was agony – I felt as if I'd been plunged underwater. My time was fast – the fastest I've ever done, at 59.103 seconds. But that was 28-hundredths of a second slower than Arnaud.

It was agonizing, but, thankfully, less in a physical than a psychological sense. It was as I crossed the line, having really suffered on that final lap, and wobbled badly on the finishing straight, that I felt the lack of oxygen. Again, though, here is a curious thing. I am convinced that, if I had beaten the record, I wouldn't have noticed: that I would have carried on riding round, celebrating, acknowledging the cheers of the crowd – which included the Bolivian Army band – and only later collapsed, if at all. As it was, I didn't make it round one full lap before tumbling from my bike to the grass, where Kenneth met me and stuffed the oxygen tube back in my mouth. I was gutted not to break the record, but it only took a minute or two of lying there in the grass, surrounded by a small pack of photographers, before I realized two things: one was that I could, and should, acknowledge the crowd; the other was that I could, and would, have another go at the record.

I knew I could go again without the anxiety of worrying about my possible collapse – or worse. The lack of oxygen made it an uncomfortable last lap, and a painful few minutes afterwards, but we weren't even close to worst-case scenario territory. As I recovered and reflected on the ride, I became more convinced that my fear had been a factor in my failure to beat Arnaud's time, as remarkable as it was.

Next morning, at the same early hour, I was in a far more confident frame of mind, even if the conditions still weren't exactly ideal. It was much the same as the previous morning – and therefore not nearly as favourable as that first, perfect evening in La Paz. But I had been so close 24 hours earlier: I knew I could find the 29-hundredths of a second I needed to beat Arnaud's time.

And I almost ... *almost* found them. This time, the margin was five thousandths of a second. It takes considerably longer to write that than it does for the time to elapse: but the clock, for me, stopped at 58.880 seconds. Arnaud's record, which stands to this day, was 58.875 seconds.

But you know what? I honestly don't look back on Bolivia with any regret, or disappointment, or sadness, at all. On the contrary, it was the most incredible experience to go there, with a little team, and to get the most amazing reception and support from the Bolivian people. Plus, I didn't return without a record; a few hours after my second kilo, in the beautiful late afternoon – not dissimilar to the one I'd experienced when I first arrived – I had a crack at the 500m record, set on the same track by Arnaud Dublé in 2001, during the same trip as Tournant's kilo. Dublé had done 25.850 seconds, which I felt was beatable – but I couldn't have imagined by how much. This was for the 'flying' 500 – not from a standing start, in other words – so you can't compare it to the kilo (it doesn't take you into oxygen debt, for one thing), but I know that my performance in the 500 was the best of my three efforts in Bolivia; and if I'd gone as fast, in such good conditions, earlier, I'm sure I'd have had Tournant's kilo record.

Without question, it was, at that time, the fastest I have ever gone on a bike (under my own steam, as opposed to being paced by a motorbike). I was flying: absolutely flying. After building up my speed, I attacked the start of the 500 at full whack, kept it going, and crossed the line in 24.758 seconds – more than a second quicker than Dublé. And to prove my theory that winning doesn't hurt half as much as losing, there was no collapse this time. Finally I got to do my lap of honour; and finally my team, and the local people who were still there in support, got to celebrate a world record. We had our moment – it meant a lot.

I returned without the feeling of disappointment and frustration I'd had after Stuttgart in 2003 and, to a lesser extent, Melbourne in 2006. And who knows? Perhaps it could be a blessing. If I'd broken the record, there'd be no excuse to go back. Now I have the incentive, to take care of unfinished business. I would love to return, and I would love to do another kilo. Back to Bolivia? I wouldn't rule it out.

CHAPTER 18

A Stroll in Beijing

Beijing, Tuesday 19 August 2008

… and my sprint semi-final against Mickaël Bourgain.

But before I take on Bourgain, let me reflect on what, even before that fifth and final day of the Olympic track programme at the Laoshan Velodrome in Beijing, had been an astonishing year – one that I could never have imagined.

I described, in chapter one, how I achieved my breakthrough as an individual sprinter at the Copenhagen World Cup in February 2008, when I beat Bourgain in the semi-final. I had ridden the sprint competition in all the World Cups, placing fifth in Los Angeles, third in Sydney, and fifth in the same Laoshan Velodrome as now hosted the Olympics. On that occasion I was beaten by Bourgain, but in Copenhagen it was as though I were a different rider, in control rather than intimidated. Although I lost the final to his countryman, Kévin Sireau, my victory over Bourgain was hugely significant – it dispelled a lot of the myths about sprinting, myths that had dissuaded me from making a proper attempt at the event earlier in my career.

It wasn't that I didn't like the sprint. That and the other sprint event, the keirin, had always fascinated me, largely because they were beyond my capabilities. Or so I'd always believed. From the age of about 17, when I began to specialize as a track sprinter, it had been drummed into me that I was not a tactical rider, but one who relied on pure power. Proper sprinters 'would make you look like an arse!', as one of my old mentors so memorably told me when I was 17. I was a one-speed cyclist – fast, yes, but best at riding in a straight line, and against the clock, not against other riders.

But my victory in the keirin at the 2007 world championships in Palma opened my eyes to the possibility that maybe, just maybe, I could be more than that. Admittedly my 'tactical' ability was still up for debate, given that my keirin successes tended to owe more to my kilo rider's ability to ride fast in a straight line (as long as I went from the front), over a relatively long distance, than to my ability to duck and dive, and to beat my opponents using brain rather than brawn. To use a football analogy: in sprint racing I was proving to be more of a big, bustling and very direct old-fashioned centre-forward than a skilful, Cristiano Ronaldo type. Yet it seemed to be working.

Whether a similar approach could work in the individual sprint was another question, however. In this discipline there was no getting away from it: you need to know your opponent's strengths and weaknesses, and you have to think about how to exploit those to win. You need a strategy, or a number of possible strategies, for each race.

You also need other attributes. As a sprinter you have to command the track – the whole track – and use the banking. If you keep height on the track for as long as possible, then swoop down at the optimum moment, that can make a significant difference to the speed at which you attack your opponent. And when you see how close so many sprint matches are, you realize how important every fraction is. This ability to command the track is known as 'track craft'. Over the years, the best match sprinters – from Reg Harris to Jan van Eijden – have possessed sheer speed but also this less easy to define, apparently innate, track craft. They have managed to beat people who – on paper – are faster than them by being clever, and through their ability to control the race and dominate the match sprint. There's a parallel with boxing, where 'ring craft' can enable a shrewd, smart boxer to beat a stronger, more powerful but less agile puncher.

Having Jan van Eijden on board was obviously a huge advantage. As I mentioned in the previous chapter, he shared little pieces of advice, getting me to incorporate things in my training that wouldn't make me faster, but could improve my track craft. One of his tips, as I've mentioned, was to practise riding with my head tilted back, eyes focused on the track behind me, because a match sprinter will sometimes spend virtually the entire race looking behind, watching his opponent, to prevent him from springing a surprise attack. It meant that, in warm-downs, I would ride the whole time looking over my shoulder at an imaginary opponent, using my peripheral vision to watch the lines and so check that I was going in a straight line. Initially I would do this on an empty track, and it would leave me feeling a bit wobbly as I got off my bike; but as I practised I got better.

I still had a lot of work to do to improve as a match sprinter as I prepared for the world championships in Manchester in March 2008. But a couple of weeks before them there was an incident which could have been a big setback. I suffered a heavy crash in training, though it could have been a lot worse. I'd just finished a motor-paced effort behind the motorbike, piloted by Iain Dyer. The theory behind this type of drill, which I do before every session, is that it gets the legs really spinning, and the muscles working; slipstreaming the motorbike means you can hit speeds close to 50mph, pedalling at over 200 revs per minute for 300 metres at the end of the drill, while all the time sitting about an inch behind the rear spoiler of the bike. It is potentially very dangerous, when you think about it. So you don't think about it – or, rather, you make sure you have a very competent motorcycle pilot, which, in Iain, I have.

Anyway, on this occasion I'd been spinning round the track at 50mph, no problems, before swinging off, and beginning to slow down, to stop and then start the training session proper. It was as I was slowing down, my speed having probably dropped to about 35mph, when I heard an almighty bang – my front tyre exploded, and I went straight down. Had it happened a few moments earlier, that could have been it: certainly the world championships, and maybe the Olympics, over right there. As it was, it was painful, but not catastrophic. After a couple of days' recovery, I was back in full training.

The world championships opened in Manchester with Jamie Staff, Ross Edgar and me claiming … yes, you guessed it, silver in the team sprint, behind France. It was the fastest team sprint competition ever staged, with the French recording 43.271 seconds. We recorded our fastest ever time, too, but we were half a second slower than the French. It prompted mixed emotions: you can't be too disappointed with your best ever time; but the speed and precision of the French trio – Grégory Baugé, Kévin Sireau and Arnaud Tournant – was awesome. Looking ahead to the Olympics, it was a little sobering. We had to assume they'd go faster there. So a half-second improvement wouldn't be enough for us; in Beijing, we'd need more. The consolation was that we knew our ride hadn't been perfect; that there was more to come. Partly, this was because a huge amount of work specific to the team sprint was being done in the background by the support team, led by Scott Gardner. We knew that, between now and Beijing, he would be analysing our performance, and others', to the nth degree, which could shave vital thousandths of a second from our time.

Next came the sprint. I qualified fourth, with a personal best 10.032 seconds over the 200 metres. Sireau was fastest, with 9.992 seconds – a track record. I got through to the quarter-final, which presented the highest hurdle in the tall, lean shape of Theo Bos, the world champion for the last two years, and then the world record holder for 200 metres, with 9.772 seconds.

The first round seemed only to highlight my shortcomings as a sprinter: specifically, the tendency to switch off. Speed is not enough; you need to concentrate, intently, for the three laps of the race, even if the first two are – as is often the case – taken at a snail's pace, as the two riders suss each other out. Here, Theo got me as we were crawling along, watching each other or, in my case, not watching (which was ironic, given how much work I'd been doing on my observation skills). He jumped me from behind when I looked away for a nano-second, and that was it. Game over. I began chasing, but it was futile – and a little embarrassing ('He made you look like an arse!'). One-nil Theo.

Jan spoke to me after that ride, and said it was similar to my World Cup ride against Bourgain; I had nothing to lose now, so I might as well, as he put it, 'commit'. Or, as he really put it, 'COMMIT!'

The second round was close; I watched Theo, he watched me, and neither could get the gap. On the final lap, I led out, he started to come round me with 150 metres to go, and almost made it past; but I dug deep, and held him on my outside. I threw my bike at the line, and it was just enough – I took it by a few centimetres. But I knew as soon as I came off the track that I had him now. We were level at 1–1, but I could detect in Bos an air of defeat. In a situation like this you have to forget immediately about the last round, but I could tell that Bos was smarting, and starting to doubt himself, just as he appeared to do in Palma the previous year, when he began quizzing me before the keirin. And so it proved: in the final round, Bos tried to give the impression that he was still on top, but his body language said that he was nervous, not confident. He tried to control the race by taking the front with one-and-a-half laps to go, but I kept my height on the banking, forcing him to continue to pick up the pace. At the bell he had fully committed, which gave me the 'carrot' to chase. I closed a two-length gap on the back straight, drawing level on the home straight, and by the time I crossed the line I already had my right arm in the air, celebrating the biggest scalp of my sprinting career so far. The noise inside the velodrome was as loud as I had ever experienced; it felt as though I had won a gold medal rather than 'just' a quarter-final!

I still maintain that my defeat of Bourgain, a month earlier, was my Eureka! moment as a sprinter, but there are many people who believe that this quarter-final victory over Bos was more significant.

In the semi-final I was confident, and beat Roberto Chiappa of Italy to set up a final with Sireau, the fastest qualifier. And so I would at least equal Craig MacLean's feat of two years earlier, when he won silver behind Bos in Bordeaux. The sprint, as I have said, has been seen as the holy grail of track riding – no British rider had won a world championship gold medal in 54 years, since the late, great Reg Harris.

In the first round against Sireau the many hours I'd spent riding while looking behind me came in handy. I took the front, he sat off me, and I watched him, anxious not to make the same mistake I'd made in the first ride against Bos. When Sireau made his move – early, with 350 metres to go – I saw it, and reacted with sufficient power that when he came past me, he didn't open too much of a gap. I held the gap, and then closed it, drawing level on the bend, and beating him narrowly on the line.

Again, in round two I could sense Sireau's doubts. I had the upper hand, and as I followed him around the track for the first two laps, almost stalking him, I felt huge confidence; no matter what he did, I was sure I could counter. It was an unusual feeling for me to have in a sprint – to be the rider in control. All those people who had told me, in my early years, that I didn't have the tactical instinct to control and kill off an opponent might have had a point; but I realized now, and especially looking back later, how much it depends on confidence. If I had had confidence when I was younger – rather than having it knocked – I might have ridden with a little more tactical *savoir-faire*.

When Sireau made his move – from the front – I didn't panic. Recalling Jan's instructions, I didn't just react to him; I held back a little, holding my position up the banking, making sure the gap didn't grow too much, but not being panicked into sprinting for his back wheel. When I made my move, and did approach Sireau's back wheel, he flicked out slightly, but I wasn't distracted; I put the foot down, drew level, then came past him for a far more convincing victory than in round one. I was world sprint champion, and Jan, when I met him in the track centre, was pretty emotional. The last time the championships had been held here in Manchester, in 2000, he had won – it was a nice bit of symmetry.

Successfully defending my keirin title the next day – again using the same tactic throughout the series, of going from the front – meant that my haul from the championships, two gold medals and one silver, was my best ever. And it was part of the best ever collective display by the British team: nine gold medals. As a send-off for Beijing, we couldn't have asked for more. There was a dual effect: we had given our own confidence a massive boost, and dented that of our rivals, who left Manchester knowing that they had to go away and play catch-up.

They had enough time: after the world championships there were still four months until the Olympics. But it was four months of not racing, just training, which created a challenge for all of us. While motivation was hardly a problem, the challenge was to get into peak condition in isolation, without the 'barometer' of form that racing can provide.

Inevitably there were hiccups and moments of doubt – these things are routine in an athlete's life; the test is how you deal with them. But when I went to Newport in Wales for our pre-Olympic training camp I felt that all had gone as well as it could. The goal I had set myself was to record personal bests in all the individual components of my training, from the gym to the track. In the weights room, in June, I did a personal best full squat lift (227.5kg), while on the track I felt I was capable of going faster than ever – and our final sessions on the Newport Velodrome would confirm that, with me dipping under 10 seconds for the 200 metres for the first time ever. And doing it no fewer than four times in two different sessions.

I should also mention at this point – because I believe it was an absolutely critical factor in everything going so well in training – that I was as happy as I had ever been in my personal life. I had met my girlfriend, Sarra, in 2006, on a visit home to Edinburgh. She was a friend of my mate Chris's girlfriend who had no idea about cycling, and wasn't massively interested in sport, but, when we were introduced, she said she vaguely remembered seeing me win my gold medal in Athens – though I think this might have been politeness on her part. It turned out she was a lawyer in

Edinburgh, where she was originally from; we chatted quite a lot and I thought she was great, so I made sure I got her phone number, and, a couple of nights later – the obligatory length of time to seem interested, while retaining some cool and dignity in the event of her knocking me back – I sent her a text, asking if she fancied meeting up again. We went out on our own the second time, and got on really well, mainly because we discovered we had the same sense of humour. But there was no rushing into anything; I saw her on visits home, we continued to get on well … and my visits home became curiously, and probably suspiciously, more frequent.

Which was funny, because, with my previous relationship having ended earlier in the year, I had actually decided that, between then and Beijing, I had no space in my life for a girl-friend. I wanted to be focused only on the Olympics; I didn't need any distractions. My mind was firmly closed to the idea of seeing anyone. Which, as I can testify now, is perhaps the best state of mind in which to meet someone – it certainly beats the reek of desperation!

When Sarra first came to see me race, at the Manchester World Cup in February 2007, I knew for sure that I was pretty keen on her, because I was as nervous as hell. I ended up winning three golds and one silver – my best ever performance in a World Cup. Just as well, because if I hadn't, I might have felt the urge to tell her, 'But I was really good in the past, you should have seen me in Athens!' (Not really.)

(OK, maybe.)

The hiccups in the build-up to Beijing mainly affected others in the team, with Bradley Wiggins struck down by a virus in Newport, and everyone worrying that it would spread around the rest of the team. As I write we are in the midst of a panic about a possible 'swine flu' pandemic – and it was a bit like that in the British camp in Newport in the days before we left for Beijing. It was like a gathering of OCD (obsessive compulsive disorder) sufferers rather than a cyclists' training camp, which is not uncommon. Even before Brad's illness, we had been given hand-cleaning gel, with instructions that we should use it before entering or leaving any room. Now we were truly OCD about it, washing our hands every five minutes, which continued in Beijing – but with good reason. A rowing crew was wiped out with a diarrhoea virus, as were a couple of triathletes.

I don't know how significant the hand gel was, but on this occasion we were spared. Thankfully Brad recovered, the team wasn't struck down by its own mini-pandemic, and we left for Beijing in a confident frame of mind.

When you think about it, arriving at the Olympic village must expose you to all sorts of bugs and viruses from all around the globe, so it makes sense to do all you can to prevent a last-minute illness that could ruin four years' hard work.

My reference to OCD – with no offence intended to genuine OCD sufferers – has a grain of truth, because my mum is among those who have claimed that I am a typical case. She is joking (I think), but it's true that, when it comes to training and trying to live the life of an athlete, I am quite particular. Obsessive? Maybe. But my rationale is this: when it comes to the Olympics, I don't want to have any doubts. I don't want any 'what ifs'. What if I hadn't had those beers in May? What if I had trained that tiny bit harder when I knew that I could? What if I had stayed in that night, rather than gone out? I try to pre-empt this by imposing on myself a blanket booze ban for six months, and committing to give 100 per cent in each training session. A lot of people say that a beer or a glass of wine helps them to relax, but, for me, making sacrifices like this actually helps me to relax going into a major competition. By giving 100 per cent in every effort of every training session, and looking after myself off the bike, I know there's nothing else I could have done, which gives me peace of mind and makes it easier to accept the outcome on the day.

I arrived in Beijing, then, with no 'what ifs'.

The Olympics were under way, and they were going well, with Nicole Cooke getting Team GB – and the cycling team – off to a dream start, winning the women's road race on day one. We all watched and got caught up in the drama of the finale, when, with the rain lashing down, turning the road into a virtual river, she let a gap open to her breakaway rivals on the final corner. Having ridden a tactically perfect race, she seemed to have blown it; we edged forwards in our seats, digging our nails into whatever we were gripping, and then urging her on as she pulled them back, then finally over-hauled them in the last few metres to win. In a road race, where so much can go wrong, it was a fantastic performance; the mood in the camp was already positive, and that lifted it even higher.

I watched a lot of other sports, too. I like the weightlifting because I can relate to it, as we do a fair amount of that as part of our training. I can appreciate just what some of the weights feel like, and marvel when a guy virtually half my height can lift more than me! I also enjoy track and field because it's such an iconic part of the Olympics. Then, when you hear there's a British medal chance in anything, from badminton to shooting, you tune in. It's quite weird because you watch it without the commentary; for those of us brought up in Britain, it is strange not to have the BBC describing the action.

In Beijing, following Nicole's gold, there were more and more occasions when we would tune in to watch another

British medal chance. I kept thinking, this can't go on, the bubble's got to burst ... but in Beijing it did go on, the bubble just kept expanding.

Otherwise, I settled into village life. Some people say that experience is overrated in sport, but I don't think so. The Olympics is like no other event, and they can overwhelm you if you're not mentally prepared. At my first Games, in Sydney, we had prepared for our events away from the village, then got a taste of the atmosphere afterwards. In Athens I'd been in the village for the duration, as I would be here, but the very fact that I knew what to expect, that I wasn't surprised by what I found there, meant that I settled in very smoothly, with no disruptions to my preparation.

What did I find there? Well, my room was an empty white box, with a white tiled floor, a wardrobe, a cabinet and a mirror. But the British Olympic Association deserves credit for applying little touches that made our village apartments more homely. There were pictures on the wall, done by kids from schools in the UK – drawings, paintings and cards with good luck messages. There were pictures by Chinese kids as well. And there was some furniture, supplied by one of Team GB's sponsors, B&Q. I added my stretching mat and Bose sound dock for my iPod, and my hand-pump espresso machine (though we had a proper one in the communal area downstairs, thankfully – I'm not sure how I'd have lived without proper coffee).

I also had Jamie Staff and Jason Kenny next door. Jason, at 20, had been a revelation since the world championships, where he didn't even make the team. Following that he began flying in training, and it came down to a ride-off in early July between him, Jason Queally and Craig MacLean, with Jason K getting the nod. Since then he had gone better and better, and he had now been selected for the team sprint, replacing Ross Edgar, who would ride the keirin. So it meant a new line-up for the team sprint: Jamie to lead out, Jason to go man two, and me as the third man.

But two days before the team sprint, I can now reveal, we – Jamie, Jason and I – screwed up.

It was a rest day. We had been in the village a week, and for all that the atmosphere was good, and the apartments homely, we were starting to suffer a little bit from cabin fever. It was that stage of your preparation where you're doing a minimum of training, and just polishing your form. You're fresh, ready to go. You're sitting around, trying to relax, but with as much energy and edginess as Shane Sutton after a quadruple espresso.

So I had an idea for a little trip to get rid of some of that pent-up energy and break up the routine. Oakley, who provided Jamie and me with sunglasses, had taken a house in Beijing where their athletes could go to enjoy some nice food in a relaxed environment, away from the village. And maybe – if you play your cards right – pick up a nice new pair of shades, too. So off I went, with Jamie and Jason for company.

Oakley House was next to the beach volleyball arena, we were told. It was simply a case of jumping on one of the buses that left from the village, taking athletes to their venues. The bus took us across what felt like the whole of Beijing, on a network of busy roads, with indecipherable signposts at the intersections. Eventually we emerged into 36-degree heat on a typical Beijing day: overcast, stuffy and hot.

Being über-professional, we weren't distracted by the beach volleyball, but instead asked a volunteer where Oakley House was. He didn't seem to have a clue, but directed us to the west gate. We went to the west gate, and asked there, only to be told by an equally confused volunteer to go to the south gate. From there, we were directed back to the west gate.

For almost an hour we wandered backwards and forwards, asking a succession of volunteers who didn't have a clue what, or where, we were talking about. The signposts, meanwhile, were all in Chinese. I spent a lot of time on the phone to my contact at Oakley. He said, 'I'll send someone to get you – where are you?' By which time, with us having wandered beyond the beach volleyball arena into some unknown part of Beijing, all I could say was, 'At a road, by some traffic lights ...' It was a maze.

Remember what I said in chapter one about the cyclists' code? To repeat: never walk when you can cycle, never stand when you can sit down, never sit down when you can lie down. It's why none of us took part in the opening ceremony – it would have meant a couple of hours on our feet.

Oh, the irony. Having missed the 45 minutes or so of strolling that the opening ceremony would have entailed, here we were, 48 hours before the team sprint, wandering aimlessly around deepest Beijing: lost, sweating and starting to panic. We tried hailing a taxi, then couldn't explain to any driver where we were going. We ended up just walking and walking, looking for some landmark that could help the Oakley people find us.

After two and a half hours we somehow found the house. It wasn't the cue for celebrations. We were grumpy and angry with ourselves. All of us were thinking that it could be catastrophic. For months our training plans had been mapped out, detailing each day's session, and I had pretty much followed it to the letter.

We sat at a table in silence, ate some food, and looked sheepish and guilty, as if we'd been naughty schoolboys. We agreed a pact. 'We tell no one about this. This is not going to get back to Shane, or Iain, or Jan. Because we're going to be in a lot of trouble if things don't work out.'

And we kept that pact – they never did find out. Until now, of course.

The next day was critical, though. It was our last session on the track, which is important psychologically. My legs had felt drained and fatigued the previous evening, after our marathon walk, but the next day, thankfully, they felt revived. My last session was a good one.

And then it was upon us: the Olympics. Forget World Cups and world championships, this was what had got me out of bed every morning for the last four years; what it had all been leading towards. At the Laoshan Velodrome, a big, futuristic structure on the outskirts of Beijing, we'd had glimpses of the other teams during training sessions, and gleaned some information – or, rather, people like Scott Gardner had, through watching them closely. I was told that Kévin Sireau had been talking up the French team's chances in the press. Actually, he had been talking down *our* chances, saying he didn't expect us to be as good as we'd been in Manchester. That gave me a huge boost, as it seemed to me that he was relying on that. What's more, I knew he was wrong: that it was wishful thinking on his part. Because we were going better than in Manchester – all of us.

I always find it interesting when sportsmen and women spend time trying to psych out their opponents via the press. To me it just shows they're worrying about them rather than focused on their own performance.

The team sprint, the first event, was the difficult one. That half a second in Manchester was a big gap, yet we knew from our sessions that we'd be on world record pace. The big question was, would the French?

In qualifying we had our answer. Jamie exploded out of that start gate as though he were propelled by the engine of a Formula One car. In fact, for the first half of our first revolution in the team sprint, the torque we produce is greater than a Formula One car – just under 600 newton metres.

Jason and I followed, Jason taking over for lap two – and putting in the fastest ever second lap – and me finishing off the job, also with the fastest time ever recorded for the final lap, for a time of 42.95 seconds: the first ever sub-43-second ride over the 750-metre, three-lap race. The French were half a second down – and, in that moment, I believe they were defeated. You arrive at the Olympics, having prepared in your bubble, and you just hope that what you have will be enough. If you discover that it isn't, it can be a devastating blow. Our qualifying ride was the equivalent of a knock-down in the first round of a boxing match. The French were on the canvas.

However, the way the final panned out ... well, let's just say that it didn't exactly go according to plan. Again, Jamie burst out of the start gate, setting an unbelievable pace, which Jason coped with better than I did. As those who watched the final will know, I lost Jason's back wheel. When he took over, after Jamie's lap, I was dangling a length and a half off the back, which had some people scratching their heads. What on earth is he doing? A good question. Normally we raced as a tight unit: you could barely see daylight between us.

It was down to fatigue, pure and simple. I was pretty gassed from the first two rides (in the second round we beat the USA en route to the showdown with France), mainly because riding man three is incredibly draining. It's the closest you get to riding the kilo, and this was a bit like riding three kilos in the space of a few hours, which you would never do. Plus, as man three, I was using a bigger gear than the other two, which took more effort to get up to speed.

In the final, because I knew that Jamie was going unbelievably fast, I nailed the start. Then I began to pay for that, and relaxed just a little bit, and I could see the gap between me and Jason opening. It had happened a bit in the first ride, too, but I thought, it's OK, don't stamp on it – if I reacted, and pushed hard on the pedals, requiring a huge surge of power that would create a sudden increase in lactic acid production, I wouldn't have time to recover: it would hit me on lap three. So it was actually better to let the gap open. It went to a length – a length is OK. Then it stretched, on the back straight, to a length and a half.

When Jason took over from Jamie for lap two, he went very quickly – and the gap kept growing. I thought I'd get him back on the first corner, but it was stretching beyond a length and a half as we raced down the back straight on lap two; and even as we entered the bend before the home straight it felt as though he were pulling away. Meanwhile, in my peripheral vision, as I entered the home straight, I could see the French on the opposite side of the track, and I could see they were still a unit. But what mattered was not where Jason was, but where their third man, Arnaud Tournant, was. I was racing against Arnaud, not Jason. And I was up on Arnaud.

I started to close the gap to Jason on that bend, closing it further on the home straight, and then I started pouring it on. I started my lap going faster than Jason, and then, on my own, I was fine. I admit that, while sitting a length and a half off the back of Jason, there had been a tiny element of panic – mainly due to the fact that this was a team event, and the knowledge that I could be the one to screw it up.

You could say that, in that split second, the chimp threatened to escape, but I caged it; and on my final lap I was in control. Having resisted the temptation to sprint after Jason's back wheel – which I think I would have done earlier in my career – I didn't have the horrendous lactic deficit which would have resulted from the kick; I still had enough in the tank to give it everything on that final lap, and it was enough to win, in 43.128 seconds, still half a second up on the French.

Afterwards, Jason said, 'Imagine how much faster we could have gone without our day out in Beijing!'

It was a historic moment, my second Olympic gold medal – a feat that, I found out later, got me the front-page treatment from the newspapers in Scotland – but I didn't want to get too carried away. I had two more events. At the press conference that followed I answered a couple of questions, then made my excuses and left Jason and Jamie to field the rest of them.

Next day was the keirin, in which I was the strong favourite, having won 24 consecutive races in World Cups and world championships. I lived up to that, winning – and winning quite comfortably – all three rounds: qualifying, semi-final and final. After two days I had two gold medals in my pocket: three Olympic golds in total. By now this was sparking something of a frenzy at home, of which I was completely unaware at the time. Even my contact with my parents, my six-months pregnant sister Carrie and her partner Garry, and my girlfriend Sarra, all of whom were in Beijing, was kept to a minimum. In any case, *they* didn't know about the fuss back home, either.

Just to illustrate how cocooned I was, on the evening of the keirin I wasn't celebrating, but waiting in a dingy room, trying in vain to spell the name 'Hoy' to some Chinese officials, before allowing another one to assault my arm rather clumsily with a needle. It was dope control, a process which, though sometimes time-consuming, is normally pretty straightforward. You pee in a cup. You have a blood sample taken. A form is filled in. Simple!

Not on this occasion. The rules state that an athlete can't fill in the various forms – they have to be completed by anti-doping officials; anti-doping officials who, in this instance, had as good a grasp of English as I have of Chinese. As for the official who took blood from my arm, well, all I can say is that this was the most uncomfortable and painful experience I've had in a dope control. And it was the Olympics! She fumbled, and stabbed, as though she'd never conducted the procedure before, and made a right mess of my arm, which was bruised and painful the next morning. It also took forever: I didn't get back to the village until midnight. So there was no danger of getting carried away. I had some dinner and then had a fitful night's sleep – mainly because I was buzzing after the keirin – before having to get up at 6 a.m. to eat and prepare for qualifying in the men's sprint.

But you know what happened in the first two days of that – I qualified fastest, in a personal best 9.815 seconds, with Jason second in 9.857. Again, the psychological blow this inflicted on our rivals should not be underestimated. I was delighted with a personal best time, but also left wondering how much closer to Theo Bos's world record of 9.772 seconds I might have been with a proper night's sleep.

By the fifth and final day of the track programme we, as a team, had enjoyed almost total domination. Gold in the team sprint; gold and world record in the team pursuit; gold in the men's pursuit, thanks to Bradley; gold and silver in the women's pursuit, through Rebecca Romero and Wendy Houvenaghel; gold and silver in the keirin, with Ross claiming silver.

Something special had happened – and was happening – in the Laoshan Velodrome. But some, inevitably, didn't see it like that. We became aware of veiled remarks from one or two other nations that our success was 'suspicious'. There were no outright accusations, but the implication was clear, and it had been made in the past – that there was some sinister explanation for our success.

For me, in a period when there is increased drugs testing, especially at and around the major events, it is more suspicious to be slower at the Olympics than at a World Cup or

Grand Prix meeting nine months earlier. I find it odd that people can go to the biggest race of their lives and go slower than they have gone at other times of the year. You go there fresh, motivated, tapered, and with the best equipment. The explanation for our success was very simple: we paid incredible attention to detail and we got everything spot on. We raised our game when it counted, and the others didn't. Many nations even underperformed.

Sour grapes are perhaps inevitable. But I have always given my rivals the benefit of the doubt when they produce amazing performances. Call me naïve, but I like to think that if I can win clean, then they can too.

In the arena, warming up, we were oblivious to the crowd. Actually, that's not strictly true – I was aware, as I always am, that my family and Sarra were there, because I knew they were coming. But when I was asked afterwards about the effect of having some other illustrious people in the audience, I said it hadn't registered, and that's the truth. Tony Blair was there with his entire family; Princess Anne was there; and Sir Clive Woodward; and Bernie Ecclestone. It got the journalists excited, but it made no difference to me – other than to note, afterwards, that their decision to come to the velodrome reflected fantastically well on our sport, and on the success we were having.

My sprint semi-final against Mickaël Bourgain, on the final day of competition, illustrated to me how far I had come. Whereas it had been a major breakthrough, just a few months earlier, to beat a specialist such as Bourgain, here I was the favourite, and I dominated the first heat, Bourgain in front, me behind, watching. Throughout the heat, and again in the second heat, I felt I was in control, and that Bourgain was there for the taking. Jason was similarly dominant in his two-heat win over Max Levy, and so the scenario that we had dared not speak about over breakfast was going to happen:

we would meet each other in the final.

Usually, each of us would spend time with Jan and Iain discussing our opponent's weaknesses. Not this time. Though we hadn't discussed the possibility of an all-British final, they had, the previous evening, and – as ever – they had a plan. It was this: they would shake each of us by the hand, wish us good luck, and say nothing. It was down to us.

In the first heat I forced Jason to lead it out, by suddenly slowing down on the first lap. He locked up his back wheel in an attempt to brake, but by the time he realized I was slowing down it was too late. I had him in front – where I wanted him to be. I stalked him, and when he increased the pace, I did too, maintaining the gap, keeping him in front. Given our closeness in qualifying it was always going to be tight, but I found that when I went to accelerate, I could close the gap; I drew level, came round him, and beat him to the line. One–nil. Round two was virtually identical: Jason led it out, I pulled alongside on the final bend, and then started to come round. As you come off the bend you're looking for the shortest line possible to the finish, and as I started coming out of the final bend I braced myself for a potential 'hook' from Jason. I stuck to the red line on the track, and got my elbows out to defend my position; he did move out to the red line, as I'd anticipated, and we had a slight clash, but nothing that slowed my momentum as I passed him – and realized, well before the line, that I was going to win.

It all felt surreal: it was the Olympic final, but it was against Jason, someone I saw every day in training; and then I was embracing my parents and Sarra in the stands; and then celebrating in the track centre with the people who'd supported me for the last few years – Shane, Iain, Jan, Dave Brailsford …

But I think my blubbing told the real story. When I embraced my dad, I couldn't help myself. I just kept saying to him, 'I can't believe it, I can't believe it,' and I think he replied that he couldn't believe it, either, but that it was real. It's so nice to share a moment like that with your parents; they go through so much, and make so many sacrifices, to be there supporting you. I went along the line: my dad, my mum, my sister Carrie, being careful not to put too much pressure on her 'bump,' and her partner Garry; and Sarra, whom I was finally going to be able to spend time with.

My emotional response was mainly to do with the relief of being able to let go after five days of keeping my emotions in check, and not allowing myself to celebrate my gold medals in the team sprint and keirin. I felt elated, obviously – elated that everything had gone not just according to plan, but to a plan that I could scarcely have dared to dream was feasible.

Had I known what lay ahead of me when I came home, I might also have shed a few tears for the passing of my previous life. As the journalists – many more than I had ever encountered before – thrust their tape recorders towards me, and told me things I had genuinely been unaware of (such as that the last British Olympian to win three gold medals was the swimmer Henry Taylor in 1908), I had no inkling that, back home, Olympic fever seemed to have taken over the country, and that, from the moment that I stepped back on to British soil, life would be very different indeed.

CHAPTER 19

He's Like Something from
The X Factor – the Outtakes

So, how do you celebrate three gold medals? You have the mother of all parties, right?

Wrong. In contrast to Sydney in 2000, in Beijing, on the night of my third gold, there was only a pretty low-key night out. I could say that was because I was eight years older, and more mature. But it had more to do with the fact that I was absolutely knackered, completely drained, physically and emotionally. I felt as if I had been living on my nerves for the five days of competition – though of course the mental stress started before that – and it was pretty weird now to be able to let go. In many ways it didn't feel right. I should have been demob happy; but it was too much of an adjustment to make in just a few hours.

I went out with Vicky Pendleton to meet Sarra, and we headed to a big bar in Beijing. Others in the team had gone to London House, a lakeside complex taken over by the London 2012 team, but I didn't want to go there. I just knew I wouldn't have any time to myself. With my family and Sarra I did head to London House the following evening, only to encounter a few problems trying to get in. Olympic athletes were allowed two guests, and here I was with five. As mums are wont to do, mine insisted I should produce my gold medals, but I was reluctant to do that, as it would have smacked a little of 'don't you know who I am?' In the end it wasn't necessary. An official appeared and we were all allowed in.

By now, 48 hours after my third gold medal, and four days before leaving Beijing to head back to Britain, I was becoming gradually aware that there was quite a lot of interest at home – certainly more than after Athens. My suspicions were alerted when my agent in Scotland, who for the previous two years hadn't been kept quite as busy as David Beckham's, was in touch on an hourly basis. There were offers coming in, of the kind I associated more with Beckham than with me – things like glossy lifestyle magazines for at-home photo-spreads. This was new territory. I can't say that, as I was making all those maximal efforts on a turbo trainer, putting in sessions that would often end with me spewing my guts out, I ever envisaged a day when I would don my bathrobe to be photographed in my 'plush Manchester apartment' (as I imagined such magazines might describe my distinctly mediocre Manchester flat). It made me laugh.

Those final four days in Beijing were strange: we were still in our bubble, oblivious to the outside world, but I found there were more demands on my time than there had been during the racing. Every minute was accounted for; there were press interviews and photographs, as well as official functions, and people to meet, literally from first thing in the morning to last thing at night. The big blow-out party kept being postponed, until, on the night of the closing ceremony – our final night in Beijing – it happened.

I had the huge honour of carrying the flag at the closing ceremony, meaning I led Britain's most successful Olympic team of all time into and around the magnificent Bird's Nest stadium. But my official duties didn't end there, as I shall explain in a moment.

Walking into the stadium, in front of 90,000 people who had just witnessed an unbelievable closing ceremony, is hard to describe; you're just focused, really, on trying not to drop the flag, or trip up, and so it's hard to absorb everything. The added twist for me was that, after completing my flag-bearing duties, I had been given instructions to abandon the rest of the team, make a quick exit from the track centre, change into a suit, complete with shirt and tie, and re-enter the stadium on a commuting bike, as part of the London 2012 presentation.

Easier said than done. In fact, I had to abandon the flag, and the team, before we'd finished marching into the centre. Then I had to make my way, quickly, to the other end of the stadium, and disappear into its bowels to get changed. What I encountered, however, was a human chain – Chinese security guards, arms linked, under strict instructions not to let anyone through. Looking at my watch, I saw I had only a few minutes before I was supposed to re-enter the arena on a bike, and I tried to explain that I was involved in the next part of the ceremony – that I *had* to get through.

But they wouldn't budge. So eventually I gave up on the idea of getting back into the interior of the stadium and just brushed past them to the area where the London bus was, and the bike. Dripping with sweat, I changed into a suit, when, suddenly, there was an eruption of deafening screaming right beside me. When I looked towards the bus, I realized what had happened: a large group of young Chinese girls, who were part of the official ceremony, had caught a glimpse of David Beckham. He had popped his head out, then pulled it back in, and the screaming erupted and then died, as though someone had flicked an 'Off' switch. Then he popped it out a second time. 'On' went the switch – and the screams started again.

When I was changed, I went over and had a chat with him. 'Does that always happen?' I asked. 'Over here it does,' he said. He said some really kind things in the press, saying my third gold medal had been his Olympic highlight. He'd enjoyed seeing me embrace my dad, which had reminded him of his own experiences as a footballer, his dad being his biggest supporter. Chatting to Beckham, it was hard to reconcile this really friendly guy with the Beckham legend, who only has to move to make the front pages, or to send large groups of Chinese girls into a state of frenzy.

I also met Jimmy Page, which was a thrill, because I was a late convert to, and am now a fan of, the music of Led Zeppelin, mainly thanks to those old rockers Jason Queally and Craig MacLean. Backstage in the Bird's Nest, I managed a quick text to Jason: 'Jst met beckham and jimmy page ...'

The reply came: 'Not fussed about beckham, but jimmy page: wow!'

Like a proper fan, I also managed to take a few photos with my phone, even if I drew the line at screaming in the presence of Beckham, or indeed Jimmy Page. And then, with Jamie Staff and Vicky Pendleton, I took part in the London 2012 presentation, riding along behind the London bus. Again, I can't describe how it felt to be dressed in civvies and riding bikes behind a London bus in the Bird's Nest, around the track on which, just days earlier, Usain Bolt had set new world records in both the 100 metres and the 200 metres. Suffice to say that this was another experience I could never have envisaged; but I have to say that it was immensely good fun – in the midst of all the pomp and circumstance of the closing ceremony, there was a familiar sense of liberation and freedom in our little blast around the track, which harked right back to my early days on a BMX.

That night, a party was laid on back at the athletes' village by the British Olympic Association. They set out an area in the British part of the village, though athletes from other countries drifted by and joined in. It was great, relaxed rather than raucous, but the mood, as you'd expect after our successful Olympics, was buoyant. It wrapped up around 5 a.m., a whole hour and a quarter before we had to leave for our flight. I made the mistake of lying down, thinking I'd grab a few minutes' kip. I dozed and came round a few seconds later. Well, it *felt* like a few seconds. Actually, it was an hour – and it was time to leave Beijing, with the hangover just starting to kick in.

A few of us were in first class for the flight home – Becky Adlington, Ben Ainslie, Tim Brabants, Steve Williams – oh, and Princess Anne. There was a newspaper on my seat, the front page given over to Becky. 'Bloody hell!' I said, showing her the paper. I hadn't looked inside yet – when I did, I found a big spread of photos of Sarra and me, taken in Beijing a couple of days earlier. Leaving Beijing, preparing to leave the Olympic 'bubble', I had imagined that we were returning to reality – and to normality. But seeing the paper, and the extent of the coverage, I began to wonder ...

We landed in London at 8 a.m. on the Monday morning, and emerged from the steps of the plane – I watched the video of our arrival recently, and was almost reassured to see that I looked as bad as I felt, despite sleeping the entire duration of the flight – into what resembled a frenzy. We were led, initially, into a packed press conference. And the first question was for me: 'What do you think of Sir Sean Connery's backing of the Scottish National Party's call for a separate Scottish team at the Olympics?'

Though I didn't fully realize it at the time, this was a booby trap. I had been asked the same question the previous day, on our final day in Beijing, and, in front of just a few journalists, I said what I thought, which was that, without the kind of investment we have had as Team GB, over more than a decade, it is ridiculous to think that Scotland could expect to enter a team in the Olympics and be competitive. For my sport, the facilities and backing just aren't there – which isn't the case across the board, but it certainly is for cycling. Indeed, there was irony in the fact that Scotland's only proper velodrome, Meadowbank, where I cut my teeth as a track rider, was due to be demolished to make way for housing.

I couldn't be more proud to be Scottish, but I won my three gold medals in Beijing as part of Team GB; I'd also had the support of the British set-up for years leading up to the Games. I am Scottish and British; I don't see the two as mutually exclusive. I resented that this question was being put to me now – and that, over the next 24 hours, I would keep being asked: do you consider yourself Scottish or British? To me, it's an irrelevant question, like asking Gavin Hastings whether he was more proud to represent Scotland or the British Lions. But in the press conference I said what I'd said the previous day: that it was a ridiculous proposal when we, as track cyclists, wouldn't even have anywhere to train in Scotland. With hindsight, and given some of the headlines that followed, I perhaps should have deflected the question.

After London I returned briefly to Manchester and then drove up to Edinburgh on the Tuesday evening, where, the following morning, I would take part in an open-top bus parade with the other Scottish medal winners – Ross Edgar, the rower Katherine Grainger and canoeist David Florence.

As I drove into Edinburgh I experienced two odd moments. The first almost caused me to crash my car in shock. Driving down Lothian Road, I saw, near the bottom, an enormous – and I mean half-a-football-pitch enormous – poster of yours truly, from a photo-shoot I'd done before Beijing, standing on Mons Meg, the famous cannon (and 'one o'clock gun') on the ramparts of Edinburgh Castle. 'The King of Scotland', read the strapline, in huge letters, along the bottom. It was an advert commissioned by one of my sponsors, Adidas, and had been erected the day after the Olympics finished.

As I recovered my composure I was hit by the next shock. It came as I pulled into a garage and spotted the newspapers, or rather the headlines, in the stand. I couldn't believe it. Several of the papers had headlines like 'HOY AT WAR WITH SNP' and 'HOY BLASTS SALMOND' – meaning Alex Salmond, Scotland's first minister. My response to the question about the prospect of a Scottish Olympic team had been spun into a political statement. My point, and my only interest, had been concerned with sport, but I realized now, in that forecourt in Edinburgh, that I'd stepped into a minefield – and one of the mines had blown up in my face.

I arrived at Sarra's flat feeling quite down, and very worried about the following day's bus parade. All kinds of thoughts went through my head. Would people think I'd been disloyal to Scotland? Would I be booed? It sounds ridiculous now, but this experience of being on the front page of newspapers was completely new to me, and I genuinely feared people's reaction. I also made the bigger mistake of looking at some of the comments people had posted online, after these 'Hoy at war' stories. There was some real vitriol on there, and you start to wonder: is that the general consensus? Then, helped by Sarra, I had a moment of clarity: who posts these comments? If someone began yelling insults at me in the street, would I take what he said seriously? Unlikely. Some of the posters must, I conceded, be the internet equivalent of the nutter in the street.

But another irony is that I am very patriotic. Scotland is a great nation and a beautiful place, and has produced countless amazing people. It's unfortunate that there is a minority who seem less interested in celebrating being Scottish than in being anti-English, and defining themselves in that way.

This story, or non-story, was playing into this minority's hands. I felt I'd been set up to start a political debate, which I found immensely frustrating. I will use the platform that sport gives me to discuss sport, and so, for example, I was happy to highlight the plight of Meadowbank, and to call for more facilities. It's the least I can do, having had so much help along the way. But I am still a bike rider, not a politician – and, believe me, I have no desire to become one.

I didn't sleep too well that night, and on the morning of the parade I was apprehensive. In fact, I thought: I don't want to do it. I just want to go to the wee café near Sarra's flat, or wash my car, or head out to the driving range, hit a few golf balls, and relax. I craved normality; I wanted to do something mundane. Most of all, I wanted to catch up with mates, spending time with the people who really knew me. I was seriously stressed out: Sarra could see it; my parents could see it.

And it was all for nothing. When the four of us – Ross, Katherine, David and me – got to Edinburgh Castle, where the bus parade was to start, we were led to a packed room for a press conference; and as we entered, everyone stood up and began clapping. I felt my anxiety wash away immediately; my face relaxed into a smile that stayed there for the rest of the day. At one point I was asked the dreaded Scotland/Britain question by one journalist; I responded saying that I stood by what I'd said, and we moved on.

When we walked out on to the Castle esplanade there were hundreds of people standing behind barriers, cheering. Four years previously, following Athens, we'd had an open-top bus parade, and it was good, but it was low key. This was anything but. From the Castle to the Scottish Parliament, all the way down the Royal Mile, there was a sea of people – 50,000 according to Lothian and Borders police. What was most humbling was that they had all come out to see us: they had made a special effort, many waving flags and banners with our names.

I felt silly for having worried. There wasn't a single negative comment; the very idea was ridiculous. This was euphoric; it was overwhelming; it brought tears to my eyes, and I'll remember it forever. After that I did a two-hour signing session in Jenners department store, which, pathetic as it sounds, drained the last bit of life out of me. You want to conjure up the same reaction with everyone you meet, to be as interested in them as they are in you, and it's exhausting. Sarra and I had arranged to go out that night – finally, the celebration party – but it wasn't to be. After the signing, I told Sarra that I didn't think I could face it; that I was too exhausted and we should postpone it for another night. She said that was no problem – we'd go home and take it easy.

What I didn't know was that she had secretly planned a little party, and that her mum, dad and sister were back in the flat, preparing food and drink. In the taxi, Sarra phoned her sister, Rachel, while I slumped beside her, in a semi-comatose state, and so I didn't even hear the conversation. But it led to some frantic activity in the flat. Apparently Rachel came off the phone and shouted: 'Get the food out the oven and hide the drinks!'

When I walked in, knackered, I didn't really question why the place smelt so nice. It was only weeks later that I found out what efforts they'd all gone to, in order to *not* have a party. But it is a good example of how selfless and considerate Sarra was in the post-Beijing period, which in many ways was as bizarre and as challenging for her as it was for me.

Just how bizarre was illustrated the following day. I was walking up to Sarra's flat, and there were a couple of guys working on a neighbouring roof, with one of their colleagues on the ground. 'Hey, pal,' he said as I approached, 'are you

Chris Hoy?' I nodded, and said hello, as he shouted to his mate on the roof: 'Oi, Jimmy! Look who it is!'

'Who is it?' Jimmy yelled back.

'It's Chris Hoy!'

By this time other people were starting to look, and I was turning red. I didn't want to go into Sarra's flat just then, so, after a quick chat with the guy, I walked straight past it, and did a lap of the block. I waited till the coast was clear, then sneaked in. What had the world – or my world – come to, I thought, that I was having to sneak into my girlfriend's flat?

I rationalized it by telling myself that this kind of thing would just happen in Edinburgh – my home city, but more like a big village than a major city. I was wrong: it happened in Manchester, even London: people at traffic lights, saying, 'All right Chris? Well done on those medals, mate.' It was utterly bizarre – as though I'd stepped out of the Big Brother house; as though I had become a different person.

I didn't have a problem with this attention. But there were times when it felt a bit intrusive. While standing peeing in a public toilet in Milan, for example. There I was, mid-stream, when there was a tap on my shoulder. 'Chris Hoy? Photo?' I turned round: 'Er, OK, but can I finish first?'

When I'm asked if I enjoy this attention I always say yes – as long as it's not in a public toilet – because it has all been very positive. I haven't had any negative comments (not to my face, anyway), and you can see that people take pride in their team, and in your performances, because you are representing that team – in effect representing them. Some people have seemed to be quite emotional, telling me their stories about being on holiday somewhere, finding a TV showing the Olympics in a wee bar, and feeling proud to be watching us winning. It is very gratifying. I mentioned near the start of the book that footballers seem to me to have become quite removed from the general public. Here, in what these people told me, and in their very genuine reactions, I could tell that they could relate to us as athletes – perhaps because most of us do it for the love of the sport, rather than for money. You wouldn't become a track cyclist or a swimmer for money.

But I remember after Athens saying that I was glad, then, that I didn't have to deal with what Kelly Holmes had to deal with. Kelly was *the* star of the British team in 2004, and I marvelled at her ability to cope with all the pressure she was under when she came home.

Another example of how my life had changed came with a phone call. It was a number I didn't recognize, but I answered. 'Hello, Chris?' said the voice. 'It's Max Clifford.' 'Yeah, right.' I was sure it was a wind-up, but Max convinced me he was Max. Then he explained that he thought he could help me in my dealings with the media, so, although I was a bit wary, on account of what I thought I knew about him, I travelled to London to meet him, and I had all my expectations and preconceptions blown away. To me, Max Clifford operated in an area of the media that I didn't know much about – and didn't want to know much about. But he wasn't the Rottweiler I had half expected him to be. He was really pleasant, he took a lot of personal interest, and there was a real family atmosphere in his office; it was relaxed, friendly, completely unimposing.

I worked with Max in that initial, frantic period, when my agent was unable to deal with the volume of enquiries. It was a real eye-opener in terms of learning how the media works. I got the impression that Max wanted to suss me out. But I think he picked up quite early that I wasn't going to be caught coming out of Stringfellows with a bird on each arm at three in the morning.

He wanted to find out what I wanted from the profile I now had; he said I could throw myself into the celebrity circus, and earn a lot more money doing that than cycling. But I was adamant that I wanted to continue cycling, and that I just wanted to get back to training as soon as possible. That pretty much ruled out a long-term association with Max, but I'm glad I had the experience of working with him, albeit for a brief period.

I learnt other things, too. One day, in Max's office, one of his staff, on learning that I was going to the James Bond premiere, asked whether I wanted a 'draper' for the evening. 'A draper?' I must have looked confused. Was it some kind of flower? Something you wore? 'Someone for your arm,' she said. 'Ah, no thanks – I've already got one.'

At the risk of sounding ridiculously showbiz, I also went to the National Film Awards in London, following Kylie Minogue, amongst others, on to the stage to present an award in front of 10,000 people and more A-list celebrities than you could ever imagine in one (very large) room. Later, Samuel L. Jackson came and introduced himself (a little unnecessarily). There were many more surreal moments. As I have already mentioned, I marched on to the Murrayfield Stadium pitch before Scotland played the All Blacks, carrying the match ball, wearing my three gold medals, a Scotland shirt with 'Hoy' and '3' on the back, and into a wall of noise that took my breath away. You expect a positive response at a cycling event – but this was a rugby match.

Then there was the advert I made for one of my new sponsors, Kellogg's. By November I hadn't had a single day without commitments since Beijing, and I was really looking forward to a holiday with Sarra in Thailand. But the day after the holiday I was supposed to be in Palma, Majorca, for a day's filming. Why Palma? It was the only covered velodrome available for hire at that time in Europe. Manchester, maybe partly due to the Beijing effect, was fully booked for the foreseeable future.

Thailand was just what I needed. We stayed in an idyllic little villa on the island of Phuket. I took my bike with me, and managed a couple of hours on it every morning – wheeling my bike through the complex, with staff saying, 'Olympic gold medal!' (yup, word had spread to Thailand, too) – before spending the rest of the day relaxing. And I mean Olympic standard, or Jason Queally-style, do-absolutely-nothing-but-lie-in-the-sun-and-read relaxing. I could feel my batteries recharging.

Just before the end of the holiday, though, a little metaphorical cloud appeared on the horizon with news of a protest at Bangkok airport. That cloud grew a little darker and bigger with each passing day. The relaxed mood in the complex where we were staying was soon replaced as fellow holidaymakers crowded around the one computer in reception, searching for solutions to their travel nightmares. As far as I was concerned, there was no need to panic. I even said to Sarra, 'Let's just stay, and wait till it all blows over.' Then I remembered: Majorca and the Kellogg's advert.

Back at home, British Cycling were looking at possible solutions, as was my dad. There was nothing. At one point an epic bus journey to Kuala Lumpur was proposed, but that was a non-starter. As a last resort, Dad contacted Guy Elliott, a friend, and a long-time supporter of me and of British Cycling. Guy, the chief executive of DHL in northern Europe, managed to find the final two seats on a Tiger Air flight to Singapore, which his company had booked in case any of their employees were stranded. We were able to buy these tickets, and, from there, Sarra and I flew to Frankfurt, where she caught a flight to Edinburgh, and I met a guy holding a sign with my name on it, who led me outside the airport and into a car. We drove around the corner and stopped beside a private jet, where I was greeted by the man from Kellogg's.

And then it was on to Majorca. I landed at 8.15 a.m., after travelling all night, was taken to a hotel for a shower, given a clean pair of underpants, and driven to the velodrome for 12 hours' filming. I swear that at one point, towards the end of the day, I fell asleep while standing up, with my bike over my shoulder. We finished in the evening, and I was driven back to the airport, shown to the private jet, woken up at Edinburgh airport, and almost poured into a car that took me to Sarra's at the end of what had been yet another bizarre, and exhausting, 24 hours.

That aside, much of it sounds very surreal and glamorous, but the flipside is the travel, the early starts, the permanent state of sleep-deprivation. In the 84 nights after Beijing I never slept in the same bed for more than two consecutive nights. A lot of the time you're thinking: this is amazing, I should be enjoying this, appearing on TV programmes like *Blue Peter, The Weakest Link, Would I Lie to You?, 8 Out of 10 Cats, Friday Night with Jonathan Ross*, plus numerous news and general interest shows ... But what you're actually thinking, a lot of the time, is: I'd love to just relax, and have some time to myself. It sounds pathetic, I know. And a legitimate question is: why do it? Because I didn't have to: it was a choice.

The reason was that I wanted to maximize the opportunities I was being presented with, because I knew they wouldn't keep coming. I'd spent several years not making very much money. My main source of income was the lottery; I was on £25,000 in the build-up to Beijing. With sponsorship and prize money on top of that I had enough money to be comfortable, but, in my thirties, I had to face up to the reality that I wouldn't be earning it for much longer. And it's around the time that you stop competing that you might begin to think about taking on extra responsibilities, such as starting a family. And this – so my parents tell me – isn't cheap. So I felt I owed it to myself, and to any future dependants, to make hay while the sun shone. But it was more knackering than I could ever have imagined. It became like an intensive training programme with no rest days.

And, incidentally, though I admit that I'm a bit like my dad in finding it difficult to say 'no', there was one thing I don't regret doing even though it earned me no end of stick from my friends: singing in a video to publicize Scotland's Homecoming campaign, along with Sir Sean Connery, Brian Cox, Lulu, Amy Macdonald and others. The aim of the campaign was to celebrate Scotland and encourage exiled Scots, even several generations removed, to return to their homeland. The song was 'Caledonia', from the old 1980s beer advert, and it had always resonated with me – as far as I'm concerned it's a classic, and many's the night when my mates and I have sung it coming home from the pub.

I'm the first to admit I'm not a great singer, but I thought that would be a poor excuse for turning it down – so I said yes. Besides, it didn't sound very demanding; all I had to sing was one line: '… the changes that have come over me …'

On the morning that I was due to go into a studio to record my line I woke up with the first signs of a sore throat, purely from being run down. But no excuses. I had one hour in the studio, a dozen people watching me through a glass screen; and there I was, standing there with the headphones over one ear, hanging off the other, in classic rock star pose – a bit like Bono in Band Aid – croaking my line over and over and over again. They were bringing me lemon and honey, and telling me I was doing fine, but I knew the truth, and so did everyone who saw it – or heard it – when it came out. I remember one comment about my performance: 'He's like something from *The X Factor* – the outtakes.'

The only mildly embarrassing aspect is that I come from a very musical family. My cousins, Jenny and Sarah Hoy, play in various bands, and their father, my uncle Derek, is a prominent figure on the Scottish folk scene, playing the fiddle in the band Jock Tamson's Bairns. In fact, I remember going into a music shop in Edinburgh one day shortly after Athens to buy a Bairns CD. When the guy behind the counter took my credit card, he looked at the name and did a double take. 'You're not ...?' and I thought: that's pretty cool – he's recognized me from the Olympics ... 'you're not Derek Hoy's son, are you? He's a legend.'

In the midst of all this came *BBC Sports Personality of the Year*. Obviously, after Beijing, there was talk of Rebecca Adlington, with her two swimming gold medals, and me being among the favourites. But timing can be everything. The Formula One season ended after the Olympics – handily close to *SPOTY* – and it ended in thrilling fashion, with Lewis Hamilton winning the overall drivers' championship on the final corner of the final race. Having been runner-up to Joe Calzaghe the previous year, Lewis was now the overwhelming favourite.

All the talk, beforehand, seemed to be about Lewis and Becky. I got to know Becky really well during and after Beijing, and we have become good friends. She is exactly as she appears – completely natural, utterly down-to-earth. I met Lewis on the day of *SPOTY*, at a motor racing event at Wembley Stadium, and I was impressed – he seems like a genuinely lovely guy, despite having to cope with so much attention and pressure. In keeping with her open personality, Becky didn't disguise the fact that she really wanted to win *SPOTY*, which is fair enough. I'd be lying if I didn't admit that I really wanted it, too.

It was the first time I'd made the shortlist, but I wasn't the only cyclist; Bradley Wiggins, Rebecca Romero and Nicole Cooke were all in the last 10, too. And there could have been others: Mark Cavendish, despite his four Tour de France stage wins, didn't make the final cut, and neither did another six Olympic gold medal-winning cyclists.

As I mentioned, earlier in the day I'd been taking part in the Race of Champions with Lewis Hamilton at Wembley. I'd been due to race him – me on my bike, him in his car, with some kind of handicap to make it interesting – but oil had been spilt on the track during practice, and when it started raining, it became like an ice rink. It was on-off-on-off, but in the end our head-to-head sadly had to be cancelled. In another surreal episode – though we were becoming a bit blasé about these now – Sarra and I then flew by private jet to Liverpool to attend *SPOTY*, but, ironically, we arrived quite late. Bradley and the others were arriving, all dressed up in their glad rags, as we appeared, still dressed in stinky track-suits.

We had about 15 minutes to get ready. We were rushed into the arena, shown to Gary Lineker's dressing-room – I'm not sure if he knew about this – and once again Sarra showed her true colours. Not for the first time she had been dragged somewhere and told she had 15 minutes to get ready, when, like a lot of women, she would have preferred around two hours. Here, in Gary Lineker's changing-room, she said: 'You have a shower first, then I'll look after myself.' At the end of 15 minutes, still sweating, we were ready; then we were whisked back round to the front of the arena, to make our official 'entrance' on the red carpet, in front of a big crowd, 10 minutes before the show started. I entered the arena and sat down. I was still sweating.

To be honest, what followed left me a little disappointed. The least you hope for is fair and balanced treatment, but, while Lewis and Becky got one-to-one interviews, and fairly lengthy individual profiles, we, the cyclists, including the four who'd been shortlisted, had to parade on in our cycling kit, in skinsuits and helmets, to be asked one question each. We all felt a bit like performing monkeys, and that it wasn't really necessary. People surely knew what we looked like on a bike, and I didn't see Lewis entering in his car, or Becky in her swimming costume. It was a bit patronizing. It was also extra stress, having to rush out, get changed, then changed back again, which was especially difficult for the girls. (I was glad I wasn't wearing my kilt, at least, as I'd originally intended to do.) Once on stage, I don't think we came across well as a team – more like a bunch of odd-looking folk in Lycra. The interviews didn't go that well either. But who is going to feel comfortable standing there like that? It felt as if we were the novelty act, and I thought: well, that's that then. I genuinely didn't think there was any chance of winning after that.

Then we won team of the year; and Dave Brailsford won coach of the year. But as they began to build up to the individual award, and Steve Redgrave and Michael Johnson appeared on stage with the envelopes containing the names, I turned to Sarra and said: 'At least I won't have to say anything.' Then a thought hit me, and I asked: 'If I get third, do I still have to go up on stage?' She just shrugged. How the hell would she know? A camera by my shoulder, meanwhile, meant that no matter what happened, I had to keep smiling in true Oscars fashion.

When another envelope was ripped open, and third place was announced, I felt my chest tighten. 'Rebecca Adlington.' Wow. I was shocked. I think she was, too. And I thought, my God, maybe I've got second. Then they read out second: 'Lewis Hamilton.' But I didn't think I'd won; I really didn't. In fact, I felt kind of deflated, already, at missing out on going up on stage, and collecting one of the wee replica trophies. The names I was thinking, when that third envelope was being opened, were 'Calzaghe' or 'Murray'.

Then Steve Redgrave opened the final envelope, and read out my name, and I just threw my head forward, while Sarra turned round to hug me. It was – as I think I mentioned in my acceptance speech, about 18 times – incredible. I turned to shake hands with Dave B, then Bradley, on my left, and Brian Cookson, the president of British Cycling. And then, as I stood on stage, and the applause kept going, I thought: what am I going to say? Maintaining the smile is difficult when you're nervous, but I was also studying the audience, seeing some legend of British sport everywhere I looked, and glancing at the famous TV camera trophy. It's big and handsome, but it's looking its age. It's bashed up a bit; the base is a little faded, but it's got character. And you look at the names: Jackie Stewart, Bobby Charlton, David Beckham, and think: it's been on all their mantelpieces, and now it'll be on mine.

The extended applause gave me time to compose my thoughts. First you have to thank the people who voted for you. And your family, of course. In contrast to so many major events in my life, mine weren't there; my mum and dad were with my sister, Carrie, who'd just given birth to her first daughter and my first niece, Anna. So I mentioned her, which was a nice thing to be able to do – hopefully she'll watch it when she's older. There were too many other people to thank, and I knew that if I started listing names I'd inevitably forget someone. I remember that Redgrave, during his acceptance speech in 2000, forgot to thank his wife. So I made sure I didn't make that mistake: I thanked Sarra for being with me for the last four years of the Olympic cycle. Which itself was a bit of an error: we'd only been going out for two years.

Like most people, I grew up with *Sports Personality of the Year* (*SPOTY* is a handy acronym, but it doesn't really convey the prestige of it); it was as much a fixture in our house as the *Only Fools and Horses* Christmas special, or James Bond on Boxing Day. It transcends your sport and captures the public's attention, but I don't kid myself that it's necessarily about the greatest sporting performance of the year. It's a popularity contest; it's about who the public feel deserves it the most.

I knew that winning it didn't mean I was a better athlete than Lewis or Becky, or another of the fancied contenders – and someone I greatly admire – Andy Murray. I won it, I think, because the public warmed so much to the Olympics. The Games caught their imagination, and I was seen as the figurehead of the British success simply because I won more gold medals.

But as I stood on the stage in Liverpool, with the trophy in my hands, I already knew something that wouldn't be made public for another couple of weeks, when the New Year's Honours list was to be announced.

On 2 December, as I was driving home from a press conference at Gleneagles Hotel, I got a phone call. It was an official from a government department, checking I'd received their letter. What letter? A couple of weeks earlier my Mum had got a letter from the same place, telling her she was being awarded an MBE for her services to nursing. She had retired the previous year, after 43 years working as a nurse, 20 of them in sleep medicine at the Edinburgh Royal Infirmary. I had also been made an MBE after Athens, so she was joining me, and her mother, my grandmother, Isa Reid, who had been honoured with an MBE in 1989, for her work as chairwoman of Multiple Sclerosis Scotland; the picture of her at Buckingham Palace, with my mum and her brother Jim, has pride of place in the house. Mum's MBE was a cause for big celebration, and it was nice to see someone whose work is not in the public eye receive some public recognition. It was particularly special because one of her colleagues, to whom she was very close, had died just before Mum retired. In many ways it had been a sad end to her career, but her MBE was as fitting as it was deserved. I was so pleased for her, and it seemed to complete a fantastic year for our family: my Olympic success, the arrival of my sister's baby, Anna, and my mum's honour.

Now, as I drove back to Edinburgh, I was told by this official that the letter I should have received – and which had obviously gone to my old flat in Manchester, from which I had moved since Beijing – was to inform me that I was to be knighted. Sir Chris? It hasn't sunk in, and as I told one journalist, it does seem mad. Not mad as in ridiculous, but mad in the sense that it seemed so surreal. I regard it as a huge honour, and one that gives me extra responsibilities to my sport; responsibilities that will continue long after I have stopped racing. Like the Sports Personality of the Year title, I don't think it's just for sporting achievement – it is a form of ambassadorial role that you are expected to take on, I think. I don't necessarily want to go into sports politics, but I do want to bang the drum for improved facilities and funding, and I want to try and encourage and inspire more young kids into the sport.

Mum and I received our honours on the same day, in June 2009. She almost missed my big moment, as she waited, in a different part of the Palace, for her ceremony. But as I kneeled before a sword-wielding Prince Charles, I caught sight of her out of the corner of my eye; she was standing off to the right, having been sneaked in by the Palace staff. It was an amazing day for our family, rounding off an incredible year, albeit six months after the year in question had actually ended.

Afterwards, a BBC television reporter interviewed both of us. 'He got his gong for sport,' he said to my mum, gesturing towards me, 'but you got yours for actually doing something useful, didn't you?'

An amusing postscript came some weeks later, when my mum was contacted by the fashion editor of the *Daily Telegraph*. A reader had written in, apparently 'desperate' to know where she had bought the outfit that she wore to Buckingham Palace to collect her MBE. And with that her transformation from Carol Hoy, dedicated nurse and devoted mother, seemed to be complete. Now she is Carol Hoy MBE and style icon.

CHAPTER 20

Rings and Roundabouts

Copenhagen, 14 February 2009

It was Valentine's Day, and I was racing. It had come as such a relief. From September to December I felt almost as though I were living someone else's life. But in early January I hatched a plan to escape. Perth, Australia, was my destination, for a training camp that, as it drew closer, got me more and more excited. If I had doubted, even for a second, whether I still had the appetite to train and compete, my sheer enthusiasm for getting back to work had settled it. I couldn't wait.

For five weeks in Perth I worked hard: in the gym for weight training or a two-hour road ride in the morning; a track session in the afternoon, with Shane Sutton and Vicky Pendleton; early to bed, and early up the next day to do it all again. This is the kind of simple routine, dedicated to the task of training, that I love; I was in my element, with a ten-day visit from Sarra adding to my good mood. Normally girl-friends or wives aren't allowed on training camps, but thankfully I was given special dispensation due to my situation.

From Perth I travelled straight to Copenhagen for the World Cup, my first major event since Beijing, and a reunion with all my rivals. On the first evening we picked up where we left off in the team sprint, the Olympic trio of Jamie Staff, Jason Kenny and me, riding in the Sky+HD colours of our new professional team, beating Cofidis, which was more or less the French national team, minus the now retired Arnaud Tournant.

Motivating me was the thought of the world championships in Pruszków, Poland, at the end of March. I really felt that in Perth I had got back on top of it. Of course I lost condition in the months after Beijing, when training played a distant second fiddle to all my other commitments, but I kept some basic fitness, and over those five weeks in Perth I tried to do the work needed to regain my power and speed. I accepted that my season was compromised, but I still felt I had a decent chance of doing what I had failed to do in Los Angeles, at the world championships that followed Athens. There, no Olympic champion managed to double up, i.e. add the world title to the Olympic crown. Which speaks volumes – it is bloody difficult to maintain the drive, ambition and hunger that you need to become Olympic champion. Dave Brailsford has put it well: 'The whole point of peaking when it matters is just that: you peak. You don't peak and then plateau. You peak and then come back down.'

Exactly. But whereas in LA I failed to back up my Olympic kilo with the world title largely because of post-Athens feelings of anti-climax, this time was different. There was no such anti-climax. Because my life had been transformed, with completely different challenges, and not many of them cycling-related, I relished the return to full-time training; it felt like going home.

The day after our winning team sprint ride, I lined up for the keirin. I won my two qualifying heats fairly comfortably to reach the final, playing it safe by going from the front as usual.

But in the final I wanted to try something different. The plan was not to go from the front, but to sit back a bit, be patient, to see if I could win using a different tactic. As the gun blasted, Ross Edgar and Grégory Baugé both went for the back wheel of the motorbike, while I slotted into third, with a ringside view of a fascinating tussle: diminutive Ross and man-mountain Baugé, barging shoulders as they both fought for the wheel, Ross on the inside, Baugé on the outside. Remarkably, Ross prevailed, and after a lap Grégory dropped back. And so it continued for the next couple of laps: Ross first, me second, the four others behind, all in an orderly line.

On this occasion, though, as the motorbike began to speed up, I let the gap to Ross open a bit, while I throttled back. When the bike swung off, with two and a half laps to go, I accelerated a bit, but at the same time I was aware of a presence on my right shoulder: Baugé. The Frenchman came straight past me and then past Ross, who had stalled rather than taking it on from the front, as I had expected. I couldn't delay: I also went past Ross in pursuit of Baugé, but as I sprinted for his wheel there was another presence on my right shoulder: Kévin Sireau. As he drew level, he moved in a little, and his elbow flicked, connecting with my elbow.

And I don't remember much else, other than that horrible moment when you realize you're going to fall. In fact, I don't remember some of the above – I've only managed to piece it together by watching the video of the crash, which I wouldn't say was the worst of my career, though it resulted in my most serious injuries. When Sireau and I collided, I went straight down, as though I'd been shot by a sniper in the stand, or my bike had been ripped from under me. I hit the ground at about 40mph, landing heavily on my right hip, then my shoulder, while Ross went straight into my back, cartwheeling over me, and Andre Vinokourov rode into my neck. Ross might be compact, but Vinokourov is a big unit. Put it this way: he's the last guy you'd want to ride into your neck.

Sireau went on to win the race, while it was Baugé, ironically, who was disqualified for dangerous riding. As for Sireau's move, I wasn't impressed. I'm not saying it was a deliberate attempt to knock me off – the keirin is, after all, a physical event and one in which accidents often happen. Perhaps he was trying to intimidate or distract me rather than intending me to fall – but I did feel it was an unnecessary move. It's a shame, too, because traditionally the French are considered to be amongst the fairest opponents. They don't rely on flicks or hooks, but instead on pure speed – a style of racing that I think emanates from Daniel Morelon, their coach for several years in the mid-1990s, and an eight-times world champion. So while the Australians, for example, have previously been renowned for their rough-and-tumble, win-at-all-costs approach, Morelon instilled a certain classiness in the French; and they won with their sheer speed. Whether or not that mentality has changed, one thing I am sure of is this: Sireau is a great athlete with incredible speed and can win without getting his elbows out.

I was lucky the track was in such good condition, so I didn't pick up any bad splinters – it was cuts, grazes and burns, which are painful, but largely superficial. I lay still for several minutes, as medics checked my feet, worried about a possible neck injury. I stood up, and then it was my hip that caused most concern, seizing up as I was led from the track centre by the British Cycling doctor, Roger Palfreeman, in my shredded and bloody skinsuit. I flew back to Manchester to have it assessed, but I was in for weeks of frustration. Within about a fortnight it became clear that the world championships were out of the question, though I delayed making a final decision as late as possible. As the weeks went on, the injury showed few signs of healing. When I thought it was a little better, I would go back out on my bike. But every time I did so it would become swollen and painful again. The experience was underlining only one thing: I am a very bad patient.

But it is especially difficult when you don't know what the problem is, and have no real idea of the timescale for recovery. Eventually, though, it was diagnosed – and it wasn't good news. It was a complex 'de-gloving' injury, described by Roger Palfreeman as 'quite serious and pretty rare'. The term 'de-gloving' basically means that the skin and the underlying tissue and fat have become separated from the muscle. Suffice to say, they should be knitted together. So it was a case of waiting for the tissues to re-knit – and to do nothing in the meantime. I was told I was likely to have at least eight weeks off: the longest period off my bike, I estimated, since I was a seven-year-old BMX racer.

I was asked if I wanted to go to Poland, to be part of the team, but I declined. I needed to get away from it; to have gone would have just left me feeling even more frustrated.

The enforced break from training and racing gave me time to think, and – for the first time, really – to reflect properly on Beijing, on what it had meant, and how I wanted to spend the next few years. I made a few decisions, one of which wasn't so much a decision as a confirmation that I had made the right decision in stating, consistently and forcibly, that I want to carry on to the London Olympics in 2012. I'll be 36, but I'm confident that I can be better there than I was in Beijing. Shane Sutton, after Beijing, said on a few occasions, to several journalists, 'Us coaches won't have been doing our job properly if Chris is in the team for London.' Which didn't exactly please me, but I know what Shane's doing – shooting his mouth off, yes, but also confirming that no one will be selected on reputation, or on the strength of what they've done in the past. I know that to make the team for London I'll have to be not just as good as, but better than I am now.

That, of course, is the challenge that any athlete relishes. More than that, that is the challenge that any athlete needs. Constant improvement is what you strive for; and I'm confident, despite my advancing years, that I can achieve it. After all, I'm a relative beginner in two of my events, the sprint and the keirin.

And beyond London? I definitely want to stay involved in sport. It will be hard to change from the lifestyle of an athlete – I'll miss not only the thrill of competition, but the routine of training, which, as I've already said in this chapter, I really enjoy. I love building up to major goals, and so coaching might be one way of staying involved at the sharp end. Then again, coaching is no half-way house: you have to be as committed as the riders, or you're not going to be effective. I look at Shane, Iain Dyer, Jan van Eijden – all of them are 100 per cent committed to the job, sometimes 24/7. I'm not sure I could do that; my priorities might change. The only thing I know is that I have to do something I have a passion for; not something that I'm just doing for a pay cheque.

Some people have suggested sports politics – whatever that is. In Beijing I was up for election to the IOC athletes' commission, but I had a problem. Because I was competing until almost the end of the Games, I wasn't able to lobby. And I think: well, if I wasn't able to lobby, would I be able to do a good job? It may have been a blessing that I wasn't elected – I intend to carry on as an athlete, after all, at least until the next Games.

I do have strong views on sport and on the Olympics in particular. I share the popular view that the Olympic Games should be the pinnacle in your sport, and so I have serious doubts as to whether certain sports should be included. The reputation of the Games is at stake: if a gold medal isn't regarded as the be-all and end-all in a sport, then it diminishes the Olympic gold medal. It was recently announced that golf has been recommended for the 2016 Games. But what would a golfer rather win – an Olympic gold medal or the US Open? Similarly, in football, what would a top player rather win – the World Cup or the Olympics?

As for those other big decisions … well, there was an irony, perhaps, in my Copenhagen crash happening on Valentine's Day. Was there a message? I'm not sure about that; but anyway, something momentous that I did during my enforced absence, when Sarra and I went to Prague for a long weekend, I'd had in my mind for at least two months, since I'd visited a small jeweller's near to my house in Manchester, and selected a solitaire diamond ring.

Sarra didn't know where we were going – which hadn't been that unusual in recent months, given that she'd accompanied me to so many events and engagements. But on this occasion I hoped I wouldn't be the centre of attention. I told her that, since I had been ordered off my bike for at least eight weeks, I'd use the time to book us a break. When she asked where, I said: 'It's a surprise.'

By the time we left, for Easter weekend, I think she actually had a pretty good idea where we were going, after bombarding me with questions designed to catch me out, like, 'Do they have the Euro there?' My initially puzzled reaction immediately narrowed down the list of possibilities. But she didn't know what else I had up my sleeve – or, more accurately, in my pocket.

I wanted to do the traditional thing and speak to Sarra's parents before we went. So I concocted a story, telling Sarra I was taking her parents an Easter egg to thank them for, er, giving us Easter eggs. Incredibly, she bought it. I think.

In Prague, I booked a romantic restaurant for the Saturday night. But over dinner didn't seem like the right moment; it was too public. Afterwards, Sarra suggested going to see the Charles Bridge illuminated at night. Perfect, I thought. But when we got there, again I felt there were too many people around; I suggested that we carry on wandering. It stunned Sarra, I think, my sudden interest in Prague, and its beautiful architecture, by night. 'You sure you're happy just walking around?' she asked, mindful not only of my injured hip, but also of the fact that wandering aimlessly is not really my thing. 'Yes, absolutely,' I reassured her.

We kept walking, on up to Wenceslas Square, but everywhere we went there were crowds of people. Eventually, we meandered back to the Old Town Square, which was close to our hotel. During the day the square had been packed with people; by night, with the crowds largely dispersed, it seemed even more vast, spectacular and dramatic, surrounded by the spires of the Gothic and baroque buildings; but just when I thought the time was right, a little cluster of people would appear. Normally I think I have a pretty good instinct for when to make my move – I'm talking bike racing here – but I was running out of time; if I was going to attack, so to speak, I had to do so soon. 'Sarra, I want to ask you something,' I said as we strolled across the square, approaching the huge Jan Hus Memorial monument in the centre. Then I went down on one knee (not easy, given my injured leg), produced the ring that I'd been too scared to leave in the hotel, and had thus carried in my pocket in its little box throughout the two days we'd been in Prague, and popped the question. Fortunately, she said yes immediately. And unlike so many of the moments we'd shared in recent months, it was all the more special because it was just the two of us.

Then, as we walked away, newly engaged, with our beaming smiles and our arms entwined, we were stopped by two guys.

'Are you Chris Hoy?' one of them asked, in a Scottish accent. 'You mind posing for a photograph with us?'

'Not if you don't mind taking one of Sarra and me as well,' I said. We weren't about to break our happy news to strangers, but little did they know how much that picture meant.

Chris Hoy in Numbers

Height	1.86m
Weight	93kg
Fastest 200 metres	9.815 seconds (Olympic record, Beijing, 2008)
Fastest kilometre	58.880 seconds (second fastest ever recorded, Bolivia, 2007)
Fastest kilo at sea level	1:00.711 minutes (sea level world record, Athens, 2004)
Max power generated	2483 watts on the track
Gym	227.5kg full squat
Hours' training per week	30
Daily calorie intake	3,000–4,000

DIET

General

Plenty of fresh fruit and vegetables; good-quality protein. Swear off alcohol for around six months before a major competition. Six litres of water a day.

On a typical hard training day

Breakfast	Big bowl of bran flakes and cornflakes mixed together, with honey and bananas on top, probiotic drink, coffee, smoothie, multi-vitamin tablet, glass of water and protein shake
After gym session	Protein recovery drink
Lunch	Tuna or turkey sandwich or beans on toast
During afternoon training session on track	Electrolyte or caffeine drink
After session	Protein or carbohydrate recovery drink
Early evening dinner	Chicken and vegetables with noodles or rice
Late evening	Breakfast cereal or toast or scones; protein shake before bed

Palmares

Full name: Christopher Andrew Hoy
Date of birth: 23 March 1976

OLYMPIC GAMES MEDALS

Gold 1km time trial, 2004, Athens
Gold team sprint, 2008, Beijing (with Jason Kenny and Jamie Staff)
Gold keirin, 2008, Beijing
Gold sprint, 2008, Beijing
Silver team sprint, 2000, Sydney (with Craig MacLean and Jason Queally)

WORLD CHAMPIONSHIP MEDALS

Gold 1km time trial, 2002, Copenhagen
Gold team sprint, 2002, Copenhagen (with Craig MacLean and Jamie Staff)
Gold 1km time trial, 2004, Melbourne

Gold team sprint, 2005, Los Angeles (with Jason Queally and Jamie Staff)
Gold 1km time trial, 2006, Bordeaux
Gold keirin, 2007, Palma
Gold 1km time trial, 2007, Palma
Gold sprint, 2008, Manchester
Gold keirin, 2008, Manchester

Silver team sprint, 1999, Berlin (with Craig MacLean and Jason Queally)
Silver team sprint, 2000, Manchester (with Craig MacLean and Jason Queally)
Silver team sprint, 2006, Bordeaux (with Craig MacLean and Jamie Staff)
Silver team sprint, 2007, Palma (with Ross Edgar and Craig MacLean)
Silver team sprint, 2008, Manchester (with Ross Edgar and Jamie Staff)

Bronze team sprint, 2001, Antwerp (with Craig MacLean and Jason Queally)
Bronze team sprint, 2003, Stuttgart (with Craig MacLean and Jamie Staff)
Bronze team sprint, 2004, Melbourne (with Craig MacLean and Jamie Staff)
Bronze 1km time trial, 2005, Los Angeles

COMMONWEALTH GAMES MEDALS

Gold 1km time trial, 2002, Manchester
Gold team sprint, 2006, Melbourne (with Ross Edgar and Craig MacLean)

Bronze team sprint, 2002, Manchester (with Ross Edgar, Marco Librizzi and Craig MacLean)

Bronze 1km time trial, 2006, Melbourne

WORLD RECORDS

500m, 24.758 seconds, Bolivia, 2007
Sea level 1km, 1 minute, 0.711 seconds, Athens, 2004

OLYMPIC RECORDS

200 metres time trial, 9.815 seconds, Beijing, 2008
750 metres team sprint, 42.950 seconds, Beijing, 2008 (with
     Jason Kenny and Jamie Staff)
1km time trial, 1 minute, 0.711 seconds, Athens, 2004

AWARDS

BBC Scotland Sports Personality of the Year, 2003
BBC Sports Personality of the Year, 2008
Sports Journalists Association Sportsman of the Year, 2008

Appointed MBE for services to cycling, 2005
Created Knight Bachelor, 2009

Honorary Doctor of Science, University of Edinburgh, 2005
Honorary Doctor of Science, Heriot-Watt University, 2006
Honorary Doctor of Science, University of St Andrews, 2009
Inducted to University of Edinburgh Sports Hall of Fame, 2009

Chris Hoy is also an ambassador for the 2012 Summer
Olympics in London and the Scottish National Veldodrome
which is being built for the 2014 Commonwealth Games in
Glasgow.

Acknowledgements

When I was awarded BBC Sports Personality of the Year I had about a minute to gather my thoughts and try to remember all those who have helped me. In the end I didn't dare reel off a list of names – mainly because I was terrified I'd miss someone important.

Now, though, I am grateful to have the opportunity to properly thank all those people who have helped me in some significant way over the years. Of course there are still far too many to mention individually, but I remain indebted to you all.

In some kind of chronological order, I'd like to thank George Swanson for spotting my cycling potential as a seven-year-old kid and for asking me to join the Scotia BMX team; and thanks to Matt Boyle and all my other arch-rivals for inspiring me to work harder.

To Murdo Montgomery, Rob Calder, Graham Glen, Stephen and Ali Hall, Kirsty Robertson, Caroline Robb, Rhona Robinson (and her son Hector, my godson), Mike Hunter, Chris Mackie, Colin Miller and all my other mates whom I see so little of, but will definitely catch up with sooner or later.

To my old rowing mates: Grant Florence, Peter Robertson, James Hayden, Steven McCloghry, Duncan Stewart, Alistair 'Mac' Macgregor, Simon Mungall, Chris Warwick and Ben Roberts, plus all the other boat club members.

A big thank-you to Ray and Doreen Harris and everyone from Dunedin Cycling Club. To the Meadowbank Track League crew and to the City of Edinburgh Racing Club; my old clubmates Nicky Hall, Derek Smith, Jamie Henderson, Peter Jacques, Anthony Stirrat, Steve Paulding, Graeme 'Grambo' Herd, Martin Williamson and the rest of the black, blue and white squad. I am also grateful to my early sponsors, Sir Tom Farmer, and to Keith Miller CBE of the Miller Group. Keith has been, and continues to be, a great supporter and friend.

To my sporting heroes for their inspiration: Gavin Hastings, Graeme Obree, John Robertson and Chris Boardman.

Special thanks to everyone at British Cycling, especially Shane Sutton, Jan van Eijden, Iain Dyer, Dave Brailsford, Steve Peters, Doug Dailey, Scott Gardner and all the support staff of whom there are too many to name check. I've no doubt in my mind that without all of your help and hard work I wouldn't have one Olympic gold medal, never mind four. At the Scottish Institute of Sport, thanks to strength and conditioning guru Dave Clark. To our old sprint coach, Martin 'Marv' Barras, 'You're The Man, Marv!' And to Peter Keen, for his vision and drive in setting up the World Class Performance Plan in 1997.

To Diane Evans at the Manchester Velodrome reception, thanks for always having a smile and a story.

To Ivor Reid, Alasdair Maclennan, Louise Martin and everyone involved with the Scottish Commonwealth Games Team, from Kuala Lumpur '98 through to the present day.

Thanks to all of those who were part of the Bolivia record attempt; it was a unique experience and one I look back on with real fondness. Maybe we can go back there one day to have another crack …

There are so many team-mates I'd like to thank. You know who you all are, but special mentions must go to my sprinter team-mates Craig MacLean, Jason Queally, Jamie Staff, Ross Edgar, Matt Crampton, Marco Librizzi, Jason Kenny and Vicky Pendleton. To those of you who have helped to keep my body in one piece over the years: Roger Palfreeman, Chrissie O'Connor, Gavin King, Garry Beckett, Sylvan Richardson, Phil Burt, Gavin Thomas, Luc de Wilde, Heidi Collishaw and James Watson, to name but a few. And to Terry Dolan, for his help and support over the last fifteen years. I would also like to thank Richard Moore, an old team-mate and now journalist, for his help with this book.

Thank you to all of my sponsors over the years for showing belief and faith in me, for making it possible for me to pursue my ambitions. To Chris Murray and Ricky Cowan for helping me find those sponsors.

To Charlie Reid for her tireless work in making sure I turn up at the right place at the right time, for dealing with journalists, autograph requests, for arranging appearances and events and generally making my life easier to manage since the Beijing Games.

I suppose, given that this list was supposed to be chronological, that my mum and dad should have come first. But I decided to leave the most important thank-you's to last. My mum and dad have been unstinting in their support for me and my sporting endeavours for over a quarter of a century, from when I was a seven-year-old BMX racer. I've never felt any pressure or expectation from them, simply unconditional love and their desire to see me happy.

They, and my sister Carrie, with her husband Garry, have been ringside for many of my biggest competitions and I can honestly say that I wouldn't have achieved a fraction of what

I have achieved without their backing. Beyond the BMX tracks, rugby pitches, rivers and velodromes, I am grateful to my family for their love and support. I know how lucky I have been to be able to pursue my dreams and ambitions with their blessing. To my extended family, aunties, uncles, cousins, soon-to-be in-laws and baby niece Anna: I owe many thanks to you and your 'dee dees'! I'm sorry that you travel the world to cheer me on and yet I get so little time to spend with you all.

Finally, special thanks to my fiancée, Sarra Kemp. You have made me realize there is much more to life than just riding a bike around in anti-clockwise circles. And yet, ironically, since meeting you I have never performed better or enjoyed my cycling more. Thank you for making me laugh and for saying, 'Yes'.

Index